Institutions and Institutional Change in the Federal
Republic of Germany

*Also by Ludger Helms*

EXECUTIVES IN WESTERN DEMOCRACIES

PARTEIEN UND FRAKTIONEN: EIN INTERNATIONALER VERGLEICH *(editor)*

WETTBEWERB UND KOOPERATION: ZUM VERHÄLTNIS VON REGIERUNGSMEHRHEIT UND OPPOSITION IM PARLAMENTARISCHEN GESETZGEBUNGSVERFAHREN IN DER BUNDESREPUBLIK DEUTSCHLAND, GROßBRITANNIEN UND ÖSTERREICH

# Institutions and Institutional Change in the Federal Republic of Germany

Edited by

Ludger Helms
*Assistant Professor of Political Science*
*Humboldt University of Berlin*

First published in Great Britain 2000 by
**MACMILLAN PRESS LTD**
Houndmills, Basingstoke, Hampshire RG21 6XS and London
Companies and representatives throughout the world

A catalogue record for this book is available from the British Library.

ISBN 0–333–73663–X

 First published in the United States of America 2000 by
**ST. MARTIN'S PRESS, INC.,**
Scholarly and Reference Division,
175 Fifth Avenue, New York, N.Y. 10010

ISBN 0–312–23001–X

Library of Congress Cataloging-in-Publication Data
Institutions and institutional change in the Federal Republic of Germany / edited
by Ludger Helms
p.   cm.
Includes bibliographical references and index.
ISBN 0–312–23001–X
1. Germany—Politics and government—20th century.   I. Helms, Ludger.

JN3971.A58 I594   1999
306.2'0943'09045—dc21

99–052034

This book is printed on paper suitable for recycling and made from fully managed and sustained
forest sources.

10   9   8   7   6   5   4   3   2   1
09   08   07   06   05   04   03   02   01   00

Printed and bound in Great Britain by
Antony Rowe Ltd, Chippenham, Wiltshire

# Contents

# List of Figures

# List of Tables

# Preface

Since unification, German politics has clearly become one of those subjects that have attracted growing attention among foreign scholars of comparative politics. While international research on the Federal Republic has significantly prospered over the past decade, the German-language literature on the German system of government and the somewhat smaller English-language body of research on the Federal Republic are still marked by a kind of 'co-existence' rather than un-restricted mutual exchange – a fact that can at least partly be explained by the continuing language barriers.

This volume contains a collection of original essays written by German specialists, many of whom have long dominated the debate in their respective area of research at home without presenting their insights to a larger English-speaking community of scholars. The common perspective of the individual chapters is on continuity and change of the core institutions of the German polity. What general developmental direction have German political institutions taken during the past half-century? Does it appear reasonable to consider the political system of the Federal Republic as an island of institutional stability, as many foreign observers suggest? And what impact has unification had on the working of German political institutions?

As the initiator and editor of this volume I have probably accumu-lated more debts than any other participant in this project. In particular I would like to thank Klaus von Beyme and Manfred G. Schmidt for their comments on earlier drafts of the introductory chapter. Parts of Chapters 1 and 5 were written during my time as a Visiting Researcher in the Department of Government at the London School of Economics and Political Science, August 1997–June 1998. I feel indebted to the German Academic Exchange Service for granting me an unusually gen-erous post-doctoral research scholarship. The editorial work on this volume would not have been finished on time without the kindness and patience of my former colleagues in the Department of Political Science at the Institute for Advanced Studies, Vienna. My special thanks go to Niken Sri Mastuti who undertook the main body of typing work for this volume and worked tirelessly checking the numerous revisions.

*Berlin*                                                    LUDGER HELMS

ix

# List of Abbreviations

| | |
|---|---|
| BdL | Bank Deutscher Länder (Bank of the German Länder) |
| BDI | Bundesverband der Deutschen Industrie (Federal Association of the German Industry) |
| BND | Bundesnachrichtendienst (Federal Intelligence Service) |
| BVerfGE | Entscheidungen des Bundesverfassungsgerichts (Decisions of the Federal Constitutional Court) |
| CDU | Christlich Demokratische Union (Christian Democratic Union) |
| COREPER | Committee of Permanent Representatives of the National Governments |
| CSU | Christlich-Soziale Union (Christian-Social Union) |
| DBB | Deutsche Bundesbank (German Federal Bank) |
| DBD | Demokratische Bauernpartei Deutschlands (Democratic Peasants' Party of Germany) |
| DDP | Deutsche Demokratische Partei (German Democratic Party) |
| DGB | Deutscher Gewerkschaftsbund (Federation of German Trade Unions) |
| DNVP | Deutschnationale Volkspartei (German National People's Party) |
| DP | Deutsche Partei (German Party) |
| EMU | European Monetary Union |
| ESCB | European System of Central Banks |
| EU | European Union |
| ECB | European Central Bank |
| FCCA | Federal Constitutional Court Act |
| FDP | Freie Demokratische Partei (Free Democratic Party) |
| GDR | German Democratic Republic |
| JCC | Joint Constitutional Convention |
| KPD | Kommunistische Partei Deutschlands (Communist Party of Germany) |
| MP | Member of Parliament |
| NDPD | National-Demokratische Partei Deutschlands (National Democratic Party of Germany) |
| NSDAP | Nationalsozialistische Deutsche Arbeiterpartei (National Socialist German Workers' Party) |

| | |
|---|---|
| OECD | Organistion for Economic Co-operation and Development |
| PBC | Political Business Cycle |
| PDS | Partei des Demokratischen Sozialismus (Party of Democratic Socialism) |
| PPBC | Partisan Political Business Cycle |
| SED | Sozialistische Einheitspartei Deutschlands (Socialist Unity Party of Germany) |
| SPD | Sozialdemokratische Partei Deutschlands (Social Democratic Party of Germany) |
| USPD | Unabhängige Sozialdemokratische Partei Deutschlands (Independent Social Democratic Party of Germany) |
| LDP | Liberal-Demokratische Partei (Liberal Democratic Party) |
| VAT | Value Added Tax |
| ZBR | Zentralbankrat (Central Bank Council) |

# Notes on the Contributors

**Klaus von Beyme** is Professor of Political Science at the University of Heidelberg and former president of the International Political Science Association. He has written extensively on comparative European and German politics as well as political theory. His publications include *The Political System of the Federal Republic of Germany* (1983), *The Transition to Democracy in Eastern Europe* (1997), *The Legislator: German Parliament as a Centre of Political Decision-Making* (1998), and *Parlament und Regierung: Die Demokratisierung der parlamentarischen Systeme* (1999).

**Ludger Helms** is Assistant Professor of Political Science at the Humboldt-University of Berlin. He has published widely in journals and books on various aspects of German politics and comparative politics. His main publications include *Wettbewerb und Kooperation: Zum Verhältnis von Regierungsmehrheit und Opposition im parlamentarischen Gesetzgebungsverfahren in der Bundesrepublik Deutschland, Großbritannien und Österreich* (1997), (editor) *Parteien und Fraktionen: Ein internationaler Vergleich* (1999), and *Executives in Western Democracies: A Comparative Study of the United States, Great Britain and Germany* (forthcoming).

**Eckhard Jesse** is Professor of Political Science at the University of Chemnitz. He has published extensively in the areas of German politics and political extremism in Western democracies. Among his major publications are *Elections: The Federal Republic of Germany in Comparison* (1990), (co-editor) *Die Gestaltung der deutschen Einheit* (1992), (editor) *Totalitarismus im 20. Jahrhundert* (1996, 2nd edn 1999), (co-editor) *Wahlen in Deutschland* (1998), and *Die Demokratie der Bundesrepublik Deutschland* (8th edn, 1997). He is also co-editor of the annually published *Jahrbuch Extremismus & Demokratie*.

**Karlheinz Niclauss** is Professor of Political Science at the University of Bonn. He has published widely on German politics, German post-war history and comparative politics. His major publications include *Kanzlerdemokratie. Bonner Regierungspraxis von Konrad Adenauer bis Helmut Kohl* (1988), *Das Parteiensystem der Bundesrepublik Deutschland* (1996), and *Der Weg zum Grundgesetz: Demokratiegründung in Westdeutschland 1945–1949* (1998).

**Oskar Niedermayer** is Professor of Political Science at the Free University of Berlin. He has published extensively on political parties in Germany and Western Europe. Among his main publications are *Europäische Parteien?* (1983), *Innerparteiliche Demokratie* (1989), (co-editor) *Stand und Perspektiven der Parteienforschung in Deutschland* (1993), (co-editor) *Public Opinion and Internationalized Governance* (1996), and (co-editor) *Parteiendemokratie in Deutschland* (1997).

**Wolfgang Rudzio** is Professor of Political Science at the University of Oldenburg. He has published widely in the field of German politics. He is the author of *Die organisierte Demokratie: Parteien und Verbände in der Bundesrepublik Deutschland* (2nd edn, 1982), *Die Erosion der Abgrenzung: zum Verhältnis zwischen der demokratischen Linken und Kommunisten in der Bundesrepublik Deutschland* (1988), and *Das politische System der Bundesrepublik Deutschland* (4th edn, 1996).

**Martin Sebaldt** is *Privatdozent* at the University of Passau. His major publications are *Die Thematisierungsfunktion der Opposition. Die parlamentarische Minderheit des Deutschen Bundestages als innovative Kraft im politischen System der Bundesrepublik Deutschland* (1992) and *Organisierter Pluralismus: Kräftefeld, Selbstverständnis und politische Arbeit deutscher Interessengruppen* (1997).

**Roland Sturm** is Professor of Political Science at the University of Erlangen-Nuremberg. Most of his published work has been concerned with comparative politics; policy studies; political economy; and European, British and German politics. Among his most recent books are *Großbritannien: Wirtschaft – Gesellschaft – Politik* (2nd edn, 1997), (co-author) *Koalitionen and Koalitionsvereinbarungen: Theorie, Analyse und Dokumentation* (1998), and *Public Deficits* (1999).

**Uwe Wagschal** is Assistant Professor of Political Science at the University of Bremen. He specialises in comparative politics and public policy research. His major publications include *Staatsverschuldung: Ursachen im internationalen Vergleich* (1996) and *Statistik für Politikwissenschaftler* (1999).

# 1
## Introduction: Institutional Change and Adaptation in a Stable Democracy

*Ludger Helms*

## Introduction

Institutions have been at the centre of the discipline of comparative politics in Western Europe for most of the past 50 years. Contrary to the situation in the United States, there was a considerable number of countries on the Continent which did not experience a behaviouralistic revolution drawing scholarly attention away from institutional matters of politics. Germany was among those countries in which the classical institutionalism concentrating on the constitutional architecture of a system and the formal dimension of individual institutions remained particularly strong due to the tradition of *Allgemeine Staatslehre*.[1] Early works on political institutions written by German political scientists often tried to gain an independent profile against the strong legacy of constitutional law by looking at institutions through the lenses of specific normative or idealistic concepts.[2]

Since the 1980s, institutions have been 'rediscovered' on both sides of the Atlantic. 'New institutionalism' in its various forms[3] became a highly influential, if not the dominant paradigm in the field of comparative politics with a strong impact especially on public policy research. In contrast to the 'old institutionalism' predominant during the first two decades after the Second World War, these approaches normally treat institutions as independent variables for explaining public policies and administrative behaviour. At least as far as the amount of theoretical debate among scholars of comparative politics is concerned, political research concentrating on political institutions as dependent variables has not been revived to the same extent. 'Structural institutionalism' appears to be the only variation of

1

neo-institutionalism that looks at institutions in their own right and the internal power balance within institutional systems.[4] Compared to the old institutionalism, the focus of structural institutionalism is not confined to analysing the formal or constitutional structure of a given polity or an individual institution. Informal aspects of institutions as well as the interaction between different institutions in a given system are considered more systematically. The 'veto points'-approach with its concentration on institutional barriers against majority rule within a system can be seen as the most sophisticated theoretical concept of this modern school of institutionalism.[5]

The interdisciplinary debate over political institutions has been significantly hindered by the lack of consensus among scholars over an appropriate definition of the subject of research. In a number of early works, almost any regular pattern of behaviour – be it habit, routine or convention – was classified as an institution.[6] In this volume we stick to a much more traditional and restrictive understanding of political institutions as formal institutions structuring the political decision-making process.[7] This leads us to concentrate our attention on three different kinds of political institutions: constitutional organs, other public institutions with an explicitly political character, and political actors who have achieved a degree of institutional consolidation that makes it reasonable to refer to them as political institutions.

The individual chapters of this volume provide a perspective on the German polity concentrating on the historical development of institutions and institutional change. A systematic approach to studying institutional change should first distinguish between different *levels* of institutional change. It is possible to discern changes of individual institutions on the one hand, and changes in the relationship between institutions (e.g., a change of the institutional system) on the other. Admittedly, this is a mere analytical differentiation, as a significant change of an institution is unlikely to leave its relationship with other institutions untouched.[8] Secondly, institutional change may be classified according to the *degree* of change (stretching from incremental to revolutionary change). As for the *causes* of institutional change, international factors may be separated from domestic ones. In reality these different dimensions result in *concrete forms* of institutional change, the most important domestic manifestations of which will be briefly outlined in the next paragraph.

Constitutional reform and other legal reforms represent the two most obvious ways of altering the profile of political institutions. However, there are a number of more subtle ways by which political institutions can change. Among them a change in the composition of the political elite working within and through political institutions seems to be of particular importance.[9] This kind of change is usually felt most strongly in institutions which are made up by only one incumbent, as in the case of the top positions within the executive branch (e.g., the office of prime minister and/or president). As Bert Rockman has remarked with regard to the American presidency, 'the incumbent is the institution'.[10] Changing behaviour of political institutions may be classified as another form of institutional change. In liberal democracies a significant change in the behaviour of political institutions tends to reflect altered public expectations towards political institutions. Usually, single incumbent institutions do respond most sensibly to significant changes in the public mind. Empirical evidence for this can best be found in the area of governmental institutions, as has been revealed particularly by more recent research on the American presidency and the so-called 'expectations gap'.[11] Of course, changing public expectations towards a political institution sometimes also stimulate formal institutional reforms. This may take different forms. As it is mainly the parliamentary party elite that decides on what wishes or proposals of institutional reform are to be implemented, most public demands for institutional reform are directed at the political parties represented in parliament. Still, the institutions seen as being in need of reform do not necessarily have to be the parties or parliament itself. For instance, the parties in parliament may respond to a growing demand for direct participation rights of citizens by introducing plebiscitary instruments at the constitutional level, as has been observed in the German Länder.[12]

As one of the most respected scholars of political institutions in Western democracies has emphasised, 'in the absence of adequately developed theory that explains how political and administrative institutions change, we need careful historical–institutional descriptions and analyses of actual transformation processes'.[13] This is what this book is about. While the individual chapters of this volume deal with the most important political institutions as they have developed over recent decades, the aim of this introduction is to give an overview of institutional change and adaptation at the level of the German political system as a whole.

In the following subsections we shall first look at the historical conditions of institutionalising democracy in the Federal Republic half a century ago and the main principles of the constitutional order. We will then analyse the most important changes within the institutional system which have occurred over recent decades accounting both for domestic and international stimuli to institutional change. This historical appraisal will then be followed by a more theoretical assessment of the German polity focusing on the overall performance of institutions in terms of political representativeness and governance.

## Institutionalising democracy in post-war Germany

The history of political regimes in Germany from the foundation of the first German nation-state in 1869/71 until the end of the Second World War was characterised by a very low degree of stability. The two regimes that followed the Empire – the Weimar Republic (1919–33) and the authoritarian Third Reich (1933–45) – both lasted for less than 15 years. On two occasions, the implosion of the existing political regime was at least partly a direct result of the preceding crushing military defeat. Even more than in the case of the Weimar Republic, the pre-history of the Federal Republic started with the 'unconditional surrender' of the old regime.

The process of re-institutionalising democracy in the Western part of Germany developed against a political background very different from that to be found in the two other 'axis powers' (Italy and Japan) and Austria (which had formed part of the German Reich between 1938 and 1945). While the Italians were allowed by the Western Allies to draw up a completely new republican constitution virtually free of any external intervention, the post-war constitution-building process in Japan was dominated, if not monopolised, by the leading Western power, the United States. With regard to the influence the allied forces exerted over the constitution-building process, (West) Germany takes a medium position between Italy and Japan (probably with somewhat lesser distance from the Italian case). However, the situation in the Western parts of Germany was certainly very different from that in Austria where constitutional re-democratisation was brought about by simply re-introducing the old republican constitution of the 1920s.

The deliberations in the Parliamentary Council (*Parlamentarischer Rat*), created to draft a new constitution for the Western territory of post-war Germany, were marked by the search for compromise rather than prevalence of confrontational strategies. The rather careful and consensus-seeking style of negotiation within the Parliamentary Council was favoured by internal as well as external factors. Both an exact numerical balance of the two major parties (SPD and CDU/CSU) in the Parliamentary Council and the specific ratification procedure which asked for the confirmation by two-thirds of the Länder prompted a co-operative style of constitution-building. This was further intensified by the insecure international background against which the constitutional deliberations took place. Until the ratification of the Basic Law it remained a real possibility that the three Western allied forces would give up the idea of a West German state in favour of an all-German compromise with the Soviet Union. In contrast to some other issues, such as the exact definition of the economic and social order, most issues regarding political institutions in the more narrow sense were agreed upon rather quickly. Federalism, and the nature of the envisioned second chamber in particular, marked the most important exception provoking much debate among the framers.[14]

The founding fathers of the Basic Law established a democratic model characterised by an extremely large number of institutional 'checks and balances', referred to by Peter Katzenstein as a 'semisovereign democracy'.[15] Probably the most important check against unfettered majoritarian government is provided by the federal system and the Bundesrat, which was designed to represent the interests of the Länder (rather than those of the political parties in government and opposition) in the decision-making process at the federal level. Moreover, the power of German governments has been restricted significantly by other independent powerful institutions, namely the Federal Constitutional Court and – until 1999 – the Bundesbank. Another important feature of the democratic model realised in the Basic Law is the almost complete absence of plebiscitary rights at the national level.[16] In contrast to more recent reservations about the compatibility of plebiscitary devices with the system of representative government, the most important argument against the introduction of direct democratic instruments at the time of writing the Basic Law was the negative experience with plebiscites in the Weimar Republic. The same holds true for the construction of the office of president in the Basic Law. With regard to his election as well as his actual powers in the political decision-making process the federal president represents the complete opposite to the extremely powerful and directly elected Weimar *Reichspräsident*.

To what degree has the institutional system established by the Basic Law changed over the past half-century? It seems adequate for a critical assessment to divide the last 50 years of the Federal Republic's history into two periods, namely the four decades before unification and the period since 1990.

In a historical appraisal of the Federal Republic's institutional development published on the eve of German unification Gordon Smith pointed to 'the absence of significant developments' and 'the stability, even inertia, of the basic institutions'.[17] At first sight there seems little to add to this authoritative judgement, especially if the focus is on the institutional system as a whole in terms of the inter-relationship between the basic institutions. The reform of the federal system in 1969 – introducing a new finance system and the so-called 'joint tasks' of the federation and the Länder which strengthened the position of the former – probably marks the most far-reaching institutional reform of the first four decades of the Federal Republic.[18] It established what has become known as 'interlocking federalism' or 'intergovernmental decision-making'.[19] The formal relationship between the five constitutional organs – Bundestag, Bundesrat, federal government, federal president, and Federal Constitutional Court – remained virtually unchanged, although the role of the Bundesrat in relation to the Bundestag and the federal government gradually increased due to the growing proportion of public bills that were considered to need the approval of both the Bundestag and Bundesrat (*Zustimmungsgesetze*).[20] Even minor reforms, such as the early abolition of the possibility of the federal president to seek judicial advice from the Federal Constitutional Court, remained an exception.

The dominant tendency of institutional development during the first four decades of the Federal Republic seems to have been towards gradual 'concentration' and 'centralisation'. This is certainly true for the internal dynamics of the federal system.[21] While scholars have argued as to whether a tendency towards centralisation has already been foreshadowed in the Basic Law or only developed later due to a number of very different factors, it is practically unanimously agreed among observers that the general developmental tendency of German federalism since the early days of the Federal Republic has been towards strengthening the role of the federation.[22]

The development of the party system up to the 1980s was also characterised by a clear tendency to concentration. Whereas no less than 11 parties were represented in the first Bundestag, their number declined to three (CDU/CSU, SPD, and the smaller FDP) in 1961. Only in 1983 was this 'two-and-a-half party system' challenged successfully by the Greens. As Moshe Maor[23] has argued, the *societal* dimension of party competition referring to changes in the party preferences of the electorate is not the only way by which a party system may be transformed. There also exists a *political* dimension of party competition which is related to the competition strategies and programmatic profiles of the parties which may alter a system's character without direct involvement of the electorate. Interestingly, this second dimension of party competition in the Federal Republic has also moved the whole system towards the centre. The single most important manifestation of this tendency was the Godesberg Programme of the Social Democrats passed in 1959 which scrapped the last remaining Socialist confessions in the SPD's programmatic profile. As in other Western democracies, the Social Democrats' centrist movement in economic, foreign and military policy was paralleled by comparable programmatic alterations in other policy areas, such as social policy, on the part of the Christian Democrats.[24]

The two-fold concentration process of the party system was accompanied (although not caused[25]) – by gradual reforms of the electoral system designed to make it more difficult for small parties to gain representation to the Bundestag. In 1953 the 5 per cent hurdle was tightened by applying it to the share of votes gained by a party at the national level instead of in any one of the Länder; in 1956 the number of direct mandates needed to gain seats, even without jumping the 5 per cent hurdle, was increased from one to three.

Within the Bundestag a tendency towards concentration manifested itself in the growing cohesion of the parliamentary party groups (*Fraktionen*). During the first decades after the war, the SPD was the only party marked by a considerable degree of '*Fraktion* discipline' (*Fraktionsdisziplin*).[26] Apart from that, the numerical definitions of *Fraktionen* were significantly tightened.[27] During the first years of the Federal Republic only 10 deputies were needed to form a *Fraktion*, which meant just 2.5 per cent of the total of members of the Bundestag. Between 1952 and 1969 the quorum was set at 15 deputies, which according to the growing number of members meant 3.7 and later about 3.0 per cent. In 1969 the parliamentary standing orders finally set the quorum at 5 per cent of the total of members of the Bundestag. Also the internal coherence of the governing majority – the so-called 'coalition-discipline' (*Koalitionsdisziplin*) – developed only gradually. It remained particularly low among the Liberals throughout the 1950s.[28] However, it has become part and parcel of German parliamentarism since the early 1960s.

Still, the tendency towards 'centralisation' has not been a ubiquitous phenomenon in the German system. An important area in which there were signs of 'concentration' as well as 'de-concentration' was the field of public administration. There was a marked development towards concentration through a series of territorial reforms at the local level.[29] However, territorial centralisation was accompanied by contradictory developments at the functional level of the public administrative system. Both the proliferation of para-government institutions and a marked tendency towards 'internal privatisation' of the public sector since the 1980s have challenged the legal and organisational coherence of the administrative state.[30] Nevertheless, Germany does still belong to an intermediate category of models of public administration to be found in Western democracies, combining a strong tradition of professional bureaucratic administration with a medium-strong degree of delegation of administrative powers to autonomous authorities.[31]

A modest tendency towards de-centralisation also characterises the field of interest group/government relations, although the dominant pattern of interaction between the administration and interest groups in Germany has always tended to be of a sectoral rather than a cross-sectoral nature. Attempts at establishing a neo-corporatist mode of interest group/government relations culminated in the late 1960s and early 1970s. After the breakdown of the so-called 'concerted action' (*Konzertierte Aktion*) in 1976 no comparably successful tripartite negotiation structure has emerged again, although the economic difficulties in the aftermath of German unification led to a significant revival of tripartist ideas.[32] A different kind of decentralisation or pluralisation in the field of interest group politics concerns the numerical increase of political players. The number of interest groups registered officially with the German Bundestag doubled within the period 1974–90 and has further increased since.[33] This development was accompanied by the proliferation of a wide range of so-called 'new social movements' since the 1980s challenging both the established political parties and major interest groups.[34]

The dominant developmental tendency within the German polity towards 'concentration' and 'centralisation' was complemented by what could be called 'informalisation' of the governmental decision-making system. While there had been various attempts at establishing informal channels of intra-governmental decision-making since the early days of the Federal Republic,[35] this development peaked under the chancellorship of Helmut Kohl (1982–98). Under Kohl the 'coalition committee' (*Koalitionsrunde*) – consisting of the chancellor, the head of the federal chancellery, the chairmen and secretary-generals of the coalition parties as well as the *Fraktion* leaders, chief parliamentary whips, and a number of ministers – became the centre of intra-governmental decision-making.[36] The extensive use of the 'coalition committee' as a genuine decision-making body not only replaced the older system of cabinet committees and inter-ministerial committees (which were still an important part of the governmental decision-making system during the early years of the Federal Republic) but also weakened the principle of individual ministers' authority in their given policy field (*Ressortprinzip*).[37] Under Chancellor Gerhard Schröder the chancellery was significantly strengthened at the expense of informal coalition networks. Moreover, Schröder not only kept some distance from his own party, but also showed less consideration for the smaller coalition partner than his predecessor – a fact which was facilitated by the very favourable position of the SPD in the post-1998 election party system (see below).[38] Still a 'red–green' coalition committee was established, and some observers felt that the tendency towards a 'de-parliamentarisation' of the decision-making process continued under the new government.[39] Policy negotiations between government and opposition outside the parliamentary arena and the creation of inter-party working groups of the Länder and the federation constitute further components of an 'informalised parliamentarism'.[40]

## German unification as a watershed of institutional reform?

For quite some time it seemed as if German unification could bring about major constitutional change. Given the then party political majorities in the Bundestag and Bundesrat, the opportunity to write a completely new constitution for unified Germany was closed by the decision to bring about unification on the basis of Article 23 of the Basic Law. By this, contrary to the alternative of activating Article 146 of the Basic Law which would have meant setting up a constitutional convention, the German Democratic Republic (GDR) became part of the existing Federal Republic under the terms of the Unification Treaty on 3 October 1990. Although the deliberations of the Joint Constitutional Commission (JCC), set up in 1992 comprising equal numbers of representatives from the Bundesrat and Bundestag, covered almost every major area of German constitutional law, only a very small proportion of reform proposals discussed there were passed as official recommendations of the JCC. More importantly, the majority of recommendations and actual constitutional changes did not affect the institutional system.[41] The federal system was the only institution that was partly reformed, although the most important reform of the federal system concerned the rights of the Länder in European affairs rather than their position in the domestic decision-making process. In domestic politics the potential for somewhat more diversity between the individual Länder was increased by substituting the old constitutional stipulation committing the federation to striving for a 'uniformity of living conditions' throughout the territory of the Federal Republic by a new pledge to an 'equality of living conditions' in the Länder – a seemingly minor change that has, however, considerable relevance, as it went hand in hand with a redefinition of the preconditions under which the federation is allowed to intervene in legislative matters concerning the Länder.[42] The extreme difficulties of changing existing institutional (or more precisely territorial) structures in Germany became clear once more with the failed attempt at fusing Berlin and Brandenburg – a measure suggested in Article 5 of the Unification Treaty. While the merger treaty was accepted by the parliaments of Berlin and Brandenburg, it was dismissed in the ensuing referendum on 5 May 1996.[43]

The judgement of 'non-reform', formulated with regard to the federal system[44] seems to suit even better the development in the area of direct democratic instruments. The introduction of various plebiscitary institutions at the federal level was clearly among the issues causing the most extensive and heated debate throughout the deliberations of the JCC. Still, in stark contrast to the situation in the Länder,[45] the parties at the federal level did not respond to the public mood, which strongly favoured the introduction of plebiscitary instruments. In the end not a single reform proposal concerning the expansion of direct democracy achieved the necessary two-thirds majority support in the JCC, although many measures were supported by a simple majority in the JCC.[46] Thus, despite the ongoing debate over the pros and cons of direct democratic instruments, the Federal Republic has kept its 'super-representative constitution'[47] established by the founding fathers half a century ago.

The more recent discussion of institutions and institutional change in the German political science community has centred on assessing the specific problems which have accompanied the 'transfer of institutions' (*Institutionentransfer*) from the West to the East.[48] According to the mainstream judgement on the state of transformation in the Eastern parts of unified Germany, there has been a remarkable degree of institutional consolidation. Nevertheless, the social anchoring of political institutions has remained considerably weaker than in the West, with a significantly lower organisational density of political parties and interest groups and lower scores of trust in, and support for, the established democratic institutions.[49] It would go far beyond the scope of this historical overview to tackle the crucial aspects of institutional transformation in the Eastern parts of unified Germany in detail. What seems clear is that so far post-unification Germany remains an 'asymmetrical system' based on the general structure of the 'old' Federal Republic.[50] Possibly the most interesting developments relate to those institutional areas which could not simply be exported by expanding the Basic Law to the territory of the former GDR, namely the system of parties and interest groups.

Despite a mixed performance of the parties in a number of areas, such as membership recruitment or electoral turnout, it would seem inappropriate to speak of a general crisis of the German party state in the 1990s.[51] The process of institutional adaptation in the aftermath of unification was by no means restricted to the territorial expansion of Western party organisations to the East but included the parties' willingness to meet the challenge of a changing political culture. Both major parties responded to the growing public demand of direct democratic participation rights by introducing plebiscitary forms of intraparty democracy in the first half of 1990s. At the level of the party system there has been some regionalisation but no fragmentation.[52] The two major parties proved more or less able to defend their dominant position against a growing number of smaller parties. A crucial new feature of the German party system of the 1990s must be seen in the emergence of a 'two-block system' (CDU/CSU and FDP vs. SPD, the Greens and PDS) putting party competition on a more symmetrical basis than in the past.[53] This new structural balance of the party system prepared the ground for the first major change of government in the Federal Republic's history brought about directly by the electoral result. It remains to be seen if the quite unusual 5.7 per cent lead of the SPD over the CDU/CSU marks an historical turning point in the development of the party system substituting the traditional 'CDU-bias' of the German party system by a longer lasting Social-Democratic hegemony. What seems clear is that the FDP has lost its traditional role as 'kingmaker' in the new bipolar party system structure, while the PDS – in notable contrast to its position in the Eastern Länder – remains an actor without any coalition-building potential at the federal level. Perhaps the most important feature of German party politics at the governmental level, which survived unification and the 1998 landslide election completely unscathed, is the continuing need to form coalition governments.

In the field of interest group representation and industrial politics the changes brought about by German unification have been even more significant than in the area of party politics. Interest groups in the five new Länder developed much better in terms of early (although not enduring) successes in membership recruitment and democratic performance than many observers had expected.[54] However, the formal institutional integration has neither led to the emergence of a functionally integrated all-German economy nor to a uniform system for negotiating socio-economic issues between the social partners. To many scholars of institutional change in post-unification Germany, the 'crisis of the German Model' represents the most critical development of the 1990s, although this crisis is rarely seen as being a completely home-made problem.[55]

## Continuity and change – a second glance at institutional change in Germany

The aspects discussed above seem to suggest that there has been more continuity than change within and between the basic political institutions of the Federal Republic, at least when constitutional or other formal reforms of institutions are taken as a yardstick. However, it must be remembered that the profile and overall performance of political institutions depends on a number of additional factors. In this subsection we concentrate on two groups of those factors, namely the social composition of the political elite and the impact of changes in party control of political institutions.

### Changing features of the German political elite

As mentioned above, the profile of political institutions is significantly dependent on the people working within them. While this correlation is most evident in the case of leadership positions held by a single incumbent, it holds true for all other political institutions too. There are at least two significant developmental tendencies in this field which we refer to as 'professionalisation' and 'feminisation'.

Professionalisation of the political class has become one of the most widely discussed features of the German system of government since the 1980s. As in most other West European democracies, the proportion of people in Germany who not only live for politics but also from politics (to use a classical distinction introduced by Max Weber) has significantly increased. The parliamentary allowances of members of the German Bundestag are among the highest in the Western world.[56]

Especially the share of members of the German political elite who do not have significant professional experience in other areas has increased dramatically over recent decades. In the 13th Bundestag (1994–98) a quarter of the total of deputies had a maximum of just two years working experience outside the area of politics.[57]

The tendency to professionalisation of the political elite has been accompanied by a somewhat less marked, yet considerable development towards 'feminisation' of the core institutions. While Germany still seems far away from Scandinavian standards of female representation in the political arena, the proportion of women represented in the core institutions – such as the Bundestag, the cabinet, the Federal Constitutional Court or the parties – has been on the increase at least since the 1980s. However, women have been represented very unevenly in different institutions. While the first female judge at the Federal Constitutional Court was elected the same year the Court was established, almost half a century ago, there were only three female federal ministers during the first 25 years of the Federal Republic, the first of whom was nominated as late as 1961. Moreover, female representation in politically influential top positions has altogether remained very modest. Most importantly, there has so far been no female chancellor, in fact not even a female chancellor candidate since 1949. The same holds true for the office of federal president, although there has been at least a small number of female candidates since the late 1970s. The first female president of the Bundestag was elected in 1988, and since 1994 the Constitutional Court has also been presided over by a woman.[58] The female representation rate in the Bundestag developed from 6.8 per cent in 1949 to 26.3 per cent in 1994, and 30.9 per cent in 1998, although it is important to note that the 10 per cent margin was not crossed until 1987. Last but not least, the proportion of women in political parties – at the level of party members as well as within intra-party organs – has risen steadily since the early 1980s. The remarkable increase in female representation among parliamentary candidates and within intra-party bodies in the major parties was favoured significantly by a number of intra-party reforms, namely the introduction of female quotas in the 1990s.[59]

There has been much discussion (though comparatively few empirical findings) concerning the possible effects of these changes in the social composition and career backgrounds of the German political elite. The question as to whether a high share of female representation in political institutions does matter in terms of political performance and policy outcomes has mostly been answered in the affirmative, especially but not exclusively in the works of feminist scholars. Female members of the Bundestag are seen as having somewhat stronger post-materialist orientations and employing different communication strategies. Moreover, female members of the political elite are considered as being more sensitive to 'female issues', such as abortion. However, as the findings of more recent studies suggest, the growing numerical proportion of female deputies by no means automatically entails adequate consideration of female views in the parliamentary decision-making process.[60]

Most authors would agree that the strong tendency towards professionalisation of the parliamentary elite has also had a crucial impact on how the Bundestag performs and interacts with other political institutions. Again, the exact effects of this development have rarely been studied empirically. Still, it may be assumed that a high degree of professionalisation among parliamentarians does not only affect the relationship between the political elite and the public.[61] It seems likely that a high degree of professionalisation among parliamentarians also affects the way candidates behave in the parliamentary arena, and the relationship between parliament and government. A prominent assumption maintains that, especially in systems with a proportional electoral system based on party lists, the position of the parties towards individual deputies is strengthened significantly if the latter are professional politicians lacking alternative career opportunities outside the world of politics. This general expectation can be considered to be valid also in the German case, although recent empirical research has revealed that parliamentary 'dissenters' are hardly ever punished by their parties with exclusion from the party list.[62] Furthermore, a strong degree of professionalisation of the parliamentary elite may also strengthen the role of the head of government in the parliamentary arena, as has been demonstrated for the British case by Anthony King. As members of a professionalised parliamentary elite have a vital interest not only in securing their professional status but also in further advancing their career, the patronage power of the prime minister, who decides cabinet appointments and the distribution of other secondary governmental positions, is significantly strengthened by increasing professionalisation.[63] Although the constitutional and political position of the chancellor in the German system is to a much lesser extent a bastion of unfettered executive power than that of a British prime minister, the general thrust of this argument also seems to fit the German case.[64]

As mentioned above, the influence of individual incumbents is strongest in political institutions represented by a single person, such as the office of chancellor or federal president. Clearly, incumbents are most likely to leave their mark on an institution when the office they occupy has just been created, as was the case with Adenauer and Heuss, the first chancellor and federal president of the Federal Republic respectively. The constitutionally strong position of the chancellor in the German system was further broadened by Adenauer's expansive interpretation of his powers of office which also strengthened the structural position of his successors in the chancellery.[65] The extremely long-lasting chancellorship of Helmut Kohl provides another case in point for the thesis that aspects of personality are important for the structural development of institutions. Much of what has been high-lighted as specific mechanisms for problem-solving within the executive territory was owed to Kohl's specific leadership preferences.[66] Even more obvious is the impact of an incumbent's personality and specific political style in the case of the German federal presidency, which must be seen as a result of the rather modest presidential office powers. The presidency of von Weizsäcker, for example, made the whole institution of federal president appear much more political than in the preceding decades. Nevertheless, expectations that the incumbency of von Weizsäcker could mark the beginning of a 'higher-profile presidency'[67] in unified Germany have not come true under the presidency of von Weizsäcker's successor, Roman Herzog.[68]

## Change in party control as a variable of change

Modern parliamentary democracies are party democracies. It is the parties which act as gatekeepers to political offices and dominate the political decision-making process. As parliamentary democracies are based on the principle of majority rule, with parties competing with each other on the basis of specific electoral manifestos, it may be assumed that a change in party control of political institutions constitutes another key aspect in explaining changing institutional performance.

The usual consequences of a change of government for the Bundestag appear as rather limited, at least when compared with the situation in legislatures of Anglo-Saxon democracies.[69] Parliamentary business in Germany is organised on the principle of proportional representation, guaranteeing the opposition a certain share of chairs in the legislative committees and representation within the Bundestag's legislative steering committee, the so-called 'Council of Elders' (*Ältestenrat*). Even at the governmental level itself, the virtually unbroken existence of coalition governments has moderated structural innovation in the aftermath of changes of government.[70] Also the repercussions of government change on the career civil service appear as rather modest judging by American standards.[71]

In the more recent past the debate on institutional change by changes in party control of institutions has centred on the Bundesrat or – more precisely – the relationship between the Bundesrat and Bundestag. There have been significant variations with regard to the Bundesrat's position in the political decision-making process which reflect the impact of different party political constellations. The periods during which the Bundesrat more often than not vetoed important bills passed by the Bundestag largely correspond with those intervals in which the opposition parties in the Bundestag had a majority in the Bundesrat.[72] When, on the other hand, the same parties controlled both the Bundestag and the Bundesrat, the decision-making system worked much more smoothly in general. The developments during the last term of Helmut Kohl's chancellorship (1994–98) in particular provided much support for the party politicisation thesis. Against the background of significantly restricted financial options in the aftermath of German unification and important structural changes in the party system, the SPD – controlling the Bundesrat – almost completely abandoned co-operative strategies towards the Christian Liberal government.[73]

Still, it seems necessary to take into account two qualifications of the party politicisation view of the Bundesrat. First, there have been occasions on which the Bundesrat in fact acted as a chamber representing the views of the Länder, as provided for in the Basic Law. More recent examples include the all-German redistribution of income between the individual territorial entities of the German federal state (*Bund, Länder* and *Gemeinden*), and the lengthy wrangling over the reform of parliamentary allowances for members of the Bundestag.[74] What these examples demonstrate is that the federal decision-making process has become more complex since unification. One of the main reasons why the parties in the Bundestag can no longer take for granted the support of their party fellows in the Bundesrat is to be seen in the much more diverse spectrum of governing coalitions in the Länder in the 1990s.[75] This is aggravated by the growing gap between the poorer and the better-off Länder.[76]

Second, and more important, even if decision-making in the Bundesrat is not free of party political considerations, many cases in which the Bundestag and Bundesrat took an opposite view in the early stages of the parliamentary decision-making process could finally be solved through extensive co-operation between the relevant political players. This strong inclination to negotiate complex issues until a measure is eventually agreed upon by both government and opposition constitutes an important aspect of a prominent characterisation of the Federal Republic as a 'Grand Coalition state'.[77] While the institutional structure of the Federal Republic is not the only factor responsible for generating political compromise – being supported by a generally consensus-oriented political culture and the absence of deep-running social rifts – it must be seen as what Gordon Smith has called a 'consensus-inducing mechanism'.[78] According to some scholars, the impact of the Federal Republic's institutional system is not restricted to the legislative arena but also constitutes a core variable influencing the long-term strategies of political actors: 'The adoption of the Godesberg Programme of the German SPD in 1959 mirrors not only the ambition to mobilise new voters, it is also a response to state structures which require a considerable amount of co-operation from each of the office-seeking parties'.[79]

## The impact of European integration

Like any other Western democracy, the Federal Republic has not been immune to challenges from the international arena. On the contrary, the degree to which the German post-war democracy has been influenced by external factors has been exceptionally high. During the first decades of its history the Federal Republic was a 'penetrated system',[80] mainly due to the considerable co-determination powers of the allied forces in the field of foreign affairs and German–German relations. While this kind of international 'penetration' gradually declined in importance, and eventually ceased to exist with German unification, the impact of European integration on the German polity has continuously increased over recent decades. The precise amount of institutional change following from European integration is difficult to assess as most changes are of a rather indirect nature. Still, a number of observations can be made concerning the development of the German polity against the background of an emerging 'ever-closer union'.

First of all, there have been very few formal changes of individual institutions due to the European integration process, such as the creation of a Standing Committee on European Union Affairs both in the Bundestag and the Bundesrat. Perhaps the most important institutional reform of this kind can be found in the area of German federalism. Through a reform of Article 23 of the Basic Law the position of the Länder in European matters has been strengthened significantly.[81] Second, although European integration potentially restricts the political power of all domestic institutions to the extent to which sovereignty rights of the nation-state are delegated to the supranational level in Brussels, some institutions have been more affected by this development than others. Quite obviously, the process of deepening the political dimension of European integration has increased the power of the executive. However, not all parts of the executive have profited from Europeanisation equally. According to Beate Kohler-Koch, it is the chancellery and the Foreign Ministry that have gained most in the more recent stages of European integration, mainly at the expense of the Treasury.[82] Also the Länder have come to profit from the European project. The shift of power from the federation to the Länder has been accompanied by an intensification of inter-Länder co-ordination and co-operation concerning EU-related matters. As Klaus Goetz has argued, 'these adaptive reactions have not, however, challenged any of the defining characteristics of German federalism. Rather, adjustments have tended to bolster existing features of the intergovernmental system.'[83]

The main 'losers' of the European integration process are comparatively easier to identify. After Germany's decision to participate in the European Single Currency project, most observers agree that the Bundesbank is the key political institution that suffered most severely from European integration.[84] The second major political institution for which further deepening of European integration has meant a gradual loss of power is the Federal Constitutional Court. With a steady increase in European legislation, more and more important legislative measures belong to the European Court of Justice's area of responsibility, consequently restricting the jurisdiction of constitutional courts in the single member states. As the Federal Constitutional Court has often – perhaps too often – been the institutional focal point in the process of settling political disputes in Germany, this silent transformation of judicial review may have an even deeper impact on the German polity as a whole than the recent sweeping reforms of the Bundesbank.[85]

## Representativeness and governance

Two paradigms have dominated the more recent debate over different institutional configurations of liberal democracies in the more recent past. The first one relates to differences between presidentialism and parliamentarism.[86] The second, somewhat more complex, one distinguishes 'consensus democracies' and 'majoritarian democracies'.[87] While this discussion has greatly enhanced our understanding of political institutions and the institutional conditionality of democratic polities, there is still a scarcity of more sophisticated theoretical concepts suitable to assess the character of institutions and institutional systems beyond mere classifications of different kinds of democracies.

One of the most rewarding theoretical perspectives on political institutions has recently been put forward by Bert Rockman.[88] Drawing on a concept developed by Richard Rose[89] and Kenneth Shepsle,[90] Rockman distinguishes between two general functions of political institutions in democratic regimes. In all liberal democracies representativeness and governance represent two competing values which political institutions are expected to provide for the political system. It is important to realise that these two possible effects of institutions constitute a trade-off: if the institutions in a given system are mainly designed to account for fair representation of all relevant social groups in the decision-making process, this will necessarily have negative side-effects on the structure of governance of this system. If, on the other hand, the main ambition of those responsible for designing the institutional system is to facilitate governance, the degree to which different actors (especially those representing minorities) are included in the political decision-making system is likely to be significantly lower than in the first group of systems.

How does the German system fare regarding the competing values of representativeness and governance when compared with other Western democracies? In a sweeping comparative judgement Richard Rose[91] classified the United States as a political system based on the principle of 'putting government before politics', while the ranking of both aspects in the major democracies on the Continent was the other way round. From this perspective, democratic regimes in Western Europe are seen as being more likely to generate governing authority at the expense of accessibility and representativeness than to induce a high degree of political access of different actors to the decision-making process at the cost of authority.

What seems clear is that the German polity is much less oriented to the goal of facilitating governance than, for instance, the political systems of Great Britain or France. At almost all levels and within the majority of political institutions there are signs of a high degree of representativeness and political inclusion of different actors and social forces. Above all, the very existence of federalism – and the powerful position of the Bundesrat in particular – strongly supports this view. The organisation of parliamentary business in the Bundestag, based on a fair representation of the different *Fraktionen*, as well as the two-thirds quorum in the Bundestag and Bundesrat required for changes of the Basic Law may be mentioned as two other crucial components of the German 'power sharing'-system. The overall impression that dissenting minorities are by no means simply excluded in the German polity is further enhanced by the strong position of the Federal Constitutional Court and the system of interest group representation in the governmental arena. Even the German electoral system – marked by a rather high 5 per cent threshold – has been judged as being 'very sensitive to political changes'.[92] The German electoral system tries to combine the virtues of a high degree of representativeness with specific rules militating against a high degree of fragmentation of the party system. Although the structure of the party system can by no means be explained by the impact of the electoral system alone, the combination of proportional representation with a 5 per cent threshold has helped prepare an institutional background for party politics in Germany flexible enough to give new parties a reasonable chance to gain parliamentary representation without making the government-building process as difficult as in some other Western countries, such as Italy or the Netherlands.[93] Last but not least, with the prevalence of virtually permanent coalition government, political power in the Federal Republic is shared even at the very centre of the government machinery.[94] Among West European parliamentary democracies, only the Netherlands and Luxembourg had an even more impressive experience with coalition government than Germany.[95]

Still, Rose's thesis of a strong orientation towards governance within the West European democracies finds a considerable amount of support also in the German case. First of all, the reality of German federalism is marked by an extremely strong tendency towards centralisation.[96] A second crucial aspect is the strong constitutional position of the government, and the chancellor in particular, towards parliament, mainly due to the 'constructive' vote of no-confidence and the Bundestag's lacking power to topple individual ministers. Moreover, the chancellor's position is strong within the core executive. While most observers agree that the more recent tendency within the core executive has been towards weakening the system of 'chancellor democracy',[97] the chancellor is still more than 'primus inter pares'. In a comparative assessment of the role of chief executives in Western democracies Germany was the only system with virtually permanent coalition government which was classified as having a strong 'chief executive'.[98] Third, the parliamentary standing orders in the Bundestag also leave very little room for manoeuvre for individual deputies or groups lacking the official *Fraktion* status.[99] In the Bundesrat, at least the legislative decision-making process in the more narrow sense is marked by a complete absence of initiatives of individual members, as votes are to be cast for each Land as a whole. Furthermore, one could also count the structure of the party system to those institutional structures facilitating rather than hindering governance in the Federal Republic. The new much more balanced 'two-bloc system' that emerged in the 1990s largely compensates for the growing number of parties represented in the Bundestag. Finally – and to many critics of the present democratic model the most serious institutional flaw of the Basic Law – there are no plebiscitary devices at the federal level at all which in many other Western countries allow citizens to participate directly in the democratic decision-making process.

## Conclusions

After a historical period marked by an extremely high degree of regime instability, Germany has become one of the most stable democratic polities within the group of Western countries. It is important to note, however, that this quite remarkable stability of constitutional democracy in post-war Germany cannot be explained by institutional factors alone. To be sure, there have been specific constitutional safeguards in the Basic Law – such as the principle of so-called '*wehrhafte Demokratie*' laid down in Article 79, 3 – but these institutional devices would have been rather powerless had it not been for a number of other background conditions all of which favoured the process of democratic consolidation in the Federal Republic. Among these supportive factors, the altogether favourable economic development and the firm commitment of the German postwar political elite to the liberal-democratic spirit of the Basic Law merit particular attention.[100] The institutional order itself had an important secondary effect on democratic stability as it was a major source of influence shaping the political culture of post-war Germany.[101]

While scholarly judgements on the German polity continue to represent a wide range of opinions it remains a remarkable feature of the study of German politics that the overall performance of the German system tends to be judged more favourably by foreign scholars. Positive endorsements include firm belief not only in the Federal Republic's democratic stability but also in the system's potential for reform. To Lewis J. Edinger and Brigitte L. Nacos it seems 'that the very features of Germany's political institutions and arrangements that work in favor of continuity and incremental change in normal times have at the same time the attributes needed for adopting major reforms in the face of extraordinary problems and looming crises'.[102] Other foreign observers have even judged the occurrence of the problematic split party dominance in the Bundestag and Bundesrat, characterising most of the 1990s, as 'a felicitous combination of stability and flexibility'.[103]

Among German commentators, there has been much more harsh criticism regarding the overall performance of the German system in the 1990s. Many observers have come to perceive the remarkable stability of the German system as inflexibility. Often, the lack of reform in many major fields of public policy has been blamed on the institutional system, its alleged inability to produce significant policy changes in a reasonable period of time.[104] However, the findings of more sophisticated research into the German system of public policy-making seem to suggest that purely institutional explanations of legislative gridlock rest on rather feeble ground. While the institutional system of the Federal Republic makes major policy changes a matter of incrementalism rather than spectacular U-turns, the Federal Republic's history bears witness to the fact that policy change is by no means impossible to achieve under the existing institutional conditions.[105]

As some scholars have rightly emphasised, Germany's apparent inability to reform may have more to do with a fatal lack of willingness to reform traditional structures among the governing political elite than with institutional obstacles.[106] The 1998 change of government provides an excellent opportunity to study the impact of this factor on the federal decision-making process in the years to come. However, it may well turn out, as some observers have maintained, that the Federal Republic's immobility is even deeper rooted among the electorate than among members of the political elite.[107] The 1998 electoral experience does not provide the worst example of this tendency. Most observers of the 1998 electoral campaign agree that the majority of voters wanted a new government but not a completely new set of policies.[108] As in the British general election of 1997, 'turning the rascals out' was facilitated by a moderate alternative government that minimised the voters' anxiousness about radical political change.

Pointing to the necessity to look for additional factors in order to explain the decision-making process in post-unification Germany is not to say that carefully designed reforms of German institutions should remain off the political agenda. Among the potential areas of institutional reform, a more than cosmetic reform of the federal system – above all, a thorough revision of the financial equalisation system (*Finanzausgleich*) – remains an issue of particular importance. There are other issues worth considering in the future debate over institutional reform in Germany. First of all, the introduction of certain plebiscitary instruments at the federal level – such as the popular initiative or the abrogative referendum – could significantly increase the responsiveness of the political system without undermining the principles of representative government or paralysing the established governance structure. Also, in the area of executive–legislative relations minor reforms (which would only have to adopt the constitutional practice in the parliamentary arena) seem desirable. Providing the Bundestag with the right of self-dissolution when governing majorities are lacking could put a stop to the highly problematic practice of using the question of confidence as a functional equivalent to the lacking dissolution power.[109] Finally, a serious reform of the public administrative system should no longer be shelved. A reduction in the number of federal ministries as well as ministerial senior staff are considered to be among the most pressing issues in this field.[110]

Still, a realistic assessment of the perspectives of future institutional reform in post-unification Germany can hardly dismiss the fact that the chances for large-scale institutional reforms are less than optimal. The fact that the unique 'window of opportunity', created by the immediate aftermath of German unification, was left unused for the initiation of major institutional reforms, makes it difficult to conceive under what conditions such reforms could be achieved.[111] However, this assessment seems only to apply to major constitutional reforms of political institutions. There is much room for institutional change taking place below the level of constitutional reform, including rather subtle forms of institutional change, such as changes in the composition of the political elite. Even without a 'masterplan' for institutional reform, institutional change and adaptation are likely to happen. The German polity remains a 'constitution in flux',[112] and indeed institutional change and adaptation must be seen as vital preconditions of continued stability of the German constitutional democracy.

# Notes

1  Bo Rothstein, 'Political Institutions: an Overview', in Robert E. Goodin and Hans-Dieter Klingemann (eds), *A New Handbook of Political Science* (Oxford: Oxford University Press, 1996), p. 137.

2  See Axel Murswieck, 'Parlament, Regierung und Verwaltung. "Parlamentarisches Regierungssystem" oder "Politisches System"?', in Stephan von Bandemer and Göttrik Wewer (eds), *Regierungssystem und Regierungslehre: Fragestellungen, Analysekonzepte und Forschungsstand eines Kernbereichs der Politikwissenschaft* (Opladen: Leske & Budrich, 1989), pp. 151–2.

3  See Vivien Lowndes, 'Varieties of New Institutionalism: a Critical Appraisal', *Public Administration*, 74 (1996), pp. 181–97; Peter Hall and Rosemary Taylor, 'Political Science and the Three New Institutionalisms', *Political Studies*, 44 (1996), pp. 936–57.

4  See B. Guy Peters, 'Political Institutions, Old and New', in R. Goodin and H.-D. Klingemann (note 1), pp. 212–13.

5  See André Kaiser, 'Types of Democracy: from Classical to New Institutionalism', *Journal of Theoretical Politics*, 9 (1997), pp. 419–44.

6  For a discussion of different concepts and definitions of institutions see James G. March and Johan P. Olsen, *Democratic Governance* (New York: Free Press, 1995).

7  See Wolfgang Seibel, 'Historische Analyse und politikwissenschaftliche Institutionenforschung', in Arthur Benz and Wolfgang Seibel (eds), *Theorieentwicklung in der Politikwissenschaft – eine Zwischenbilanz* (Baden-Baden: Nomos, 1997), p. 363.

8  See Gerhard Göhler, 'Wie verändern sich Institutionen? Revolutionärer und schleichender Institutionenwandel', in Gerhard Göhler (ed.), *Institutionenwandel* (Leviathan Sonderheft 16/1996) (Opladen: Westdeutscher Verlag, 1996), p. 27. For a more detailed discussion of the following classifications see also Andrew P. Cortell and Susan Peterson, 'Altered States: Explaining Domestic Institutional Change', *British Journal of Political Science*, 29 (1999), pp. 177–203.

9  Dietrich Herzog, 'Der moderne Berufspolitiker. Karrierebedingungen und Funktion in westlichen Demokratien', *Der Bürger im Staat*, 49 (1990), p. 48.

10  Bert A. Rockman, 'Entrepreneur in the Constitutional Marketplace: the Development of the Presidency', in Peter F. Nardulli (ed.), *The Constitution and American Political Development: An Institutional Perspective* (Urbana/ Chicago: University of Illinois Press, 1992).p. 100.

11  Jeffrey E. Cohen, *Presidential Responsiveness and Public Policy-Making: The Public and the Policies that Presidents Choose* (Ann Arbor: University of Michigan Press, 1997).

12  See Susan Scarrow, 'Party Competition and Institutional Change: the Expansion of Direct Democracy in Germany', *Party Politics*, 3 (1997), pp. 451–91.

13  Johan P. Olsen, 'Analysing Institutional Dynamics', *Staatswissenschaften und Staatspraxis*, 3 (1992), p. 266.

14  See Karlheinz Niclauss, *Der Weg zum Grundgesetz: Demokratiegründung in Westdeutschland, 1945–1949* (Paderborn: Schöningh, 1998).

15  Peter Katzenstein, *Policy and Politics in West Germany: The Growth of a Semisovereign State* (Philadelphia: Temple University Press, 1987).

16  Referendums at the national level may be held only in order to confirm the adoption of a new constitution or in cases of territorial reconstruction of the federal state (Articles 146 and 29 of the Basic Law).

17  Gordon Smith, 'Structures of Government', in Gordon Smith, William E. Paterson and Peter H. Merkl (eds), *Developments in West German Politics* (London: Macmillan, 1989), p. 39.

18  See Wolfgang Renzsch, *Finanzverfassung und Finanzausgleich: die Auseinandersetzungen um ihre politische Gestaltung in der Bundesrepublik Deutschland zwischen Währungsreform und deutscher Vereinigung (1948–1990)* (Bonn: Dietz, 1991); Heiderose Kilper and Roland Lhotta, *Föderalismus in der Bundesrepublik Deutschland* (Opladen: Leske & Budrich, 1996), pp. 183–98.

19  Fritz W. Scharpf, Bernd Reissert and Fritz Schnabel, *Politikverflechtung: Theorie und Empirie des kooperativen Föderalismus in der Bundesrepublik*, 2 vols (Kronberg/Ts.: Scriptor, 1976/77).

20  In stark contrast to the intentions of the founding fathers the share of *'Zustimmungsgesetze'* has come to account for nearly 60 per cent in the 1990s. This has mainly been brought about by the successful expansive interpretation of Article 84 of the Basic Law by the Länder which were supported in their view by the Federal Constitutional Court.

21  See Heidrun Abromeit, *Der verkappte Einheitsstaat* (Opladen: Leske & Budrich, 1992); H. Kilper and R. Lhotta (note 18), pp. 151–5.

22  However, as Braun has argued, there have been signs since the early 1980s of a latent challenge to the dominant tendency towards unitarism. Firstly, the more affluent Länder have developed a more self-assured strategy in pursuing their preferences in a number of policy fields. Furthermore, federal governments since the late Schmidt era have lost their former interest in using 'interlocking federalism' as a means of expanding their steering potential. The latter development signalled the farewell to Keynesianist concepts in the areas of social and economic policy and their gradual replacement by an adoption of supply-side economics. See Dietmar Braun, 'Der bundesdeutsche Föderalismus an der Wegscheide. Interessenkoalitionen, Akteurskonflikte und institutionelle Lösungen', *Staatswissenschaften und Staatspraxis*, 7 (1996), pp. 110–12.

23  Moshe Maor, *Political Parties and Party Systems: Comparative Approaches and the British Experience* (London: Routledge, 1997), p. 44.

24  See Eva Kolinsky, 'Das Parteiensystem der Bundesrepublik: Forschungsthemen und Entwicklungslinien', in Oskar Niedermayer and Richard Stöss (eds), *Stand und Perspektiven der Parteienforschung in Deutschland* (Opladen: Westdeutscher Verlag, 1993), pp. 46–7; Manfred G. Schmidt, 'Allerweltsparteien in Westeuropa? Ein Beitrag zu Kirchheimers These vom Wandel des westeuropäischen Parteiensystems', *Leviathan*, 13 (1985), p. 382.

25   As von Beyme has argued convincingly, the 'cleavage approach' is best suited to explain the structural development of the German party system after 1945. See Klaus von Beyme, *Das politische System der Bundesrepublik Deutschland*, 8th edn (Munich: Piper, 1996), pp. 118–21.

26   See Thomas Saalfeld, *Parteisoldaten und Rebellen: Eine Untersuchung zur Geschlossenheit der Fraktionen im Deutschen Bundestag (1949–1990)* (Opladen: Leske & Budrich, 1995), chapter 6.

27   See Ludger Helms, *Wettbewerb und Kooperation: Zum Verhältnis von Regierungsmehrheit und Opposition im parlamentarischen Gesetzgebungsverfahren in der Bundesrepublik Deutschland, Großbritannien und Österreich* (Opladen: Westdeutscher Verlag, 1997), pp. 56–7.

28   See Gerhard Loewenberg, *Parlamentarismus im politischen System der Bundesrepublik Deutschland* (Tübingen: Wunderlich, 1969), p. 384.

29   For figures see Wolfgang Rudzio, *Das politische System der Bundesrepublik Deutschland*, 4th edn (Opladen: Leske & Budrich, 1996), pp. 384–6.

30   See Klaus H. Goetz and Peter Cullen, 'The Basic Law after Unification: Continued Centrality or Declining Force?', in Klaus H. Goetz and Peter J. Cullen (eds), *Constitutional Policy in Unified Germany* (London: Frank Cass, 1994), p. 27; Klaus König, *Modernisierung von Staat und Verwaltung* (Baden-Baden: Nomos, 1997).

31   See Manfred G. Schmidt, 'Germany: the Grand Coalition State', in Josep M. Colomer (ed.), *Political Institutions in Europe* (London/New York: Routledge, 1996), pp. 81–2.

32   See Heidrun Abromeit, *Interessenvermittlung zwischen Konkurrenz und Konkordanz* (Opladen: Leske & Budrich, 1993), pp. 166–71. There were early signs that the newly elected Schröder goverment put much effort into establishing something of a tripartist negotiation structure in the field of employment policy, the so-called 'alliance for employment' (*Bündnis für Arbeit*).

33   See Martin Sebaldt in this volume.

34   See Roland Roth and Dieter Rucht (eds), *Neue soziale Bewegungen in der Bundesrepublik Deutschland*, 2nd edn (Bonn: Bundeszentrale für politische Bildung, 1991).

35   See Wolfgang Rudzio, 'Informelle Entscheidungsmuster in Bonner Koalitionsregierungen', in Hans-Hermann Hartwich and Göttrik Wewer (eds), *Regieren in der Bundesrepublik II* (Opladen: Leske & Budrich, 1991), pp. 125–41.

36   See Waldemar Schreckenberger, 'Veränderungen im parlamentarischen Regierungssystem: Zur Oligarchie der Spitzenpolitiker der Parteien', in Karl Dietrich Bracher, Paul Mikat, Konrad Repgen, Martin Schumacher and Hans-Peter Schwarz (eds), *Staat und Parteien: Festschrift für Rudolf Morsey zum 65. Geburtstag* (Berlin: Duncker & Humblot, 1992), pp. 133–57; W. Schreckenberger, 'Informelle Verfahren der Entscheidungsvorbereitung zwischen der Bundesregierung und den Mehrheitsfraktionen: Koalitionsgespräche und Koalitionsrunden', *Zeitschrift für Parlamentsfragen*, 25 (1994), pp. 329–46.

37   See Philip Manow, 'Informalisierung und Parteipolitisierung – Zum Wandel exekutiver Entscheidungsprozesse in der Bundesrepublik', *Zeitschrift für Parlamentsfragen*, 27 (1996), pp. 96–107; Gerhard

Lehmbruch, *Parteienwettbewerb im Bundesstaat: Regelsysteme und Spannungslagen im Institutionengefüge der Bundesrepublik Deutschland* (Opladen: Westdeutscher Verlag, 1998), pp. 57–8.

38   See also Günter Bannas, 'Adenauers "Geschwätz von Gestern" heißt bei Schröder "Alles hat seine Zeit"', *Frankfurter Allgemeine Zeitung*, 29 January 1999, p. 3.

39   See Gunter Hofmann, 'Die Versuchs-Regierung', *Die Zeit*, 28 January 1999, p. 3.

40   See Ludger Helms, 'Perspectives on Government and Opposition in Unified Germany', *Politics*, 18 (1998), pp. 151–8.

41   See K. H. Goetz and P. Cullen (note 30).

42   See also Roland Sturm in this volume.

43   See Joanna McKay, 'Berlin–Brandenburg? Nein danke! The Referendum on the Proposed *Länderfusion*', *German Politics*, 5 (1996), pp. 485–502.

44   See Charlie Jeffery, 'The Non-Reform of the German Federal System after Unification', *West European Politics*, 18 (1995), pp. 252–72.

45   See S. Scarrow (note 12).

46   See Andreas Klages and Petra Paulus, *Direkte Demokratie in Deutschland: Impulse aus der deutschen Einheit* (Marburg: Schüren, 1996), pp. 21–143.

47   Ernst Fraenkel, *Deutschland und die westlichen Demokratien*, 7th edn (Frankfurt a.M.: Suhrkamp, 1991), p. 202.

48   For an extensive overview of the more recent literature see Thomas Bulmahn, 'Vereinigungsbilanzen. Die deutsche Einheit im Spiegel der Sozialwissenschaften' *Aus Politik und Zeitgeschichte*, B 40–41/1997, pp. 29–37. and Rolf Reißig, 'Transformationsforschung: Gewinne, Desiderate und Perspektiven', *Politische Vierteljahresschrift*, 39 (1998), pp. 301–28.

49   See Dieter Fuchs, 'Wohin geht der Wandel der demokratischen Institutionen in Deutschland? Die Entwicklung der Demokratievorstellungen der Deutschen seit ihrer Vereinigung', in G. Göhler (note 8), pp. 253–84.

50   K. von Beyme (note 25), p. 11.

51   See for discussion Ludger Helms, 'Gibt es eine Krise des Parteienstaates in Deutschland?', in Wolfgang Merkel and Andreas Busch (eds), *Demokratie in Ost und West: Festschrift für Klaus von Beyme* (Frankfurt a.M.: Suhrkamp, 1999), pp. 435–54.

52   The phenomenon of regionalisation is most obvious at the level of the party systems in the Länder. See Ute Schmidt, 'Sieben Jahre nach der Einheit. Die ostdeutsche Parteienlandschaft im Vorfeld der Bundestagswahlen 1998', *Aus Politik und Zeitgeschichte*, B 1–2/1998, pp. 37–53. For a more detailed assessment of the most recent developments from a historical perspective see Oskar Niedermayer in this volume.

53   See Gordon Smith, 'The Party System at the Crossroads', in Gordon Smith, William E. Patterson and Stephen Padgett (eds), *Developments in German Politics 2* (London: Macmillan, 1996), pp. 64–8.

54   See Stephen Padgett, 'Interest Groups in the Five New Länder', in G. Smith, W. Paterson and S. Padgett (note 53), pp. 233–47.

55   See Roland Czada, 'Vereinigungskrise und Standortdebatte. Der Beitrag der Wiedervereinigung zur Krise des westdeutschen Modells', *Leviathan*, 26 (1998), pp. 24–59; Georg Simonis (ed.), *Deutschland nach der Wende: Neue*

*Politikstrukturen* (Opladen: Leske & Budrich, 1998); Rolf G. Heinze, *Die blockierte Gesellschaft: Sozioökonomischer Wandel und die Krise des 'Modell Deutschland'* (Opladen: Westdeutscher Verlag, 1998).

56   See Klaus von Beyme, *Die politische Klasse im Parteienstaat* (Frankfurt a.M.: Suhrkamp, 1993), pp. 141–6, Table 7.

57   See Lutz Golsch, *Die politische Klasse im Parlament: Politische Professionalisierung von Hinterbänklern im Deutschen Bundestag* (Baden-Baden: Nomos, 1998), p. 129.

58   However, compared to the influence of the Chief Justice at the US Supreme Court or the Speaker of the Swedish *Riksdag* both positions are marked by a rather modest amount of actual decision-making power.

59   See Beate Hoecker, 'Zwischen Macht und Ohnmacht: Politische Partizipation von Frauen in Deutschland', in Beate Hoecker (ed.), *Handbuch Politische Partizipation von Frauen in Europa* (Opladen: Leske & Budrich, 1996), pp. 65–90.

60   See Brigitte Young, 'The Strong German State and the Weak Feminist Movements', *German Politics*, 7 (1998), pp. 128–50.

61   Critics have often argued that the high degree of professionalisation may have negative effects on the political elite's performance in terms of democratic responsiveness. See Günther Rieger, '"Parteienverdrossenheit" und "Parteienkritik" in der Bundesrepublik Deutschland', *Zeitschrift für Parlamentsfragen*, 25 (1994), p. 464.

62   See Th. Saalfeld (note 26), pp. 290–7.

63   See Anthony King, 'The British Prime Minister in the Age of the Career Politician', in G. W. Jones (ed.), *West European Prime Ministers* (London: Frank Cass, 1991), pp. 25–47.

64   See Ludger Helms, 'Das Amt des deutschen Bundeskanzlers in historisch und international vergleichender Perspektive', *Zeitschrift für Parlamentsfragen*, 27 (1996), pp. 708–9; L. Helms, 'Executive Leadership in Parliamentary Democracies: the British Prime Minister and the German Chancellor Compared', *German Politics*, 5 (1996), pp. 101–20.

65   See Wolfgang Jäger, 'Von der Kanzlerdemokratie zur Koordinationsdemokratie', *Zeitschrift für Politik*, 35 (1988), p. 17.

66   See Clay Clemens, 'Party Management as a Leadership Resource: Kohl and the CDU/CSU', *German Politics*, 7 (1998), pp. 91–119; Karl-Rudolf Korte, 'Kommt es auf die Person des Kanzlers an? Zum Regierungsstil von Helmut Kohl in der "Kanzlerdemokratie" des deutschen "Parteienstaates"', *Zeitschrift für Parlamentsfragen*, 29 (1998), pp. 387–401.

67   Stephen Padgett, 'Introduction: Chancellors and the Chancellorship', in Stephen Padgett (ed.), *Adenauer to Kohl: The Development of the German Chancellorship* (London: Hurst & Company, 1994), p. 18.

68   See Ludger Helms, 'Keeping Weimar at Bay: the German Federal Presidency since 1949', *German Politics and Society*, 16 (1998), pp. 62–3.

69   See also Klaus von Beyme in this volume.

70   A notable peculiarity of the German system is to be seen in the fact that until 1998 there was no complete exchange of government and opposition parties at all. This was mainly due to the specific position of the FDP. The first complete exchange of the governing elite was brought about by the most recent federal election of September 1998 by which the

Christian Liberal governing coalition was replaced by a new 'red–green' coalition (SPD and Green Party).

71  See Hans-Ulrich Derlien, 'Repercussions of Government Change on the Career Civil Service in West Germany: the Cases of 1969 and 1982', *Governance*, 1 (1988), pp. 50–78.

72  It is however important to note that there have been intervals, such as the period 1972–82, which were marked by a considerable amount of co-operation despite split party dominance in the Bundestag and Bundesrat. See Camilla Werner, 'Das Dilemma parlamentarischer Opposition', in Dietrich Herzog, Hilke Rebenstorf and Bernhard Weßels (eds), *Parlament und Gesellschaft: Eine Funktionsanalyse der repräsentativen Demokratie* (Opladen: Westdeutscher Verlag, 1993), p. 208.

73  See L. Helms (note 40), pp. 155; G. Lehmbruch (note 37), pp. 171–5.

74  See Wolfgang Renzsch, 'Föderative Problembewältigung: Zur Einbeziehung der neuen Länder in einen gesamtdeutschen Finanzausgleich ab 1995', *Zeitschrift für Parlamentsfragen*, 25 (1994), pp. 134; L. Helms (note 27), pp. 62.

75  See Sabine Kropp and Roland Sturm, *Koalitionen und Koalitionsvereinbarungen: Theorie, Analyse und Dokumentation* (Opladen: Leske & Budrich, 1998), Table 1, pp. 23–9.

76  See Roland Sturm in this volume.

77  M. G. Schmidt (note 31).

78  G. Smith (note 17), p. 29.

79  Manfred G. Schmidt, 'The Parties-Do-Matter-Hypothesis and the Case of the Federal Republic of Germany', *German Politics*, 4 (1995), p. 10.

80  Wolfram F. Hanrieder, *West German Foreign Policy, 1949–1963: International Pressure and Domestic Response* (Stanford: Stanford University Press, 1967), p. 228.

81  See Rudolf Hrbek, 'Die Auswirkungen der EU-Integration auf den Föderalismus in Deutschland', *Aus Politik und Zeitgeschichte*, B 24/1997, pp. 12–21.

82  Beate Kohler-Koch, 'Bundeskanzler Kohl – Baumeister Europas: Randbemerkungen zu einem zentralen Thema' (Mannheim: mimeo, 1998).

83  Klaus Goetz, 'National Governance and European Integration: Intergovernmental Relations in Germany', *Journal of Common Market Studies*, 33 (1995), p. 111.

84  See Uwe Wagschal in this volume.

85  See Ludger Helms in this volume.

86  See Arend Lijphart (ed.), *Parliamentary versus Presidential Government* (Oxford: Oxford University Press, 1992); Fred W. Riggs, 'Presidentialism versus Parliamentarism: Implications for Representativeness and Legitimacy', *International Political Science Review*, 18 (1997), pp. 253–78.

87  Arend Lijphart, *Democracies: Patterns of Majoritarian and Consensus Government in Twenty-One Countries* (New Haven/London: Yale University Press, 1984).

88  Bert A. Rockman, 'Institutions, Democratic Stability, and Performance', in Metin Heper, Ali Kazancigil, and Bert A. Rockman (eds), *Institutions and Democratic Statecraft* (Boulder/Col.: Westview Press, 1997), pp. 11–34.

89  Richard Rose, 'Governments Against Sub-Governments: a European Perspective on Washington', in Richard Rose and Ezra N. Suleiman (eds),

*Presidents and Prime Ministers* (Washington, D.C: American Enterprise Institute, 1980), pp. 284–347.

90 Kenneth A. Shepsle, 'Representation and Governance: the Great Legislative Trade-Off', *Political Science Quarterly*, 103 (1988), pp. 461–84.

91 R. Rose (note 89), p. 288.

92 Dieter Nohlen, *Elections and Electoral Systems*, 2nd edn (New Delhi: Macmillan India Ltd, 1996), p. 87.

93 Over recent decades there have been several failed attempts to change fundamentally the German electoral system. In the 1990s, despite the electoral gains of the post-Communist PDS, support among both politicians and scholars in favour of introducing a plurality system has remained rather modest. See Eckhard Jesse in this volume.

94 The only somewhat more extended period of single-party government in the Federal Republic dates back to 1960/61. There were three other occurrences of single-party government in 1962, 1966 and 1982, all of which lasted for just a few weeks.

95 See Wolfgang C. Müller and Kaare Strøm, 'Koalitionsregierungen in Westeuropa – eine Einleitung', in Wolfgang C. Müller and Kaare Strøm (eds), *Koalitionsregierungen in Westeuropa: Bildung, Arbeitsweise und Beendigung* (Wien: Signum, 1997), p. 10.

96 See H. Abromeit (note 21).

97 What is often overlooked is that 'chancellor democracy' can be and actually has been operationalised in different ways. A general weakening of 'chancellor democracy' characterises the developments within the core executive; see W. Jäger (note 65). However, if 'chancellor democracy' is defined as a model of the political system as a whole – including more general aspects, such as the structure of the party systems – there is much less reason to judge the concept as obsolete; see Karlheinz Niclauss in this volume.

98 See Anthony King, '"Chief Executives" in Western Europe', in Ian Budge and David McKay (eds), *Developing Democracy: Comparative Research in Honour of J. F. P. Blondel* (London: Sage, 1994), p. 153.

99 This becomes particularly clear when the legislative procedure in the Bundestag is studied in comparative perspective. See Ingvar Mattson, 'Private Members' Initiatives and Amendments', in Herbert Döring (ed.), *Parliaments and Majority Rule in Western Europe* (Frankfurt a.M./New York: Campus/St Martin's Press, 1995), pp. 448–87.

100 See Hans-Ulrich Derlien, 'Institutionalising Democracy in Germany: from Weimar to Bonn and Berlin', in M. Heper, A. Kazancigil and B. Rockman (note 88), pp. 145–170. Moreover, the experience of democratic consolidation in the Federal Republic seems to support the thesis that consensual constitution-building reinforces the chances of long-term stability of democratic institutions. See Ali Kazancigil, 'Connecting Political Institutions to Democracy', M. Heper, A. Kazancigil and B. Rockman (note 88), p. 303.

101 See M. Rainer Lepsius, *Interessen, Ideen und Institutionen* (Opladen: Westdeutscher Verlag, 1990), pp. 63–84.

102 Lewis J. Edinger and Brigitte L. Nacos, 'From the Bonn to the Berlin Republic: Can a Stable Democracy Continue?', *Political Science Quarterly*, 113 (1998), p. 190.

103 Stuart Parkes, *Understanding Contemporary Germany* (London/New York: Routledge, 1997), p. 70.
104 See Herbert von Arnim, 'Reformblockade der Politik? Ist unser Staat noch handlungsfähig?', *Zeitschrift für Rechtspolitik*, 31 (1998), pp. 138–47; Werner Patzelt, 'Deutsche Politik unter Reformdruck', in Robert Hettlage and Karl Lenz (eds), *Deutschland nach der Wende: Eine Zwischenbilanz* (Munich: Beck, 1995), p. 80. A critical review of the older literature shows that this tendency to blame the institutional arrangements for the lack of policy innovations is not a new phenomenon of the 1990s. Very similar arguments were put forward in the mid-1980s to explain the absence of a conservative revolution in Germany. See Heidrun Abromeit, 'Mehrheitsdemokratische und konkordanzdemokratische Elemente im politischen System der Bundesrepublik Deutschland', *Österreichische Zeitschrift für Politikwissenschaft*, 18 (1989), p. 165.
105 See Manfred G. Schmidt, 'Learning from Catastrophes. West Germany's Public Policy', in Francis G. Castles (ed.), *The Comparative History of Public Policy* (Cambridge: Cambridge University Press, 1989), pp. 56–99; M. G. Schmidt, *Regieren in der Bundesrepublik Deutschland* (Opladen: Leske & Budrich, 1992).
106 See H. Abromeit (note 105), pp. 178; Joachim Jens Hesse and Thomas Ellwein, *Das Regierungssystem der Bundesrepublik Deutschland*, 8th edn (Opladen: Westdeutscher Verlag, 1997), pp. 434–5.
107 See Peter Pulzer, 'Stabilität und Immobilität', in Wilhelm Bleek and Hans Maull (eds), *Ein ganz normaler Staat? Perspektiven nach 40 Jahren Bundesrepublik* (Munich/Vienna: Piper, 1989), p. 126; Werner Jann, 'Politische Willensbildung und Entscheidungsstrukturen im Prozeß der deutschen Einigung – Im Osten nichts Neues?', in Gerhard Lehmbruch (ed.), *Einigung und Zerfall: Deutschland und Europa nach dem Ende des Ost-West-Konflikts* (Opladen: Leske & Budrich, 1996), pp. 60–1.
108 See for instance Matthias Jung and Dieter Roth, 'Wer zu spät geht, den bestraft der Wähler. Eine Analyse der Bundestagswahl 1998', *Aus Politik und Zeitgeschichte*, B 52/1998, pp. 3–18, Franz Urban Pappi, 'Die Abwahl Kohls. Hauptergebnis der Bundesagswahl 1998?', *Zeitschrift für Politik*, 46 (1999), pp. 1–29.
109 See Hans-Peter Schneider and Wolfgang Zeh, 'Koalitionen, Kanzlerwahl und Kabinettsbildung', in Hans-Peter Schneider and Wolfgang Zeh (eds), *Parlamentsrecht und Parlamentspraxis in der Bundesrepublik Deutschland* (Berlin/New York: de Gruyter, 1989), p. 1309.
110 See Thomas Ellwein and Joachim Jens Hesse, 'Thesen zur Reform der öffentlichen Verwaltung in Deutschland', *Staatswissenschaften und Staatspraxis*, 7 (1996), p. 473.
111 See D. Fuchs (note 49), p. 282.
112 See W. Jann (note 107), p. 66.

# 2
# The Bundestag – Still the Centre of Decision-Making?

*Klaus von Beyme*

## The Bundestag in the institutional setting of the German system

From a comparative perspective the Bundestag has been called the 'most powerful legislature in Europe'.[1] In this context it has been emphasised that the structure of the German parliament became more similar to the American Congress. Indeed, the Bundestag has copied some of the American features of the legislature: the hearings, strong powers of inquiry for parliament, and a sophisticated infrastructure for parliamentary work by increasing the staff which works for the committees. Certainly, the German Bundestag approached the American Congress in creating one of the best documentary and statistical services of parliamentary activities to be found in Western Europe.

But the similarities with the American Congress have limits: 'unelected representatives' with an important impact on the content of the bills did not develop in Germany. More important, the Bundestag works in a parliamentary system. As the government is dependent on parliamentary votes – and, in contrast to most other West European democracies, even formally elected by the parliamentary majority – there has been no strict division of powers in the German parliamentary system. Another crucial difference compared with the American system relates to the powerful position of the parliamentary party groups (*Fraktionen*) in the German Bundestag. Contrary to the situation in the US Congress, the room for manoeuvre for individual deputies is extremely limited, at least as far as the legislative decision-making process and the intra-parliamentary organisation is concerned. The standing orders of the Bundestag do not provide for legislative initiatives of individual members of parliament. Bills emanating from parliament can be introduced only by a parliamentary party group or a group of deputies representing at least 5 per cent of the total of members of the Bundestag (which has been the numerical minimum requirement for parliamentary party groups since 1969).

The German system is – similar to the British system – governed by close co-operation between the majority parliamentary groups and the government. On the one hand this widens the range of governmental action; on the other hand it limits parliamentary control over the government because only in cases of scandals and corruption will the parliamentary majority be prepared to support parliamentary sanctions against individual ministers or the government as a whole. Moreover, individual ministerial responsibility barely exists: there are votes of no-confidence against individual ministers, but they remain meaningless in a system in which the chancellor is the only actor directly responsible to parliament. Ministers are dependent on him and on the coalition agreements. Even strong chancellors, such as Adenauer or Kohl, were frequently unable to dismiss a minister from government if he had the support of the coalition partners or of strong factions within the CDU. The chancellor on the other hand – reluctant to dismiss a minister unpopular with the Bundestag – can rarely be toppled: the 'constructive' vote of no-confidence protects him against parliamentary revolts which even strong British prime ministers have faced from time to time. Moreover, an existing government as well as parliament are protected by the lack of sanctions against negative votes from the parliamentary majority. This contributed to the fact that Germany has one of the most stable governments in the world. In terms of the number of months governments stayed in power (1946–94) Germany (31.8) is only below the level of government stability in some small consociational democracies, such as Luxembourg (43.2) and Austria (32.6).[2] German parliaments – with the two exceptions of 1972 and 1982 when a chancellor asked the question of confidence (Article 68 of the Basic Law) – completed their legal term. Dissolution of parliament was possible, but the negative vote was manipulated in both cases, as the government had to ask parts of the existing majority (approved by a recent majority in a 'constructive' vote of no-confidence) to abstain in order to clear the way for a premature dissolution of the Bundestag. The vote of no-confidence as well as the question of confidence in the German system are distorted because they invite manipulation and carry psychologically detrimental consequences: parts of a coalition seeking to leave the government have to conspire behind the back of the acting chancellor in order to build a new government.

German parliament – according to the wisdom of comparative textbooks – became more American than the British House of Commons because it has been increasingly organised as a 'working parliament'. Plenary sessions play a less important role than in Britain. The entrenched system of parliamentary committees – mostly organised parallel to the ministerial departments since the late 1960s – is the centre of decision-making and opens a lot of influence to networks of interest groups. On the other hand, the Bundestag differs from the American Congress because there is – as in the electoral formula – no principle of 'winner takes all'. The chairpersons of legislative committees are nominated according to the proportional strength of the parliamentary groups. Important committees – and always in the case of the financial committee – are presided over by members of the opposition. Moreover, the standing committees in the Bundestag still generally deliberate legislative measures behind closed doors, although they were authorised in 1969 to decide whether or not to deliberate selected issues publicly. These rules were further relaxed in the latest reform of the parliamentary standing orders in 1995. Since then it has been possible to hold the concluding session of committee deliberations on a particular bill in public.[3]

Contrary to all Anglo-Saxon systems, tendencies of 'co-government' between the governmental parliamentary groups and the opposition have developed. This is at least partly due to the fact that in some policy areas the views of the two major parties – Christian Democrats and Social Democrats – do not differ to the same extent as, for example, the views of the Conservatives and Labour in Britain. Furthermore, a comparative relationship between government and opposition is significantly favoured by a political culture characterised by strong reservations about harsh political disputes and, even more important, an unusually favourable institutional opportunity structure of the political opposition.[4]

As for the latter, the impact of the federal system merits special attention. In comparative textbooks Germany is listed as a two-chamber system, although legally the Bundesrat as the representation of the Länder is not a parliamentary chamber (Article 77,1 of the Basic Law). As a bureaucratic body it is composed of representatives of the Länder governments. Nevertheless, the other chamber has an influence on more than half of the bills which affect the interests of the Länder, and even governmental initiatives in the Bundestag are first transferred to the consideration of the Bundesrat before the Bundestag starts its deliberations. This is one of the reasons why – especially after unification – the government has introduced many bills via its parliamentary groups in order to avoid the time loss caused by a mandatory stage of deliberation in the Bundesrat. Federalism weakens the powers of parliament in Germany. There were periods, such as under the administrations of Schmidt (SPD) and Kohl (CDU), during which the opposition had a majority in the Bundesrat enabling them to block major bills of the Bundestag majority.

The procedure of mediation between the two dissenting legislative bodies has also been copied from the United States. Conference committees served as a model for the German committee of mediation (*Vermittlungsausschuß*). Frequently it manages to find a compromise. But in times of polarisation when the Bundesrat is used by the opposition as an instrument of obstruction of governmental policy (instead of one advocating the interests of the Länder), the deadlock can be virtually permanent. This happened with a number of recent major projects, such as the reform of the tax system or the social insurance system in 1997/98. With the access of the East German Länder, the potential for this politics of obstruction has certainly increased.

To sum up the crucial features of the political setting in which the Bundestag is embedded: it is a powerful legislature despite the fact that Germany with one exception (1957–61) was always forced to accept coalition governments. This is mainly due to the structure of the party system, characterised by comparatively few groups producing clear parliamentary majorities. However, the Bundestag is powerful only when there is 'business as usual'. In major crises it proved to be rather weak. In the spring of 1972, in a situation of deadlock between two equally strong party camps, the Bundestag was virtually powerless. A select committee (*Enquetekommission*) of the Bundestag for constitutional reform came to the conclusion: 'The Bundestag for several months almost did not exist and was not able to fulfil its duties as a steering and controlling institution'.[5] The unification process provided another example of a helpless parliament in Germany.

## Changes of the role of the Bundestag in the balance of powers after unification

*Prima facie*, unification seemed to have had little impact on the role of the Bundestag. Those who had expected that unification would lead to a completely revised constitution with many concessions to the views of the GDR parliamentary majority were disappointed. Not even long-debated changes which former select committees had proposed[6] were possible. The architect of the treaties with the GDR, then Minister of the Interior Wolfgang Schäuble, made it clear from the outset that unification was not to be considered as a good occasion for changes 'which had not been carried through under normal conditions'.[7] Parts of the SPD and the Green Party demanded a referendum on the agreements and blamed the process of unification as a mere process of 'uniting two governmental teams and the fraternisation of two parliaments'.

The constitutional reform of 1994 barely affected the powers of parliament. The West German system was wholesale exported to the East. With a small minority of 18 votes the East Germans were at least able to carry a decision that Berlin and not Bonn became the capital of unified Germany. The debate on this question in June 1991 provided one of the few examples of a high-quality parliamentary debate in the course of German unification, not dominated by party discipline.

Nevertheless, the Bundestag was indirectly affected by three changes in the wider political system: (1) changes in the party system caused by the unification; (2) changes in the balance of powers in the federal system by the access of five new Länder; (3) increasing powers of the executive.

(1) The changes in the party system were not as big as expected. The East Germans had a fairly good knowledge of the parties in the West. Party identification was far lower than in the West, but contrary to other former Communist countries no completely new party system developed in the East.

- The Christian Democrats (CDU/CSU) in Bonn remained in power for two more full legislative terms (until autumn 1998), in a coalition with the Liberals (FDP).
- Between 1983 and 1990 a major shift in the internal power balance of the Bundestag was caused by a new parliamentary player, the Greens. The Green Party in the West failed to conclude an agreement with the Green Alliance (*Bündnis '90*) of the East and did not enter the 11th Bundestag (1990–94). The inexperienced little Eastern Green group was barely able to exert any influence on the policies in Bonn. But in 1994 the Green Party came back more powerful.
- Until the change of government in 1998 there were two main opposition parties, the SPD and Alliance '90/the Greens. Their relationship was marked by competition and rare systematic co-operation at the parliamentary level. After 1994, the Greens were optimistic that the party would be able to increase its potential. But on the Länder

level they failed in some states to pass the 5 per cent threshold and remained weak throughout East Germany. This has also contributed to strengthening the more realistic wing at the expense of the fundamentalists in the party.

- The PDS, the post-Communists, which developed out of the ruling party SED in the GDR, entered the Bundestag after all three post-unification elections. However, only since 1998 has it owned the important official *Fraktion* status which is reserved for parliamentary party groups representing at least 5 per cent of the total of (regular) members of the Bundestag. Still, the PDS is the only party which is not yet considered as being acceptable for a coalition in Bonn or Berlin and, indeed, has looked rather isolated also within the new Conservative-led opposition camp. On the Länder level so far the party was only able to gain some importance in Saxony–Anhalt and, most recently, in Mecklenburg-West Pomerania (where it has formed part of the governing coalition with the Social Democrats). But even the SPD does not consider this as a possibility at the federal level.
- The right-wing extremist parties have never been represented in the Bundestag since the early 1950s, though they cause alarm from time to time in international public opinion by obtaining parliamentary representation in the Länder parliaments. But even there they remained without influence and usually failed to re-enter the diet in the next election.

(2) The role of the Länder increased, altering the balance between Bundestag and Bundesrat. In the 1970s there was the rule that the coalitions in the Länder mainly follow the model at federal level. There used to be few major deviant cases (such as the one-party government in Bavaria) alongside replicas of the Bonn coalition. After 1990 the variety of coalitions increased to eight different models.[8] The majorities in the Bundesrat became less calculable. Not only did the obstruction of SPD opposition governments in the Länder grow; even CDU-led states in the process of unification sometimes developed common interests with the SPD states and obstructed governmental policies which threatened to weaken the Länder.

The bureaucratic nature of the Bundesrat, comprising members of the Länder executive and the strength of bodies outside parliament based on the party state, from coalition committees to round tables with the opposition, have contributed to the deparliamentarisation of the decision-making process. This development was strengthened during the unification process. Concerning the 'solidarity pact' (1993) for East Germany, the federal government had to admit, in the answer to a deputy's question: 'The closed round table for the solidarity pact was an informal meeting for political consensus-building which preceded the parliamentary legislative procedure'.[9] Some authors have postulated that the competition between the parties has been undermined by the competition of the Länder.[10] Unification showed, however, that federalist competition is increasingly used for party purposes.[11] Only in a few decisions, as in the case of constitutional reform, have Länder interests, independent of the party composition of governments, prevailed over party interests. In August 1994 constitutional reform was rejected with the votes of all the 16 Länder which had agreed that they wanted to extend their competencies in legislation on this occasion. The Christian Democrats in power were forced to return to a former compromise with the Christian Democratic Länder governments, and Article 72 of the Basic Law was changed. The federal competence of legislation was accepted 'so far as the creation of equivalent conditions of life on the federal territory or the safeguarding of legal and economic unity [...] makes a federal regulation inevitable'. Even the SPD-governed Länder finally agreed, because the opposition did not want to enter the electoral campaign under the stigma of having vetoed constitutional reform.[12]

The more the legislative competence of the Länder declined, the more active became the federal units in the national legislative process. Amendment proposals by the Länder are an important indicator of this attempt to intervene in the federal legislation. They are most visible in cases of governmental bills and less frequent in cases of parliamentary bills. Quite a few proposals from the Länder are not based on party interest because they are carried by Länder governed by different party constellations.

(3) German unification was the 'hour of the executive'. The national legislator was overburdened. The federal administration had to hand over responsibilities to the Länder bureaucracies. In other cases, when the Länder refused to accept a higher share of the costs of unification, the federation had to take over responsibilities normally vested in the federal units, such as in the field of culture or education. The process became a kind of Keynesianism of unification – against the will of the actors involved. Many tasks were left to parastatal actors such as the trusteeship organisation (*Treuhand*). Other fields were left to non-statal societal actors among the major interest groups, such as the social

security system, health and investment policies of the entrepreneurs and the transformation of large research units of the former GDR.

All the treaties and international agreements to prepare unification were worked out by the federal government. The Bundestag was insufficiently informed.[13] Other changes in the balance of powers were only indirectly shaped by the needs of the integration process of the two Germanys: the Federal Constitutional Court has always had a strong impact on federal legislation. The doctrines of the Constitutional Court have increased not only the number of laws but also the amount of work combined with legislation. The legislator is obliged:

- to investigate the consequences of a law (BVerfGE 50, 334, 65, 55),
- to respect scientific knowledge at any given time, which is problematic in the case of new technologies (BVerfGE 49, 90),
- to offer prognoses about future developments,
- to accept the duty to amend a law after unintended consequences have been recognised (BVerfGE 49, 50).

These principles seemed to strengthen parliament, but in reality increased the influence of the administration and of certain 'think-tanks' advising policy-makers.

Of the key decisions of the Bundestag in the period of 1949–94 about 40 per cent underwent judicial review.[14] But even in cases which did not end up before the Court, the Bundestag showed some 'anticipated obedience' to possible Court sentences.[15] Normally the opposition threatens the coalition government with the announcement that it would 'carry the case to Karlsruhe'. In the accelerated process of unification laws the Court exercised largely 'judicial restraint'. But in many important cases (such as electoral law or certain legal and social measures) the Court intervened on behalf of the East German interests.

The complicated fragmented system in Germany has been dubbed a 'semisovereign state',[16] and specialists of federalism, such as Scharpf, have time and again denounced the incapacity of the German state for innovative action because of the 'traps of intergovernmental decision-making'.[17] Compared to these doomsday scenarios the German system reacted quite efficiently to the new needs after unification. But this was hardly due to a leading role of parliament.

## Changes in the working style of the Bundestag

So far it is difficult to say whether the working style of the Bundestag has been changed by unification. Only in some respects is the answer clearly 'yes'. As a consequence of the emergence of new parties the seniority of the deputies decreased. The trend will probably prove to be transitory. More parties caused more conflicts: roll-call analysis reveals that after 1990 there were more controversial decisions and fewer unanimous votes on laws. Recently there have been more personal declarations before votes are taken. But all these trends started as early as 1983 when the Green Party entered the Bundestag.

*Prima facie* the Bundestag was deeply involved in the process of integration of the former GDR. In the 12th legislature (1990–94)[18] the number of bills which became law (507) almost reached the level of the 1st Bundestag (1949–53) under Adenauer's government, which had to substitute most of the Nazi legislation (545). One-fifth of these laws were proposed by parliamentary party groups, which was above the average for the 1980s. But the formal procedure confounds the interpretation. There was little truly parliamentary initiative behind these parliamentary proposals. The government used its parliamentary groups to avoid delays in the Bundesrat (for the reasons see above). The German figures in the statistics of the Interparliamentary Union – widely used in comparative studies – are also misleading because of the peculiarities of the 'one-and-a-half-chamber-system'. The number of laws increased after unification. But Germany is still in the middle field of Western countries – far behind the United States, Italy and even small countries such as Austria, Denmark, the Netherlands or Sweden, but above the United Kingdom.[19]

If we look at the subjects of regulation by the Bundestag the greatest proportion dealt with regulations of the integrational process after unification. The Bundestag has rarely initiated one of these measures. It frequently served as a rubber-stamp institution for accelerated governmental action. The speed of legislation in the aftermath of German unification was quite unusual. Rarely have so many bills been promulgated within a few days as in the case of the unification laws.[20] Only in the case of the law on recompensations, a law with redistributive aspects not only for East Germans but also for West Germans, was the speed of legislation lowered. Many measures taken in great haste proved to be symbolic legislation which did not really work out. Thus, the type of 'speeding up-legislation' (*Beschleunigungsgesetze*) – which developed first in the field of immigration and anti-terrorism legislation in the 1980s – was increasingly applied. Moreover, parliament in these cases rarely had time to plan and to deliberate pending decisions.

The usual practice of innovative legislation to schedule public hearings was – most notably in the field of foreign policy – frequently suspended. Supposedly there were no experts who could recommend how integration of two social systems of great divergence was best to be achieved. Indeed, the unusual transformation process encouraged executive decision-making without careful scientific policy advice. Frequently the experts in this process were wrong in their forecasts: almost all economists, for example, agreed that the sudden transfer of the West German currency to East Germany would cause an economic collapse (which was partly correct for the Eastern industries, but not for the West) and enormous inflation in the whole country. The latter assumption proved to be wrong. Eight years after unification, German inflation came down to the quite unusual figure of 1 per cent.

German unification in its impact on parliament cannot really be isolated from another process which weakens the Bundestag, namely European integration. Germany deliberately tried to pacify the critics of the speedy unification process by becoming a torchbearer of the Maastricht round of European unification. In spite of this deliberate option, German policies do not always comply with European norms. To an increasing extent, parliamentary laws have to be changed because of judgements of the European Court of Justice.

The impact of Europe is also felt by the increasing influence on parliamentary initiatives and governmental bills. As early as in 1987 (11th legislature) one-fifth of the laws were actually initiated in Brussels; during the 12th legislature the figures reached 100 per cent in communication and service, 75 per cent in environmental policy.[21] If this tendency of Europeanisation was slightly declining after 1990 it was only a statistical artefact due to the circumstance that, after unification, the number of purely national regulations rose for a limited period of time.

Since 1990 the growing number of parties in the Bundestag has favoured increased internal conflicts in parliament. The times until 1983, when a three-party system worked fairly smoothly, were already gone before unification. New parties and new types of conflicts in a budding national state – not accepted by all the deputies – created new patterns of oppositional legislative behaviour. The SPD was torn to pieces in the decision-making process concerning the Unification Treaty (1990), the federal electoral law, and other major bills. 'The economic and social union' of the two German states (1990) even caused 25 negative votes in the SPD.[22] The strain on the SPD caused by the Green co-opposition was not even mitigated by the fact that the West German Green Party failed to be represented in the 12th Bundestag because it missed its chance to find an ally for a list of coalitions.

The Christian Democrats also had some problems with German unification: 13 CDU members voted against the Unification Treaty (1990). The SPD failed to vote unanimously in the decisions on asylum-seekers (1993) and the 'structural reform of the health care system' (1992). In the 12th legislature (1990–94), the PDS usually acted as the fundamental opposition unanimously voting against the unification laws. This forced the SPD in some cases to reduce its own misgivings and to carry the Christian Democrats' legislation. In such cases as the 'investment and privatisation law' the SPD helped the government by abstention, though it did not approve the basic neo-capitalist tendency of the bill. In questions of *Weltanschauung* (capital Berlin 1991; abortion 1992, 1994), even the post-Communist PDS did not achieve unanimity.

The times when the SPD, according to the Lowell index, achieved a score of 100 per cent (6th and 9th Bundestag) were gone. The Christian Democrats had a similar degree of cohesion in the 9th and 10th legislatures (1980–87). Even the 93.6 per cent achieved by the CDU in the history of the Bundestag since 1957 and the 96 per cent homogeneity of the SPD up to the 10th legislature (1983–87), according to the Rice index, were no longer possible after unification.[23] But on the whole – and especially when compared to the United States – party discipline is still remarkably high and even among the Liberals never fell below 87 per cent. Therefore there is no justification for taking declining party discipline as a symptom of crisis. In some respects the recent trends are a unique consequence of unification. In other respects it could be said that Germany, which found it difficult after the Second World War to accept deviant behaviour and to learn to live with a higher degree of 'disorder', came more into line with other democratic political systems.

## Interest group regimes and parliamentary decisions

Like other democratic parliaments the Bundestag has a highly specific network of decision-making. In Germany there is not only a 'cosy triangle' of parliamentarians, interest group representatives and bureaucrats, but an 'uncosy pentangle' which includes the representatives of the Länder making party leaders the most important link in the process of legislative decision-making.

The existence of interest group regimes means that Germany as a whole cannot be categorised as a corporatist country. In some policy areas there is indeed 'symmetric dualism' as described in corporatist textbooks. Most of the time class politics in Germany, however, leads to 'asymmetric dualism' (for instance, in the area of economic, housing and environmental policies). In some fields there is even a double corporatism of the partners of class conflict as well as of major status groups (property owners vs. tenants, privileged status groups vs. clients of social groups and organisations of the damaged and handicapped underprivileged in society). In some areas pluralism and corporatism are competing as a model of interest representation. Oligopolistic status group pluralism prevails in almost one-quarter of the decisions. Pluralism with a great variety of interests and free access to many groups is fairly rare. The 'American' type of true pluralism with access even for promotional groups and weak new social movements is found only in a minority of policy decisions.[24]

In Germany, policies do not determine politics in the same way as Lowi developed it as a hypothesis for the United States,[25] although this does happen in economic policy with its preponderance of symmetrical and asymmetrical forms of corporatism. Promotional groups show their dominance in legal policy in which few interests intervene and advocacy politics is demanded for underprivileged and little-represented interests. There is an affinity between policy areas and regimes of interest representation in only about one-third of the decisions – not a very strong correlation. Among the types of decision the connection between distributive and redistributive decisions and an oligopolistic type of status politics by powerful organisations is strong. True pluralism with a dominance of promotional groups is concentrated in the field of protective measures, which regulates by distributing considerable amounts of transfers.[26]

Pressure group politics in a literal sense is rare. It was common in the consolidation phase of the Federal Republic and revived during the students' rebellion. Trade unions in Germany were important influence-seekers but were very rarely lured onto the road of pressure and politically motivated strikes.

## Parliamentary government in a changing society

The power of 'co-powers' has grown.[27] This has caused counter-movements within parliament. The capacity of parliamentary self-steering has been strengthened by the parliamentary parties. An oligarchic state of coalition parties – with elements of co-government of the opposition – was the response to the decline of direct representation of constituencies by individual deputies. The party state has increasingly been criticised. It is time to recognise its positive role for the revitalisation of parliamentary government.

The oligarchic party establishment is becoming more independent from the party members and voters, but compensates this autonomy by increasing responsiveness. Parties in power try to transform their programmes and party platforms into political reality. This does not mean, however, that politicians always follow the changing fashions of the electorate's will. In most of the innovative legislation – for example the vote against capital punishment (1952), reforms of penal law, emergency laws, national census and gene technology – the people's will, as documented in surveys, has deliberately been ignored. Social movements have been able to mobilise against a law, as occurred with the law on a national census 1987 (1985), but the boycotts were followed only by 3 per cent of the population (however, enough to distort the results). In other fields in which a great majority of the voters is really interested (for example the anti-terrorism laws; limiting the number of asylum-seekers), the legislator tended to adopt a reactive and populist attitude.

On the whole, parliament has skilfully balanced on the tightrope between the Scylla of populist reactiveness and the Charybdis of innovative activism without losing touch with the electorate. Nevertheless, the normative literature on democracy has been dissatisfied with the results of the political process and has proposed letting people decide in sub-political units – under conditions where organised interests and bureaucracies do not paternalise the 'people's will'. The danger that an extension of the decision-makers will lead to an inflation of demands for participation has not been overlooked.[28] The torchbearers of sub-politicisation, such as Ulrich Beck, are aware that 'sub-politicisation may lead to a general powerlessness'.[29] More successful was the maintenance of the central decision-making networks, but at the same time mobilising advocacy politics for those groups not represented in central decision-making.

Parliamentary democracy lives under the paradox that the capacity of the state to control society is decreasing, whilst the number of citizens who demand actions by the state is increasing. Even absolutist rulers would not have dared to intervene so frequently in the economy, and certainly they would never have considered that 'matrimonial violation' ought to be regulated by law (as Germany did in 1998). Politics is a 'forum for action under conditions of trial and error'. Parliament is best suited to serve physically as the 'forum' of tentative action under conditions of uncertainty.

The results of actions – in terms of laws – are mostly full of contra-
dictions. In disputes about the logic of a law the 'legislator's will' is
still invoked by jurists, although everybody knows that there was no
uniform will of a legislator when the law was created. But despite the
scepticism of autopoietic systems theory, the state acts continuously,
although the steering capacity of parliament is limited. To use a
metaphor of navigation: the ship of the state does not precisely drop
anchors at the provided place, but it does not bob up and down on
the same spot either. Post-modern theories consider parliamentary
decisions under conditions of uncertainty mostly as symbolic politics
which are purely and simply reactions to the demands of citizens
who think that 'the state should act'. If steering of the state is successful, parliament only sets a framework for action. In many cases
the details of controlling society are left to the courts and to the
administration.

## Conclusion

During the first four decades of its existence the Bundestag adopted
institutional features both of the American Congress (such as the
strong position of the standing committees and the sophisticated
infrastructure of parliamentary work) and the British House of
Commons (such as parliamentary question time and other devices of
parliamentary control). Altogether, institutional reforms of the
Bundestag in the 'old' Federal Republic remained rather modest, oriented towards careful functional refinement and adaptation of the
existing structures rather than sweeping institutional innovation.
Also unification brought little institutional change to the Bundestag.
The modest reduction of the total number of MPs from 656 to 598
(from 2002 onwards), passed in 1996 after lengthy discussions, stands
out as the most visible institutional reform of the Bundestag in the
more recent past. However, there was a change of party conflict and
dispute settling in the federal system which deeply affected the
working style of parliament. Some of these changes were due to
unification, some of them have developed already since 1983 when
the Green Party entered the Bundestag changing the balance of
power between the 'established' parties. Other changes are due to the
process of Europeanisation of politics which undermined the power
of the Bundestag by strengthening the Länder on the one hand and
the executive on the other hand.

# Notes

1 Joel D. Aberbach, Robert D. Putnam and Bert A. Rochman, *Bureaucrats and Politicians in Western Democracies* (Cambridge, Mass.: Harvard University Press, 1981), p. 231.

2 Data compiled after Jan-Erik Lane, David MacKay and Kenneth Newton (eds), *Political Data Handbook: OECD Countries*, 2nd edn (Oxford: Oxford University Press, 1997), pp. 123–5; Klaus von Beyme, *Parlament und Regierung. Die Demokratisierung der parlamentarischen Systeme* (Opladen: Westdeutscher Verlag, 1999), Chapter 7e.

3 See on this and other components of the latest revision of the Bundestag's standing orders Thomas Saalfeld, 'The German Bundestag: Influence and Accountability in a Complex Environment', in Philip Norton (ed.), *Parliaments and Governments in Western Europe* (London: Frank Cass, 1998), pp. 68–9.

4 For an empirical assessment of the interplay of these factors in post-unification Germany see Ludger Helms, 'Perspectives on Government and Opposition in Unified Germany', *Politics*, 18 (1998), pp. 151–8.

5 See *Beratungen und Empfehlungen zur Verfassungsreform. Schlußbericht der Enquetekommission: Verfassungsreform des Deutschen Bundestages*, vol. 1: *Parlament und Regierung* (Bonn: Presse- und Informationszentrum des Deutschen Bundestages), p. 21.

6 See *Beratungen* (note 5), vol. 2.

7 Wolfgang Schäuble, *Der Vertrag: Wie ich über die deutsche Einheit verhandelte* (Stuttgart: DVA, 1991), p. 136.

8 See Klaus von Beyme, *The Legislator: German Parliament as a Centre of Decision-Making* (Aldershot: Ashgate, 1998), p. 97.

9 See *Stenographische Berichte über die Verhandlungen des Deutschen Bundestages*, 12. Wahlperiode, p. 4649.

10 See Gerhard Lehmbruch, *Parteienwettbewerb im Bundesstaat* (Stuttgart: Kohlhammer, 1976), p. 160.

11 See Heidrun Abromeit, *Interessenvermittlung zwischen Konkurrenz und Konkordanz* (Opladen: Leske & Budrich, 1993), p. 12.

12 See Helge-Lothar Batt, *Die Grundgesetzreform nach der deutschen Einheit* (Opladen: Leske & Budrich, 1996), p. 95.

13 See K. von Beyme (note 8), pp. 117–18.

14 *Ibid.*, p. 108.

15 See Christine Landfried, *Bundesverfassungsgericht und Gesetzgeber*, 2nd edn (Baden-Baden: Nomos, 1996).

16 Peter Katzenstein, *Policy and Politics in West Germany: The Growth of a Semisovereign State* (Philadelphia: Temple University Press, 1987).

17 Fritz W. Scharpf, *Optionen des Föderalismus in Deutschland und Europa* (Frankfurt a.M.: Campus, 1994).

18 The statistics for the 13th legislature 1994–98 are not yet available.

19 See Rudy B. Andeweg and Lia Nijzink, 'Beyond the Two-Body-Image: Relations between Ministers and MPs', in Herbert Döring (ed.), *Parliaments and Majority Rule in Western Europe* (Frankfurt a.M.: Campus/New York: St Martin's Press, 1995), pp. 152–78, 171; K. von Beyme (note 2), Chapter 5.3.

20  Important examples include the change of the Foreign Trade Law, June 1990; State Treaty with the GDR, June 1990; Solidarity Law, May/June 1991; Law on the Federal Consolidation Programme, June 1993; Law on Recompensations, May–September 1994.

21  See Anette E. Töller, *Europapolitik im Bundestag: Eine empirische Untersuchung zur europapolitischen Willensbildung im EG-Ausschuß des 12. Deutschen Bundestages* (Frankfurt a.M.: Lang, 1995), p. 47.

22  See *Stenographische Berichte über die Verhandlungen des Deutschen Bundestages*, 11. Wahlperiode, 21 June 1990, pp. 17281, 17355.

23  See Thomas Saalfeld, *Parteisoldaten und Rebellen. Fraktionen im Deutschen Bundestag 1949–1990* (Opladen: Leske & Budrich, 1995), p. 109.

24  See Klaus von Beyme, 'Interest Groups in the German Bundestag', *Government & Opposition*, 33 (1998), pp. 38–55.

25  Theodore J. Lowi, 'American Business, Public Policy, Case Studies, and Political Theory', *World Politics*, 17 (1964), pp. 677–715.

26  See K. von Beyme (note 8), pp. 32–3.

27  See Heinrich Oberreuter (ed.), *Parlamentsreform* (Passau: Passavia, 1981), p. 17.

28  See Rainer Schmalz-Bruns, *Reflexive Demokratie* (Baden-Baden: Nomos, 1995), p. 250.

29  Ulrich Beck, *Die Erfindung des Politischen* (Frankfurt a.M.: Suhrkamp, 1993), p. 233.

# 3

# The Federal Presidency: Parameters of Presidential Power in a Parliamentary Democracy

*Wolfgang Rudzio*

## Introduction

The first experiment with a democratic presidency had been a traumatic one in German history. It consisted of the election of the former Field Marshall Paul von Hindenburg in 1925 as *Reichspräsident* who later used his authority in a fatal way, culminating in the appointment of Hitler as *Reichskanzler* and the enacting of the '*Reichstag* fire emergency decree' (*Reichtagsbrand-Notverordnung*) of 28 February 1933 (by which numerous basic rights were invalidated). The view predominates until today that the granting of extensive powers to the president in the Weimar Republic was a structural mistake which had 'fatal implications'.[1]

As a result, in the 1948/49 deliberations on a new German constitution the opinions converged that no powerful presidency should rise again. The framers of the Basic Law opted in favour of a pure parliamentary form of government, in which the federal president received only a weak position. This can be considered the most important institutional consequence from the fall of the Weimar Republic. In general, the federal president is viewed as a powerless figure with mere representative functions – a 'dignified part' of the constitution, as Bagehot has called it.[2]

Therefore, it could seem superfluous to deal with the German presidency at all. However, at second glance it will become clear that the widespread view of this position requires some rectification or at least differentiation. This applies to the *Reichspräsident* in the Weimar Republic as well as to the federal president in the German post-war democracy.

## The *Reichspräsident*: a fatal element in the constitution?

Under the Weimar Constitution of 1919 the *Reichspräsident* indeed had a powerful position. He was elected directly by the people and thus enjoyed a democratic legitimacy independent of parliament. He represented the state at the international level, was commander in chief, appointed and dismissed the *Reichskanzler*, civil servants as well as ministers (the latter at the chancellor's proposals). He promulgated laws and was authorised to dissolve parliament. Furthermore, he could take 'measures' for the restoration of public security and order as stipulated in Article 48.[3]

However, the president was not really free in his decisions as they had to be countersigned by the chancellor or one of the ministers (Article 50). Normally this meant only a formal role of the president. In addition, measures taken by the president on the basis of Article 48 could be overruled by parliament; a chancellor appointed by him could be dismissed by a parliamentary no-confidence vote. Hence, the Weimar Republic was a semi-presidential democracy, similar to that of the Fifth French Republic or the successor states of the Soviet Union.

The position of the *Reichspräsident* did not emerge from a 'German' authoritarian way of thinking, as its frequent characterisation as 'substitute emperor' (*Ersatzkaiser*) would suggest. On the contrary, it resulted from liberal conceptions of a constitution (Hugo Preuß, Max Weber) and was welcomed particularly by the democratic parties. It was assumed that a strong president could help to overcome the inner conflicts of the German party system and to reduce the problems arising from proportional representation. The intention was to safeguard the new democracy's ability to act.[4]

Indeed, the *Reichspräsident* had for a considerable period of time a supporting effect on the German democracy. This does not only apply to the first incumbent, the Social Democrat Friedrich Ebert (1919–25), but also – up to May 1932 – to his conservative successor von Hindenburg (1925–34). Even in 1932, at a time when the democratic parties had already been in the minority, Hindenburg at least prevented Hitler from becoming president or chancellor. Thus, the *Reichspräsident* performed functions of a 'protector of the constitution'.[5]

Facing unreliable or non-existent parliamentary majorities, both presidents guarded governments with a potential to act, but nevertheless made extensive use of their own powers. In particular they enacted emergency decrees instead of laws by interpreting the constitution liberally.[6] This was done to accomplish unpopular decisions which the government considered necessary in view of inflation or world economic crisis, for which, however, parliamentary approval could not be achieved. The *Reichstag* repealed very few of these emergency decrees.

Even the combined application of presidential powers – the appointment of the chancellor, the enactment of emergency decrees and the dissolution of parliament – had a stabilising effect initially. As early as 1924 Ebert dissolved the *Reichstag* when it objected to an emergency tax decree. After 1930, when parliamentary majorities could no longer be achieved, Hindenburg pursued this path further. He appointed Heinrich Brüning (*Zentrum*) *Reichskanzler* (1930–32), promised him to sign any decrees which Brüning should consider necessary, and was even prepared to dissolve the *Reichstag* if the chancellor requested this. Thus, Hindenburg 'performed the functions of a *Reichspräsident* in crisis', as Kaltefleiter has rightly assessed this action.[7] Even though helpful for government functioning, this meant a 'presidential regime' in which the president took up the most powerful position while the chancellor became dependent on him. The breathing space, which the threatened democracy had been given by the presidency, ended when an abrupt change occurred in Hindenburg's actions after May 1932. Then the decisions of the now 85-year-old and authoritarian inspired president actually became fatal for democracy.

In retrospect the role of the *Reichspräsident* seems to have been of a contradictory nature: on the one hand his powerful position helped significantly in facing major challenges, thereby contributing significantly to the Weimar Republic surviving for 14 years.[8] On the other hand the president's powerful position made it easier for parliament and the political parties to avoid unpopular decisions (which were consequently made by the president). In times of crisis virtually everything depended on presidential actions.

## The federal president: deprivation of power as a consequence of Weimar

As stated above, the constituent Parliamentary Council (*Parlamentarischer Rat*) decided in 1948/49 against a strong president. Certainly the federal president was granted functions of a head of state, such as representing the country at the international level, appointing (or dismissing) civil servants, officers and (at the chancellor's proposal) ministers, as well as promulgating laws. But he performs only a formal role, as he needs the countersignature (and by this the approval) of government members. Moreover, his position is reduced compared with that of the

*Reichspräsident* as he is not elected directly by the people and is neither commander in chief nor authorised to enact emergency decrees. Only in a situation in which a parliamentary majority does not exist, can the president make decisions by himself (Articles 54–61, 63–64, 65a, 67–68, 81–82 of the Basic Law).

Despite the weak office powers the position of federal president has been filled by the respective political majority according to partisan and coalition-political considerations. The president is to be elected by the Federal Assembly (*Bundesversammlung*), consisting of the members of parliament and an equal number of representatives of the 16 state parliaments. An overview of the incumbents since 1949 and their election is given in Table 3.1.

All of the promising candidates were politicians, and all of the elected presidents had been members of parliament and of government (the latter with the exception of Carstens[9]) before taking over the presidency. Two of the federal presidents left the position of party chairman (Heuss, Scheel) when elected to the presidency, three the position of ministers (Lübke, Heinemann, Scheel). Two incumbents (Rau and Weizsäcker) had been head of a state government before being elected, one (Carstens) president of the Bundestag and one (Herzog) president of the Federal Constitutional Court. Thus, only Carstens, Herzog and, in a way, the present incumbent Rau – who retired as minister president of North Rhine-Westphalia as early as spring 1998, a full year before the presidential election of 1999 – were elected from positions which stood out from the daily political struggle.

Perhaps the most remarkable feature of the 1999 presidential election was the nomination by one of the two major parties of a candidate not belonging to any party. The Christian Democrats nominated Professor Dagmar Schipanski, a respected scientist from Thuringia who was not a member of the CDU. Observers were divided over the motives behind this nomination. While some praised the CDU's courage to support a female 'outsider' from one of the new Eastern Länder, others dismissed this as a populist strategy taking into account the very low likeliness for a CDU candidate to be elected by a 'red-green'-dominated Federal Assembly.

In general the presidents owe their first election to a government majority (1969: *in statu nascendi*), and in many cases they defeated their opponents only by a whisker. The 1979 presidential election marked the only occasion an opposition candidate was elected, since at that moment the opposition had the majority in the Federal Assembly. Quite out of the ordinary was the situation in 1984 when Weizsäcker

Table 3.1    Incumbents and candidates for the federal presidency
(1949–99)

| Election year | Elected candidate | Number of votes (ballot) | Members of the Federal Assembly | Major opponent |
|---|---|---|---|---|
| 1949 | Prof. Theodor Heuss 1884–1963, FDP, publicist/lecturer | 416 (2nd ballot) | 804 | Dr Kurt Schumacher, SPD |
| 1954 | (re-election) | 871 (1st ballot) | 1018 | Prof. Alfred Weber |
| 1959 | Heinrich Lübke 1894–1972, CDU, engineer/ secretary farmers association | 526 (2nd ballot) | 1038 | Prof. Carlo Schmid, SPD |
| 1964 | (re-election) | 710 (1st ballot) | 1042 | Ewald Bucher, FDP |
| 1969 | Dr Gustav Heinemann 1899–1976, SPD, company lawyer, manager | 512 (3rd ballot) | 1036 | Dr Gerhard Schröder, CDU |
| 1974 | Walter Scheel 1919– , FDP, chief executive | 530 (1st ballot) | 1036 | Dr Richard von Weizsäcker, CDU |
| 1979 | Prof. Karl Carstens 1914–92, CDU, professor, permanent secretary | 528 (1st ballot) | 1036 | Annemarie Renger, SPD |
| 1984 | Dr Richard von Weizsäcker, 1920–,CDU, legal adviser, manager | 832 (1st ballot) | 1040 | Luise Rinser (for the Green Party) |
| 1989 | (re-election) | 881 (1st ballot) | 1038 | — |

Table 3.1 Continued

| Election year | Elected candidate | Number of votes (ballot) | Members of the Federal Assembly | Major opponent |
|---|---|---|---|---|
| 1994 | Prof. Roman Herzog 1934– , CDU, professor | 696 (3rd ballot) | 1324 | Johannes Rau, SPD |
| 1999 | Johannes Rau 1931–, SPD, publisher | 690 (2nd ballot) | 1338 | Prof. Dagmar Schipanski (for the CDU/CSU) |

*Sources:* Peter Schindler, *Datenhandbuch zur Geschichte des Deutschen Bundestages, 1949–1982* (Baden-Baden: Nomos, 1983), pp. 934–5; Peter Schindler, *Datenhandbuch zur Geschichte des Deutschen Bundestages 1983–1991* (Baden-Baden: Nomos, 1994); pp. 1215; Ludger Helms, 'Keeping Weimar at Bay: the German Federal Presidency since 1949', *German Politics and Society,* 16 (1998), pp. 55; *Munzinger Archiv.*

met no serious opponent. As for the re-election of a president, it can be stated that in general these men received a wide majority, which may be attributed to the aura surrounding this office as well as to tactical motives. In 1964 the Social Democrats in opposition supported the CDU candidate Lübke, intending to pave the way for a Grand Coalition.

## The federal president in normal times: no more than a rubber stamp?

The considerable interest in this office which the parties have shown to have may be attributed to the fact that the president is usually held in high public esteem. Regarding his political influence the answer is more difficult. Whereas – at least according to the (somewhat simplified) assessment of some observers – the first president, Heuss, showed 'bad nerves' during the term of the powerful Chancellor Konrad Adenauer, so that the federal president was considered a friendly public speaker without any powers,[10] subsequent presidents filled the position differently and tested its limits. The question arises to what extent there exist presidential powers.

We will first analyse the president's role in normal times, i.e. when clear parliamentary majorities exists. In principle all his orders and decisions need to be countersigned by members of government, who in this way take parliamentary responsibility for political decisions.

Moreover, the president cannot nominate any candidate for the chancellery independently, as no-one can become chancellor without being elected by parliament. The Bundestag even may elect a candidate who has not been nominated by the president. The appointment and dismissal of a chancellor depend on preceding parliamentary elections. Thus the president essentially functions as a 'state notary' (Roman Herzog) or an 'attester' (Klaus Stern).[11]

This fits well into the model of parliamentary government. The role of the German president seems to be similar to that of the English queen. However, the question arises: Does the federal president really have to sign everything that is put before him, just like a rubber stamp? Or may he refuse to sign a document and in this way block decisions?

His refusal could cause a delicate situation, because he may be sued at the Federal Constitutional Court. Nevertheless, on some occasions in the history of the Federal Republic presidents tried to exceed the limits outlined above. The arguments they raised fall into one of the following categories:

- *Formal–legal objections against a decision*: in principle these are undisputed and have been raised successfully in some legislative cases.

  In this way the president may refuse to appoint a chancellor who was not elected in compliance with electoral regulations or is an enemy of the constitution;[12] the same applies to federal ministers and civil servants. Such cases have not occurred so far, but there have been some bills the president refused to sign: in 1962 Lübke refused to sign a special law concerning trade (because it violated the basic right to free choice of profession); in 1976 Scheel dismissed a bill facilitating conscientious objection (because the Bundesrat had not approved it);[13] and in 1991 Weizsäcker did not promulgate a bill on privatisation of air traffic control, arguing that this subject was a sovereign task to be met by civil servants.[14] In all these cases the Bundestag and Bundesrat accepted these refusals without raising objections, and refrained from filing suit with the Constitutional Court. The laws were not enacted.[15]

- *Moral objections*: there is much controversy and disagreement about repudiations on grounds of moral principles and style.

  At the political level only one precedent case has occurred: in 1953 President Heuss objected to the re-appointment of Thomas Dehler (FDP) as Minister of Justice, arguing that he had attacked the Federal Constitutional Court in an impertinent, rude way. As a result of this Chancellor Adenauer gave up Dehler. In addition to this the first two presidents successfully prevented promotions of some civil servants and a judge by raising political and moral objections; most of the nominees had a National Socialist past.[16]

More recently there have been no examples of the president acting in the capacity of a protector of political style.[17] It seems that this function has decreased in importance to the same degree as the distance from the Third Reich has increased.

- *The president may not refuse to sign a bill for simple political reasons.* This is regarded as exceeding his powers.

Of course, in confidential talks the federal president is free to raise political objections. If he is on good terms with the chancellor he may exert some political influence this way. However, when in 1961 and 1963 President Lübke persistently refused to sign the appointment of Gerhard Schröder (CDU) as Foreign Minister on grounds of his 'atlantic' orientation (in contrast with an orientation towards Gaullist France), as well as the appointment of Werner Schwarz (CDU) as Minister of Agriculture, arguing the latter favoured specific interests, he had to give in at last and sign the appointments. There were also other occasions on which Lübke tried to exceed his authority: he made several attempts (which also affected the chancellor nomination) to bring about a Grand Coalition (CDU/CSU-SPD).[18] He gained only a consolation prize in 1965/66 when achieving some choice in the appointment of members of the advisory Education Council.[19]

Hence Lübke must be considered the incumbent who sought most eagerly to participate in decision-making and eventually failed. This must not be attributed to his limited rhetorical gift, or signs of advanced age, but rather to the principle of parliamentary government ruling out such presidential claims. Since then, presidents have refrained from making similar attempts. The task of the president in the promulgation procedure continues to be restricted to formal and legal aspects.

## The federal president as a reserve power in times of crisis

However, as also the explosiveness of the *Reichspräsident*'s powers became apparent only in times of crisis, the question as to which role the federal president could come to play, in a crisis, is of great importance.

In the Basic Law a distinction is made between two types of 'crises':

- An external state of emergency, in which parliament is unable to assemble. Then the powers of the Bundestag and Bundesrat are transferred to a 'Joint Committee'. Contrary to the Weimar Republic, the president stays out of the political process in such a situation.
- The lack of parliamentary majorities. If this situation arises, i.e. if the heart of parliamentary government stops beating, the president becomes a powerful political player.

Two instances of such a parliamentary crisis are mentioned in the Basic Law:

- In the third ballot the candidate for the chancellorship has only achieved a relative majority in parliament. In this case the president makes the free decision whether to appoint him as chancellor or to dissolve the Bundestag (Article 63 of the Basic Law).
- An incumbent chancellor asks for a vote of confidence in parliament, which is refused. If the Bundestag does not immediately elect a successor, and the chancellor suggests the dissolution of parliament, it is for the president to decide whether or not to follow this suggestion (Article 68 of the Basic Law).

In both cases the president has to decide what is more likely to lead the country out of the crisis: premature elections or a government led by a minority chancellor. If political situations such as those in 1930–33 were to arise again, the president would have to make major political decisions.

So far such critical situations have not occurred in the Federal Republic. Nevertheless, there have been two instances of a vote of confidence, both of which were rejected. In 1972 Chancellor Brandt's majority in parliament had crumbled but the chancellor candidate of the CDU, Barzel, did not achieve a majority vote either. Brandt (SPD) sought the following way out: he asked for a vote of confidence and induced the members of government to abstain, thus bringing about his own defeat. Then he suggested to the president that parliament should be dissolved. Certainly this was somewhat tricky, but considering the parliamentary stalemate this procedure could appear acceptable. Hence, the decision of President Heinemann (SPD) to dissolve parliament provoked little criticism. In the following election the government secured a clear majority.

The situation in 1983 was a more problematic one. Chancellor Kohl (CDU), who had just come to power by means of a constructive vote of no-confidence, also brought about his own defeat in a vote of confidence by deliberate abstention of his supporters. Consequently he suggested to the president the dissolution of parliament, arguing that, with an opposition in the parliamentary group of the CDU's coalition partner, the FDP, his government would be no longer able to act. Although such sentiments actually existed among the Liberals, the government had not yet suffered a parliamentary defeat. President Carstens (CDU) accepted Kohl's view and dissolved parliament. His decision – which was a matter of controversy in the public and among scholars – was facilitated by the fact that the Social Democrats (forming the opposition) also demanded premature elections.[20] The following federal election of 1983 confirmed and strengthened the Christian–Liberal government.

This precedent set in 1983 may have paved the way for premature new elections not intended by the Basic Law. At least this applies to the case of an interplay between chancellor and president. The explosive aspect about this is that the president becomes evident as a political decision-maker even if there is only a hint of a crisis, or if a crisis has not yet occurred. The limits of the presidential scope of action seem to be expanded significantly.

Moreover, although it was attempted to exclude the possibility of another presidential regime like that of 1930–33, in times of crisis even under the Basic Law the president assumes a position with crucial powers. If there is no parliamentary majority he can appoint a minority chancellor and – in the event that parliament refuses a question of confidence[21] – he can promise him to dissolve parliament (which equals a threat to parliament). Presidential powers in such a situation extend even further: if a government bill was not approved by parliament the president can – at the request of the government and with the approval of the Bundesrat – declare a 'legislative state of emergency' which enables the government and the Bundesrat to pass a law even without parliamentary approval (Article 81 of the Basic Law).

Admittedly, the president cannot pass laws without the Bundesrat as well as he may maintain a 'legislative state of emergency' only for a limited period of up to six months within the incumbency of one chancellor. But the combination of presidential powers, such as the appointment of the chancellor, dissolution of parliament and passing laws without parliamentary approval, may lead to a limited form of a presidential regime in times of crisis. A chancellor without majority and appointed by a free presidential decision probably could not counterbalance the president. President Carstens, an expert on constitutional law, stated correctly that the federal president had 'extensive powers' in times of crisis.[22]

## Integration or mental leadership?

Looking back at 'normal' times, the question arises as to what influence a federal president might exert even without relevant legal authority.

In this context the president's public-representative functions are interesting: his appearance in public at festive occasions, his representing Germany at the international level, and his awarding decorations. Public speeches and addresses are of particular importance as the president may use them to morally admonish, recommend or demand popular ideas or views that can rarely be disputed without being responsible for the implementation of his exhortations.[23] In this way a president can gain popularity and exert influence.

His scope of action in this field is wide because his speeches are not subject to government approval or 'precensorship'.[24] However, the issues he can address are limited: he must not exceed his role as 'symbolic unification figure';[25] and the president must always act as an office-holder who is not responsible to parliament. From this, constitutional lawyers have concluded that the president should keep a defensive position in politically controversial issues[26] and is, at any rate, not authorised to counteract governmental policies.[27] In general the presidents acted within these limits. If a president overstepped them he would run the risk of being publicly criticised and reprimanded, e.g. when Lübke advocated a Grand Coalition, when Heinemann condemned former governmental policies or when Weizsäcker pleaded for Berlin to become the new capital of unified Germany.

Nevertheless, the question remains whether a president may assume a role which points the way ahead, and take over a kind of mental leadership. Weizsäcker is considered the incumbent who not only performed the public function in a masterly way, but also spoke for views not universally approved.

Examples of this are two speeches in which he addressed fundamental issues and which sustainingly affected the political climate in Germany. His 1985 speech on the 40th anniversary of the German surrender on 8 May 1945,[28] in which he referred to this day of defeat – although it involved death and expulsion for millions of Germans (which he mentioned too) – as a 'day of liberation'. Looking at the course and ending of the Second World War from a protestantmoralising perspective[29] Weizsäcker strove to give a meaning to it which – at that time – neither Germans nor Western victors had discerned. For example, the American directive addressed to the occupation forces declared in 1945: 'Germany is not occupied for the purpose of its liberation but as a defeated enemy state'.[30] It might be questioned whether a president's bold interpretation, certainly not the only one possible, should have gained a semi-official character. However, the historical point of view was changed, irritations were accepted.

The second comment of von Weizsäcker, which had a lasting effect, was his fundamental criticism of political parties and politicians which he expressed in talks with journalists in 1992 and which were made public in book form. Weizsäcker had moved into politics from the side (with help of Kohl) without working his way up from the bottom of party politics. He blamed the parties for 'making the state a prey' by office patronage, making decisions in coalition talks over the MPs' heads, and for creating a type of politician who is a 'generalist' without any expert knowledge (who only has a 'special knowledge of how to combat political opponents'), unable to solve problems.[31] Weizsäcker drew much applause with this, particularly from the media which many times interpreted this as a more or less open attack on Chancellor Kohl. On the other hand, his remarks led to tensions between the president and the political elites, entailing disapproval not only from the ranks of the parties in power.[32] The criticism of von Weizsäcker was certainly justified to some extent. However, it was the superficial nature of his views, and his slogan-like suggestions for solving problems, which made them appear first of all as sensational contributions to the spread of dissatisfaction with political parties and politicians in Germany.[33]

The left-wing/liberal-oriented von Weizsäcker did not succeed in gaining influence on concrete decision-making, however. For example, his 1990 call for moderate action in the German unification process ('growing together, not growing together rampantly') went almost unheard.[34] But he repeatedly used occasions to criticise governmental policies.[35]

The line of action he pursued appeared to be a break-out from the narrow 'walls of an office',[36] an attempt to give a new prospect and a higher profile to this office, even in contrast with government. The publicist Countess Dönhoff summarised his presidency to the formula 'authority without power'.[37] Weizsäcker even advocated direct election of the president by the people,[38] thus supporting a massive increase in his legitimation. Actually, the election of the president in 1994 for the first time involved campaign-like appearances of the candidates and references to poll ratings indicating the 'majority will of the citizens' for one of the candidates.[39]

Can it be concluded that this development will lead to the 'emergence of a higher-profile presidency'[40] or even a mental leadership by the federal president? This seems to be unlikely because in the personage of von Weizsäcker several factors coincided exceptionally: an outstanding rhetoric, a left-wing liberal orientation (including dissent from government) and a positive response from the media (including a high popularity rating).[41] Heuss, who rhetorically was almost as gifted as von Weizsäcker, lacked political dissent from the government. Carstens, the only president in cohabitation with a different-coloured government (1979–82), lacked similar rhetoric skills, and his walking tours throughout Germany counteracted the left spirit of the time only in a very subtle way. Herzog, Weizsäcker's more conservative successor in office, would not receive the same support from the media.[42]

Therefore it can be expected that the federal presidency will continue to be shaped by different incumbents and political circumstances differently. Interestingly, contrary to widely held beliefs, especially among foreign observers, the party affiliation of presidents does not seem to constitute a major factor shaping the style which individual incumbents develop towards the government.[43] While Lübke and von Weizsäcker (who both had the same party affiliation as the chancellor) proved to be highly contentious presidents, Carstens (the only president who had to act under the specific conditions of cohabitation) was generally on much better terms with the federal government than most of his predecessors and successors alike.

## Conclusion

In summary, we can conclude that in the abstract neither a semi-presidential nor a parliamentary system should be deemed superior. Without a strong *Reichspräsident* the Weimar Republic probably would not have survived for a long time; on the other hand, the parliamentary system in the Federal Republic with a weak president has proved effective. Comparing presidential and parliamentary democracies in general, Sartori has stated that for an evaluation it is crucial to consider the context of a given system, i.e. the electoral system, the party system and the degree of political polarisation.[44]

Thus, the founders of the Federal Republic acted wisely, for they not only reduced presidential powers but also changed the institutional context: by creating a 'militant democracy' (Karl Loewenstein) they made it possible to exclude anti-democratic parties from parliament[45] and thus to reduce the probability of lacking parliamentary majorities. In addition to this, the 5 per cent clause was introduced in 1953, which considerably reduced the splintering effects of proportional representation. Moreover, the position of the government was strengthened by introducing the 'constructive' vote of no-confidence by means of which a government can be overthrown only by electing a new chancellor.[46] In this context a crutch in the form of a strong president became superfluous.

After Lübke's unsuccessful attempts in the 1960s to participate in political decision-making (even though there was no crisis), it was universally agreed that a president should not have such decision-making powers. Nevertheless, in times of crisis the political authority of the federal president may become important. Indeed, in a constitution not ignoring the possibility of crises, at least a restricted transfer of power to the president can barely be avoided. The dissolution of parliament in 1983 by Carstens demonstrated that a wide interpretation of the term 'crisis' could enable presidents to play a major decision-making role even if a crisis has not yet occurred seriously. Since the presidency of von Weizsäcker a new prospect of the German federal presidency has arisen: that of mental leadership, resting on media and plebiscite.

With respect to the overarching perspective of this volume on institutional change a number of conclusions can be drawn: first of all, the 'sea-change' in terms of the institutional or constitutional definition of the office of president in Germany clearly occurred in 1948/49 when the founding fathers of the Basic Law decided to replace the semi-presidential constitutional architecture of the Weimar Republic by a chancellor-dominated type of parliamentary democracy leaving no room for a constitutionally powerful head of state. Second, there has been some 'institutional change' regarding the federal presidency during the course of the Federal Republic's history insofar as individual incumbents have performed differently. Strictly speaking, however, this kind of change was related to variations of political styles of presidents rather than to changes of the office of president. Third, as far as genuine institutional change in the more narrow sense of the term is concerned, it is interesting to note that the bulk of more recent proposals of reform regarding the presidency have centred on the nomination procedure of candidates – namely the popular election of the president[47] – rather than the actual powers of office. However, even in this restricted field recurring debates have not resulted in real institutional change. Finally, the most important form of institutional change concerning the role of the presidency in the wider political system may be brought about by a number of external factors, such as a change in the party system entailing the loss of clear parliamentary majorities. Although there are few signs at the moment for developments such as these to occur, it is important to note that a significant up-grading of the presidency in times of crisis remains a real possibility fully sanctioned by the Basic Law.

## Notes

1 Karl Dietrich Bracher, cited in Udo Wengst, 'Vom Reichspräsidenten zum Bundespräsidenten', in Bundeszentrale für politische Bildung (ed.), *Deutsche Verfassungsgeschichte 1849–1919–1949* (Bonn: without publisher), p. 79.

2 Walter Bagehot, *The English Constitution* (London: Collins, 1963) (1st edn 1867).

3 See Articles 25, 41–59, 70 and 73 of the Weimar Constitution.

4 See Werner Kaltefleiter, *Die Funktionen des Staatsoberhauptes in der parlamentarischen Demokratie* (Köln/Opladen: Westdeutscher Verlag, 1970), pp. 130–4, 142–3.

5 Carl Schmitt, 'Der Hüter der Verfassung', *Archiv des öffentlichen Rechts*, 55 (1928), pp. 161–237.

6 Ebert enacted 135 and Hindenburg (1931–32) as many as 99 such decrees. See Jürgen Hartmann and Udo Kempf, *Staatsoberhäupter in westlichen Demokratien* (Opladen: Westdeutscher Verlag, 1988), pp. 18–19; W. Kaltefleiter (note 4), p. 164.

7 *Ibid.*

8 See Jürgen Kotowski and Hagen Schulze, cited in Martin Broszat, Ulrich Dübber, Walter Hofer, Horst Möller, Heinrich Oberreuter, Jürgen Schmädeke and Wolfgang Treue (eds), *Deutschlands Weg in die Diktatur* (Berlin: Siedler, 1983), pp. 37 and 168.

9 Carstens, however, had been permanent secretary for a more extended period of time.

10 See Klaus Schlaich, 'Die Funktionen des Bundespräsidenten im Verfassungsgefüge', in Josef Isensee and Paul Kirchhof (eds), *Handbuch des Staatsrechts der Bundesrepublik Deutschland*, vol. 2 (Heidelberg: C. F. Meyer, 1987), p. 542.

11 Here Herzog is cited as a specialist in constitutional law; K. Schlaich (note 10), pp. 551–2.

12 See Ingo von Münch (ed.), *Grundgesetzkommentar*, vol. 2 (Munich: Beck, 1976), p. 715.

13 See Friedrich Karl Fromme, 'Wenn der Bundespräsident nicht unterschreiben will', *Frankfurter Allgemeine Zeitung*, 29 June 1981.

14 See *Frankfurter Allgemeine Zeitung*, 15 January 1991.

15 But concerning air traffic control the Basic Law was changed appropriately in 1992 (Article 87d). The privatisation then passed in an incontestable way.

16 See Rudolf Morsey, *Heinrich Lübke* (Paderborn: Ferdinand Schöningh, 1996), pp. 236–9.

17 See Heinz Rausch, *Der Bundespräsident* (Munich: Bayerische Landeszentrale für politische Bildungsarbeit, 1979), p. 117.

18 R. Morsey (note 16), pp. 348–51 and p. 421.

19 *Ibid.*, p. 427.

20 See Günter Scholz, *Die Bundespräsidenten*, 2nd edn (Heidelberg: Decker Müller, 1992), p. 449.

21 The chancellor is the only member of government authorised to ask for a vote of confidence.

22 Carstens in a speech delivered on 24 February 1988, cited in G. Scholz (note 20), p. 446.

23 H. Rausch (note 17), pp. 111–12.

24 G. Scholz (note 20), p. 45.

25 Dolf Sternberger, cited in Matthias Rensing, *Geschichte und Politik in den Reden der deutschen Bundespräsidenten, 1949–1984* (Münster/New York: Waxmann, 1996), p. 11.

26 *Ibid.*, pp. 12–13.

27 See W. Kaltefleiter (note 4), p. 270.

28 See G. Scholz (note 20), pp. 453–62.

29 From 1964 to 1970 von Weizsäcker had been president of the protestant church convention. This had a considerable effect on his rhetoric and way of thinking. For his c.v. see among others Werner Filmer and Heribert Schwan, *Richard von Weizsäcker* (Dusseldorf/Vienna: Econ, 1984).

30 Directive JCS 1067, quoted after Rolf Steininger, *Deutsche Geschichte, 1945–61*, vol. 1 (Frankfurt a.M.: Fischer, 1983), p. 48.

31 *Richard von Weizsäcker im Gespräch mit Günter Hofmann and Werner A. Perger* (Frankfurt a.M.: Eichborn, 1992), pp. 139, 146–60, 165.

32 See Patrick Horst, 'Präsident der Bundesrepublik Deutschland', *Zeitschrift für Parlamentsfragen*, 25 (1995), p. 593.

33 See Wolfgang Rudzio, 'Der demokratische Verfassungsstaat als Beute der Parteien?', in Winand Gellner and Hans-Joachim Veen (eds), *Umbruch und Wandel in westeuropäischen Parteiensystemen* (Frankfurt a.M.: Lang, 1995), pp. 1–15.

34 See Robert Leicht, 'Die Mauern eines Amtes', *Zeit-Punkte*, 1994, no. 2, p. 7.

35 This applies to his statements against nuclear energy, reforms of rights of asylum, and the kind of financing of the reconstruction in the former GDR.

36 See R. Leicht (note 34), p. 6.

37 Marion Gräfin Dönhoff, 'Autorität auch ohne Macht', *Zeit-Punkte*, 1994, no. 2, pp. 94–7.

38 See R. Leicht (note 34), p. 6.

39 See Werner Billing, 'Der Kampf um die Besetzung des höchsten Staatsamtes', *Zeitschrift für Parlamentsfragen*, 25 (1995), pp. 615–16.

40 See Stephen Padgett, 'Introduction: Chancellors and the Chancellorship', in Stephen Padgett (ed.), *Adenauer to Kohl: The Development of the German Chancellorship* (London: Hurst & Company, 1994), pp. 17–18; Ludger Helms, 'Keeping Weimar at Bay: the German Federal Presidency since 1949', *German Politics and Society*, 16 (1998), no. 2, pp. 62–3.

41 See P. Horst (note 32), p. 591.

42   See Wolfgang Wiedemeyer, *Roman Herzog* (Munich/Landsberg: Olzog, 1994). For a more detailed assessment of the Herzog presidency see L. Helms (note 40), pp. 62–3.
43   See L. Helms (note 40), pp. 59–62.
44   Giovanni Sartori, 'Neither Presidentialism nor Parliamentarism', in Juan J. Linz and Arturo Valenzuela (eds), *The Failure of Presidential Democracy: Comparative Perspectives* (Baltimore/London: Johns Hopkins University Press, 1994), p. 110.
45   See Wolfgang Rudzio, 'Freiheitliche demokratische Grundordnung und wehrhafte Demokratie', in Peter Massing (ed.), *Das Demokratiemodell der Bundesrepublik Deutschland* (Schwalbach: Wochenschau, 1996), pp. 11–12.
46   See Wolfgang Rudzio, *Das politische System der Bundesrepublik Deutschland*, 4th edn (Opladen: Leske & Budrich, 1996), pp. 184 and 236.
47   See Werner Kaltefleiter, 'Die Wahl des Bundespräsidenten durch Plebiszit?' in Günther Rüther (ed.), *Repräsentative oder plebiszitäre Demokratie – eine Alternative?* (Baden-Baden: Nomos, 1996), pp. 160–9.

# 4
# The Federal Government: Variations of Chancellor Dominance

*Karlheinz Niclauss*

## Introduction

To the political analyst the German government looks like a three-storeyed building. Generally, the observer will first of all focus his attention on its organisation, the formal decision-making process and its juridical rules and regulations. All this is to be found at the ground floor of the government. In order to understand how the German government works in practice, a look at the first floor seems to be indispensable. Here political parties and government coalitions, largely acting on terms of informal constitutional conventions, shape the political process. On the second and upper floor the role of govern-ment in the German political system is under discussion. In this context the conduct of political parties during election campaigns and the popular legitimacy of chancellors and coalitions attract the attention of political scientists.

To describe the federal government becomes more and more difficult from floor to floor. The regulations and institutions of government may easily be understood. They will be treated in the next section of this chapter. When on the first floor the dimension of political parties has to be considered, a detailed analysis becomes more intricate. These topics will be the dominant theme in the second subsection. On the second floor, in particular, the personalising and plebiscitary elements of the German 'chancellor democracy' will be dealt with. These largely unresolved questions will be the subject of the last main section of this chapter.

## Constitutional provisions in the central government territory

With regard to the formal organisation of the federal government, the Basic Law constitutes the most important source of reference. The relevant stipulations differ significantly from the corresponding rules of the Weimar Republic and most other democracies. According to Article 63 of the Basic Law the chancellor is elected by the Bundestag. The federal president proposes a candidate for the first ballot; but if his candidate fails to receive an absolute majority it is the turn of the parliamentary parties to present further candidates. Since 1949, however, the candidate proposed by the president has always received the required majority in the first ballot. In order to remove the chancellor from office the authors of the Basic Law found the elegant solution of the famous constructive vote of no-confidence: the Bundestag may overthrow the government only by electing a new chancellor with an overall majority.

According to empirical findings the effect of this regulation has been overestimated, since only one out of six chancellors lost his office following a constructive vote of no-confidence. This happened in 1982, when the Free Democratic Party (FDP) changed its coalition partner. Helmut Kohl was elected chancellor in order to replace Helmut Schmidt and to form a new government of Christian Democrats and Liberals (CDU/CSU and FDP). Nevertheless, the vote of no-confidence demonstrates the chancellor's outstanding position in the cabinet. He proposes the ministers to be appointed or dismissed by the federal president. In case he falls or resigns all ministers lose their office. As far as constitutional rules are concerned, there is only one which puts the German chancellor at a disadvantage compared to the British prime minister: the right to dissolve parliament in the British manner is not at his disposal. He can manage a dissolution of the Bundestag before its term has expired only by using the vote of confidence (Article 68 of the Basic Law). During this procedure, which was applied by Willy Brandt in 1972 and by Helmut Kohl 10 years later, the parliamentary parties of the coalition have to deny confidence in their own government. When Kohl introduced his vote of confidence in December 1982, the government parties abstained and the vote was lost by 218 to eight. Therefore the premature dissolution of parliament is highly controversial both among the judiciary and the public.[1]

One of the ministers is appointed vice-chancellor and acts as the chancellor's deputy. According to a convention, which has resulted from political practice, this position is occupied by the foreign minister who, at the same time, is the leading politician of the junior coalition partner. In the cabinets of Brandt, Schmidt and Kohl the vice-chancellorship and the foreign ministry were 'hereditary farms' of the FDP. When the Schröder government was formed, the Greens, of course, filled the vacancy with Josef ('Joschka') Fischer. The number of ministers has varied over the years from 15 under Adenauer to 24 under Kohl in 1987. At present, in May 1999, the federal government consists of 15 ministers plus the chancellor. The parliamentary secretaries of state, altogether 24, are not members of the cabinet. Their task is to support their ministers' (or the chancellor's) relationship with parliament, parties and interest groups. The parliamentary secretaries of state of the chancellor and the foreign minister are named ministers of state (*Staatsminister*). The chancellor disposes of the power of organisation in the federal government. He may determine the number and the jurisdiction of ministries and may even appoint ministers without portfolio. This competence is an implied one and not expressly conferred by the constitution. Chancellor Kohl made use of it during the German unification process when he supplemented his government with five politicians from East Germany towards the end of 1990. Immediately after unification he dissolved the Ministry for Inner-German Relations, now redundant. Instead, he established two new ministries for 'family and seniors' and 'women and youth' in order to give Christian-Democratic women a stronger representation in the federal government.

Chancellor Schröder reorganised the competence of ministries in many respects. His first Federal Minister of Finance, Oskar Lafontaine, profited most from these modifications, receiving jurisdiction over economic politics in Europe, statistics, economic research and the expert committees for economic development. According to official statements the idea behind this reorganisation was to create a treasury department comparable with other European countries, e.g. Britain and France. Commentators, however, referred to Lafontaine's position as leader of the Social Democratic Party which granted him much more power than any other minister in the government. The minister of economics had to hand over competences to the Ministry of Finance but received jurisdiction over promoting research and ventures on new technologies. Until now, the reorganisations have continued under the new Minister of Finance, Hans Eichel. The former ministries for transport and housing were merged and are headed by Franz Müntefering, the manager of the Social Democratic election campaign.

Using the 'power of organisation', German chancellors built up the Federal Chancellor's Office, which is not mentioned in the Basic Law.

Adenauer established this administration immediately after being elected chancellor in 1949. The office co-ordinates the activities of the individual ministries and prepares the government's guidelines. It is now headed by a secretary of state and enables the chancellor to lead the government. It has been continually expanding since the 1950s and today employs a staff of about 450. The policy units of the Chancellor's Office are either 'mirror-units' (*Spiegelreferate*) which are responsible for the policy field of a single ministry, or 'cross-sectional units' (*Querschnittsreferate*), whose responsibilities cut across several ministries. An example of the former is unit No. 312, named 'Ministry of Public Health'; an example of the latter is unit No. 131 dealing with the relationship between the federation and the Länder. Division 5 of the Federal Chancellor's Office has the delicate task of supervising and co-ordinating the three intelligence services of the Federal Republic. One of them, the Federal Intelligence Service (BND), works for the chancellor directly, whereas the others are attached to the Ministries of Defence and Interior.[2]

Starting with the foundation of the Federal Republic, the Chancellor's Office has been performing tasks which could not be assigned to the ministries: when, under the Occupation Statute, foreign policy was reserved to the occupying powers and the Federal Republic was deprived of a Foreign Ministry, Adenauer used his office to manage foreign relations. German rearmament, too, was prepared in the Chancellor's Office. Under its custody the '*Amt Blank*' had already grown to the size of a ministry before being officially named the Ministry of Defence in 1955. The new Chancellor Schröder followed this pattern when reorganising the competences for East Germany, the area of the former German Democratic Republic (GDR). He appointed a commissioner for the new Länder, who is a Minister of State at the Chancellor's Office. Another reorganisation measure was implemented in the field of cultural affairs: since these competences according to the Basic Law fall for the most part within the jurisdiction of the Länder, the foundation of a federal cultural ministry was not practicable. Therefore, Schröder's candidate for cultural affairs, the publisher and political outsider Michael Naumann, became Minister of State in the Chancellor's Office. Here he is attached to the chancellor directly and administers the greater part of the federation's cultural competences, in particular the 'Abteilung K.', which under Chancellor Kohl was part of the Interior Ministry. In addition to the Federal Chancellor's Office and the Federal Intelligence Service the chancellor disposes of the Federal Press and Information Office. This administration keeps the chancellor permanently informed of public opinion in Germany and abroad. On the other hand, the Press Office's task is to explain the policy of the federal government to the media. It is therefore called the speaking-tube and the ear-trumpet of the chancellor.

Within the German government a number of cabinet committees have been created. They are chaired by the chancellor and consist of a small number of ministers. The Chancellor's Office functions as a secretary's office for the committees. Although the cabinet committees place the chancellor in the same privileged position as the British prime minister, their number and their political weight is less than in Britain.[3] During Kohl's chancellorship seven cabinet committees were counted. The most important one is the Federal Security Council (*Bundessicherheitsrat*). In 1998 the 'red–green' government agreed to incorporate the Ministry of Economic Development into the Security Council, because insecurity frequently originates from social and political underdevelopment.

On the organisational level of government the Basic Law imposes three important political counterweights: the federal structure including the Bundesrat as representation of the Länder, the Federal Constitutional Court, and the Bundesbank whose competences in the near future will be taken over by the European Central Bank in Frankfurt. These three institutions function as checks and balances to the federal government and are examined in greater detail by other authors in this volume. Executive leadership in Germany from the constitutional point of view is more confined than in Britain. The German chancellor, compared with his British counterpart, seems to be acting in a 'restrictive domestic leadership setting'. The German case of leadership may therefore be called a dispersed one.[4] Nevertheless, the German government should be named 'chancellor government' rather than cabinet government, although not every chancellor is able to live up to these expectations at any time, given the strong impact of party and coalition politics.

When interpreting the text of the Basic Law, constitutional lawyers distinguish between three principles within the federal government: the chancellor principle (*Kanzlerprinzip*), the departmental principle (*Ressortprinzip*) and the cabinet principle (*Kabinettsprinzip*) (Article 65 of the Basic Law). According to the chancellor principle the chancellor determines the guidelines of governmental policy. The departmental principle enables individual ministers to conduct their department under their own responsibility. Finally, the constitution on several occasions prescribes a decision of the whole cabinet (Articles 35, 37, 65,

84–86 and 91 of the Basic Law). However, the three principles provide little guidance when it comes to understanding the political process within the government. David Southern considers them as 'a rather ill defined combination'.[5] Taking the text of the constitution separately from the political context, the chancellor principle is the dominating one. The chancellor 'bears responsibility' for government policy to the Bundestag, whereas the ministers are not individually responsible to the Bundestag. In case of conflict the chancellor could, in theory, dismiss all his ministers and appoint a new cabinet. But his success (or failure) depends less on the Basic Law and his 'personality' than many authors claim. Much more important are his position in his own party and his relationship with the coalition partner.

## Parties, coalitions and conventions

If we take into account the role of parties and coalitions the particular type of German government comes into view much more clearly. Whereas the British prime minister chairs a one-party government, virtually all governments of the Federal Republic since 1949 have been coalition governments. This applies even to the era of Adenauer's impressive electoral results: in 1953 he already won a tiny overall majority of Bundestag seats for the Christian Democrats; but he had to work for a two-thirds majority in order to get passed the modifications of the Basic Law which were linked up with the rearmament of West Germany. When Adenauer won a clear absolute majority for his CDU/CSU in 1957, he nevertheless formed a coalition government with the small German Party (DP) which kept its two seats in the cabinet.[6] Since the foundation of the Federal Republic in 1949 the Bavarian CSU has been the 'sister party' of the CDU. Both parties form a common parliamentary party in the Bundestag. The CSU deputies, however, are well organised in the Bavarian group (*Landesgruppe*) and act like a coalition partner of the CDU. They usually held three or four ministries in a Christian-Democratic headed government. In 1957 they concluded for the first time a written coalition agreement with the CDU.

The competences attributed to the chancellor by the Basic Law are significantly limited by coalition politics. According to the constitution he is free to choose his ministers. But as soon as a ministry is conceded to the coalition partner the latter decides about the appointment to the post. The succession of Foreign Minister Genscher in 1992 was a case in point: after nominating Mrs Adam-Schwaetzer for that position the Liberals suddenly changed their minds and proposed Klaus Kinkel, whom Chancellor Kohl had to accept. When the FDP in 1993 replaced its Minister for Economics, the designated Minister Rexrodt declared his appointment by the chancellor to be only a matter of form.[7] With regard to ministries occupied by the coalition partner, the 'chancellor principle' is limited and the 'departmental principle' gains importance. Since the chancellor is active in the field of foreign policy, from time to time tensions between the Chancellor's Office and the Foreign Ministry occur. This happened during the Grand Coalition (1966–69) between Chancellor Kiesinger (CDU) and then Foreign Minister Brandt (SPD) as well as during the unification process. In the numerous descriptions and documentations of this process, which were inspired by Chancellor Kohl, Foreign Minister Genscher plays only a subordinate part. The book by Elbe and Kiessler seems lightly biased in the opposite direction.[8] Generally, coalition governments constrain the activities of the political leader. They force him to act as a manager forging compromises in order to keep his coalition together. On the other hand, the coalition partner can be helpful to the chancellor. Its stubbornness may serve as a pretext to reject expectations from the chancellor's own party and to explain the failure to achieve certain political aims.

With regard to the influential interest groups there are some unwritten rules which every chancellor has to respect when composing his cabinet. The Minister of Agriculture, for example, has to come from the farmers' lobby, whereas the Minister of Labour has to be a union representative. The Minister of Justice should be trained in law and the Minister of Defence should have served in the armed forces. Significantly, Chancellor Schröder accommodated to all these demands and with Werner Müller even nominated a former industrial manager and non-party member for the Ministry of Economics.

When looking at the overthrow of chancellors we notice that in most cases problems within the government coalition or within the chancellor's party were the decisive factors. Only after long pressure by his own party and parliamentary party group did Adenauer agree to resign and to accept Erhard as his successor. Pressure also came from his coalition partner FDP, which after the raid against the news magazine *Der Spiegel* in 1962 temporarily left Adenauer's government. Erhard had to resign because his coalition with the Liberals broke down, but also because of the opposing 'Gaullists' in his own party, who demanded closer co-operation with France. Brandt's replacement by Schmidt was an intra-party exchange of the chancellor, managed by

Table 4.1   The federal government (May 1999)

Chancellor: Gerhard Schröder, SPD
Minister in the Chancellor's Office: Bodo Hombach, SPD
  *Ministers of State*: Michael Naumann, SPD; Rolf Schwanitz, SPD
Minister of Foreign Affairs and Vice-Chancellor: Joseph (Joschka) Fischer,
Green
  *Ministers of State*: Ludger Volmer, Green; Günter Verheugen, SPD
Minister of the Interior: Otto Schily, SPD
  *Parliamentary Secretaries of State*: Fritz Rudolf Körper, SPD; Cornelie Sonntag-
Wolgast, SPD
Minister of Justice: Herta Däubler-Gmelin, SPD
  *Parliamentary Secretary of State*: Eckart Pick, SPD
Minister of Finance: Hans Eichel, SPD
  *Parliamentary Secretaries of State*: Barbara Hendricks, SPD; Karl Diller, SPD
Minister of Economics and Technology: Dr Werner Müller
  *Parliamentary Secretary of State*: Siegmar Mosdorf, SPD
Minister of Food, Agriculture and Forestries: Karl-Heinz Funke, SPD
  *Parliamentary Secretary of State*: Gerald Thalheim, SPD
Minister of Labour and Social Affairs: Walter Riester, SPD
  *Parliamentary Secretaries of State*: Gerd Andres, SPD; Ulrike Mascher, SPD
Minister of Defence: Rudolf Scharping, SPD
  *Parliamentary Secretaries of State*: Walter Kolbow, SPD; Brigitte Schulte, SPD
Minister of Families, Senior Citizens, Women and Juveniles: Christine
Bergmann, SPD
  *Parliamentary Secretary of State*: Edith Niehuis, SPD
Minister of Health: Andrea Fischer, Green
  *Parliamentary Secretary of State*: Christa Nickels, Green
Minister for the Environment, Nature Conservation and Reactor Safety: Jürgen
Trittin, Green
  *Parliamentary Secretaries of State*: Simone Probst, Green; Gila Altmann, Green
Minister of Transport, Construction and Housing: Franz Müntefering, SPD
  *Parliamentary Secretaries of State*: Lothar Ibrügger, SPD; Achim Großmann,
SPD; Siegfried Scheffler, SPD
Minister of Education and Research: Edelgard Bulmahn, SPD
  *Parliamentary Secretary of State*: Wolf-Michael Catenhusen, SPD
Minister of Economic Cooperation and Development: Heidemarie Wieczorek-
Zeul, SPD
  *Parliamentary Secretary of State*: Uschi Eid, Green

the Social Democratic leadership. The vote of no-confidence against Helmut Schmidt resulted from the FDP's change of coalition partner but also from opposition within the chancellor's own party. So far only two chancellors have lost their office as a consequence of general elections: the Chancellor of the Grand Coalition, Kurt Georg Kiesinger, missed the overall majority for his CDU/CSU in 1969, and in 1998 Helmut Kohl failed in his attempt to continue his coalition with the FDP. The change of government in autumn 1998 was unique in Germany's parliamentary history. For the first time the parties in government were completely replaced by opposition parties. 'Alternative government' as in the British model has been practised only 50 years after the founding of the Federal Republic.

In Great Britain the prime minister is at the same time leader of his party and chairman of his parliamentary party group. In Germany these three posts are quite distinct from each other. No chancellor has ever been chairman of the parliamentary party. The personal union of chancellorship and leadership of the party in government is common; however, only Willy Brandt and Helmut Kohl were leaders of their parties when becoming chancellor. Adenauer, Erhard, Kiesinger, and Schröder took over party leadership during their incumbency. Ludwig Erhard, who saw himself as an expert in economics and later on as a non-partisan '*Volkskanzler*' (people's chancellor), has been described as a guest in the CDU. He became chairman of the CDU only in March 1966 and proved incapable of using his party leadership in support of his government.[9] Party leadership and chancellorship were separated during Helmut Schmidt's government because Willy Brandt continued as party leader after his resignation as chancellor in 1974. This division of labour worked fairly well until the end of the 1970s. Under the impact of controversial arguments about the deployment of middle-range missiles according to the twin-track decision and about nuclear energy the differences between the SPD and the government became more articulate during the last three years before Schmidt's overthrow in October 1982.[10] After the federal election of 1998 the chancellorship and Social Democratic party leadership were separated once again: the party's chairman Oskar Lafontaine held the influential Ministry of Finance in the Schröder government. When Lafontaine resigned, Chancellor Schröder took over the leadership of the Social Democrats without much difficulty. Whether the SPD will operate like a genuine party of the chancellor is a question to be answered by future commentators.

In order to make sure that his policy is supported by parties and parliament German chancellors face a comprehensive work of co-ordination. This work goes beyond the area of cabinet and parliament and includes, among others, state governments as well as interest groups. Outstanding examples of Adenauer's role as an intermediary are the co-determination law for the coal, iron and steel industries of

1951 and the investment promotion law of 1952. In both cases Adenauer acted independently and sometimes contrary to the intentions of his Minister of Economics Ludwig Erhard.[11] Already during the 1950s there were informal talks between members of Adenauer's cabinet and the government's parliamentary parties. Adenauer relied on his 'kitchen cabinet' including Krone, Hallstein, Globke, Blankenhorn and von Eckardt. When the FDP returned to the cabinet in 1961, a coalition agreement was signed which laid down periodical coalition talks. The chancellor, ministers, the parliamentary party whips, party politicians and politicians from the Länder took part in the conferences. During the Grand Coalition (1966–69) the partners CDU/CSU and SPD established the 'Kressbron circle' (*'Kressbronner Kreis'*) as an informal coalition committee. It was composed of government ministers and leading politicians of the parliamentary party groups from both coalition partners. Chancellor Schmidt called upon his famous trio of three advisers (*Kleeblatt*). He met weekly with Bölling, Schüler and Wischnewski in the Chancellor's Office to discuss and prepare the government's decisions. In 1977 Schmidt organised a 'Great crisis staff' together with the minister presidents of the Länder and politicians of the opposition in order to meet the challenge of terrorism. In addition to that, he established a coalition round table which included Foreign Minister Genscher alongside other ministers, the whips and the managers of the two governing parties SPD and FDP.[12]

Helmut Kohl continued the 'coalition round' which was composed in the same way as during Schmidt's chancellorship. Beginning in 1983 there were meetings every 10–14 days. The smaller governmental party FDP in particular demanded frequent meetings in order to have a greater say in preparing the government's policy. Another circle of CDU/CSU and FDP during Kohl's chancellorship was the so-called 'elephants' round' of party leaders. These meetings were intensively observed as long as CSU leader Franz-Josef Strauss, who was not a cabinet member, took part. After Strauss's death in 1988 the round became less important.[13]

The informal committees within the governmental structure decide *de facto* concerning political problems of every kind. Although not mandatory in the judicial sense, their recommendations are accepted by the cabinet and the majority parties in the Bundestag. The coalition agreement of the new Social Democratic/Green government also established a coalition committee made up of eight members from each party, designed to find a compromise in cases of conflict. Only a few weeks after the formation of the new government informal talks proved to be necessary. In view of differences over taxation within the SPD and the government the Greens demanded a meeting of the coalition committee. On the evening of 3 December 1998, seven representatives of the Greens met with six Social Democrats. From both sides three cabinet members, two or three representatives of the parliamentary party and one of the party leadership, respectively, took part in the meeting. The coalition partners agreed about weekly consultations in the future in order to improve communication between the two parties and parliamentary groups. Both sides were keen to avoid the impression that every meeting indicates major differences and tensions within the 'red–green' government.

There is no doubt that informal circles and committees work at the expense of the cabinet. Ministers, whose department is of secondary importance and who are not leading party politicians, may feel like the cabinet's backbenchers. Still, in Germany informal government seems indispensable, as powerful positions are not represented in the cabinet. This applies to the whips or even the leaders of governmental parties, but first of all to the minister-presidents and ministers of the Länder governments. Last but not least, the minor coalition partners show great interest in informal bargaining, where they can meet with the leading governmental party on equal terms.

The written coalition agreements of course cut across the chancellor's guideline competences, as David Southern remarks. But whether informal committees strengthen or weaken his political power is still debated among scholars.[14] Even in informal meetings the chancellor needs the support of parties and parliamentary groups. Coalition partners who are drifting apart cannot be held together by confidential talks. But as long as the coalition government operates, its chairman determines the agenda and the date of the meetings. Sometimes he also decides who is to be invited. We may therefore compare the German informal committees with the British cabinet committees. Both enable the head of government to transfer decisions into discrete functional units. Prime minister and chancellor take advantage of being informed earlier than other members of the circle and thus possess the key resource to co-ordinate and direct the flow of the governmental process.

The formal and informal method of decision-making from Adenauer to Schröder demonstrates the tremendous amount of co-ordinating activities which every chancellor has to perform. Therefore, to differentiate 'chancellor democracy' from 'co-ordinating democracy' appears rather misleading. The thesis that the German chancellorship has degenerated into a mere co-ordinating institution was obviously promoted by Helmut Kohl's political weakness in the years before German unification. Then Minister of Defence Rupert Scholz incautiously took over this interpretation. In an article for the newspaper *Die Welt* he reported that the 'chancellor of the guidelines' ('*Richtlinienkanzler*') had changed into a 'co-ordinating chancellor' ('*Koordinationskanzler*'). Some days later the critic found himself outside the cabinet. Obviously, the chancellor principle had been the dominating one.[15]

## Chancellor democracy: the federal government's place in the German political system

As we have seen, a description of the German government cannot be confined to the constitutional provisions and the actual decision-making process in the core-executive territory. To focus on the chancellor, his cabinet and the upper echelons of the civil service is much too narrow a perspective in understanding the role of the government and its leader. Party support is, according to Stephen Padgett, the key to the chancellor's authority and the *sine qua non* of effective government.[16] But even after taking into account the role of political parties, there remain important aspects of German government to be dealt with. This applies especially to the legitimacy of coalitions and chancellors, to elections and election campaigns and to the way the opposition and its chancellor candidate behave.

Chancellor democracy is often characterised as the chancellor's dominance over his cabinet and his coalition. In case the incumbent's fortune or competence cease, chancellor democracy collapses and, therefore, has to be replaced by 'co-ordination democracy' or some other degenerate form of government. Certainly this understanding of chancellor democracy as a synonym with effective government is a rather simple arrangement. Much more adequate would be its description as a type of government with specific attributes. The characteristics of such a systemic concept of chancellor democracy should not only account for the 'strong' chancellor, but also for the chancellor in difficulties who is about to give way to his successor. They should disclose the reasons for effective leadership as well as for the loss of power. They should also include the opposition which intends to take over according to the rules of chancellor democracy.

Looking at the course of the Federal Republic's history five specific elements of chancellor democracy can be discerned:

- The federal chancellor is at the centre of the formal and informal decision-making process. He has to secure support of his own party and the coalition partner. Therefore, he only can realise the chancellor principle in a political, not in a judicial, sense.
- Chancellor democracy means personalised political competition. The chancellor's prestige is indispensable for successful government. The exigencies of personal prestige apply also to the opposition: they have to confront the incumbent with a popular shadow chancellor.
- A close co-operation of the chancellor with the leadership of his party is necessary. Unless the chancellor himself becomes (or already is) leader of his party, he has to control his followers by indirect means.
- The contrast between government and opposition dominates the political dispute in the Federal Republic. When the Bundestag election comes into sight, the minor parties cannot withdraw from this dualism. They have to make up their mind early on the type of coalition they would prefer after the election. The difference between the two camps is a prerequisite for the so-called split vote: only if the Free Democrats, e.g., express themselves openly in favour of a coalition with the Christian Democrats, would a CDU/CSU voter 'lend' them his second vote in order to help them in crossing the 5 per cent hurdle.
- The chancellor plays a leading role in foreign policy besides the foreign minister. He represents the Federal Republic at international conferences and frequent 'summit' meetings.[17]

This concept of chancellor democracy, of course, was established under the influence of Adenauer's leadership. But it has turned out to be a valuable device for analysing the administrations of Adenauer's successors. Only the Grand Coalition under Chancellor Kiesinger (1966–69) stands out as an exception to the rule. Whereas virtually all governments were coalition governments consisting of one leading governmental party with one (ore more) minor parties, the Grand Coalition constituted an alliance of two partners with equal powers. The only opposition party in the Bundestag were the Free Democrats. They disposed of 49 seats and were hampered by the standing orders of that time. Therefore, the political dualism and the dominating role of the chancellor in cabinet and coalition were missing. Other elements of chancellor democracy, however, were present even during the Grand Coalition: Kiesinger had his own ideas of relations with the GDR and slowed down Foreign Minister Brandt's new policies towards the GDR and Eastern Europe. Kiesinger was also elected chairman of the CDU and respected as a leader, though he did not represent the typical party politician. When the differences within the Grand Coalition increased during the run-up to the federal election of 1969, the dualism of party politics returned. The Christian Democrats launched an election campaign with the slogan *'Auf den Kanzler kommt es an'* ('It all depends on the chancellor') and narrowly missed an absolute majority, obtaining 46.1 per cent of the second vote.

After the Grand Coalition had come to an end the German political system with Willy Brandt and Helmut Schmidt in office was again dominated by the elements of chancellor democracy. Helmut Kohl differed from his Social Democratic predecessor Schmidt by his uncontested leadership of his party, the CDU. On the other hand, his public prestige was inferior to that of Schmidt. According to opinion polls, support for Kohl was lower than agreement with his own party. For the first time in the Federal Republic's history the governing Christian Democrats seemed to be earning a 'chancellor malus' instead of the usual 'chancellor bonus'. When Kohl replaced Schmidt, in October 1982, he propagated the vision of an intellectual and moral turning point (*Wende*). This programme was too general to become politically effective. Although Kohl's European policy from 1985 onwards proved to be quite successful, it helped little to improve his prestige in the country. In 1989, suddenly, the state of affairs in Europe changed. The countries of the Soviet Empire freed themselves from their Communist regimes and the GDR was showing signs of decomposition.

The chancellor had a chance to realise a historical vision: German unification was imminent. During the summit conferences of 1990 Kohl acted on the same level as Bush, Gorbachev, Thatcher and Mitterand, whereas the prime minister of the GDR, de Maizière, played only a subordinate role. Kohl, up to then mainly a party politician, now governed the unification process as a statesman. His foreign policy prestige reached the same level as Adenauer's. As 'chancellor of German unity' he complied fully with the fifth element of chancellor democracy.[18]

The last change of government in autumn 1998 also took place according to the rules of chancellor democracy: the difference between the government and the opposition camp dominated discussions in public opinion and the media. The CDU/CSU and the Free Democrats declared themselves in favour of another joint coalition government under Helmut Kohl. On the other hand the Social Democrats and the Greens offered an alternative to the government in office. The chancellor, incumbent for 16 years, was challenged by Gerhard Schröder, the Social Democratic Minister-President of Lower Saxony. The election campaign was summarised well with the question 'Kohl or Schröder?'. The positive image of Schröder was, according to election analysts, a main reason for the success of the Social Democrats. So, political polarity and personalisation paved the way for a new government and a new coalition in 1998.

Compared with the British political system, where usually one party wins the majority of seats in the House of Commons, the outcome of German elections is uncertain. Because of the party system and the electoral formula, declarations on future coalition governments can only be declarations of intent. An electoral outcome with the post-Communist PDS in the key position in 1998 might have enforced a Grand Coalition of Christian and Social Democrats.

It was French political scientists who first analysed the changes in the character of modern democracies, which became basic elements of the type of government called 'chancellor democracy'. Beginning with the Fifth French Republic they observed an increasing personalisation of the political process which continued after de Gaulle's resignation in 1969. They noticed this *personnalisation du pouvoir* at first being supported by popular newspapers. Later on, television intensified this trend by creating a new intimacy (*intimité nouvelle*) and permitting politicians to enter the living rooms of the voters.[19] According to Jacques Ellul political propaganda cannot be practised in an abstract manner but only with concrete pictures: the best subject of such pictures being the man himself.[20] Against this background one could argue that politicians only pronounce those decisions to the public which in reality were prepared by committees and administrations. But in social life things tend to become what they are thought to be, as Maurice Duverger shrewdly noticed. When the public believes the prime minister to be the *chef réel* of the government, this will in any case strengthen the power of the incumbent considerably.[21] The prestige of Helmut Kohl as 'chancellor of German unity' may be adduced in this context.

The effect of mass media is not the only and decisive reason for political personalisation. The personal element has been significant in democracies from the outset. Formerly it was related to the *notables locaux*, such as the mayor or the local deputy. Those men seemed to be competent to deal with the people's grievances and wishes, whereas the president or prime minister were remote figures of symbolic meaning. With the rise of the welfare state the centre took over the jurisdiction for social and economic policies. Accordingly, the personalisation was transferred to the national government and its leader. The prerogatives of the local notables were accumulated by the *roi élu* (*president, premier ministre*) like once the rights of the *seigneurs* by the *roi-soleil* had been.[22]

Personalisation and the difference between the two camps of government and opposition together generated a plebiscitary political climate unknown to the Basic Law. Alfred Grosser had already characterised Adenauer's electoral victory of 1957 as a plebiscite. In his extensive study on the federal chancellor, Jean Amphoux described the plebiscitary elements of West German federal elections. According to his interpretation, since 1953 voters have expressed their opinion in favour of or against the incumbent chancellor and his policy.[23] The impact of this plebiscitary element changed the political system: according to the Basic Law the parliamentary groups of the Bundestag are to deliberate, after the elections, as to which coalition could be formed and who should be presented as a chancellor candidate. Political reality looks quite different: Christian and Social Democrats start their election campaigns with nominating their candidates for the chancellorship. Generally the candidate of the opposition challenges the incumbent. The minor parties adjust to this dualism. Well before election day they announce the chancellor candidate they support and the coalition they prefer. Since the Greens in 1998 were in favour of a coalition with the Social Democrats, and the FDP intended to continue Helmut Kohl's government, a bipartisan situation (*bipartisme de fait*) emerged.[24] Under these conditions elections became 'masked elections'. Officially, the voters elect the members of parliament. Actually, they elect the leader of the government by casting their vote for his party and his preferred party coalition.

## Conclusion

When we summarise the results of investigating the three storeys of the German federal government we find two aspects which are inconsistent: on the one hand the German political system is characterised by the dispersion of powers and responsibilities. The main elements of this dispersion are the Bundesrat with his far-reaching legislative competences, particularly in the field of taxes and finance, the authority of the Länder to administer the legislative decisions of the federation and the judicial review by the Federal Constitutional Court. Moreover, to find a compromise within the coalition government constitutes a permanent challenge to the chancellor. The federal structure within the party system is much underrated in this respect: the Länder-divisions of the German parties are authorised to put up the lists of candidates for general elections. Therefore, every politician on the federal level needs the support of a party unit in one of the Länder. This division of power is partly the heritage of the occupying powers' early decision to establish a federal structure, partly due to the German ideas of 'constitutional democracy' which influenced the foundation process of the Federal Republic from 1945 to 1949. From this point of view parliament, directly elected by the people, was looked upon with distrust. Its majority should be hampered by countervailing powers.[25]

On the other hand, the requirements of economic reconstruction and the social consequences of the Second World War demanded political decisions of the central government. The dispersed constitutional arrangements had to be balanced by effective leadership. This balance was brought about by the so-called chancellor democracy which supplemented the constitutional system with its conventions. In this context the structure of the party system was most important. Voters preferred two or three parties and a dualism between government and opposition emerged. Therefore, chancellor democracy is not only a type of government but first of all a 'superstructure' added to the rules of the Basic Law from 1949. This structure is the reason for inaction not being a feature of the German leadership process. The chancellor may, supported by conventions, 'impose a coherent leadership strategy upon the system as a whole'.[26]

Personalisation, dualism and plebiscitary elements became characteristics of several modern democracies. Generally, executive leadership has to compromise with a constitutional division of power. France can even afford a division of power within the executive. The British system, with alternating governments, majority voting and without federalism and judicial review, seems to be best of all adjusted to the requirements of modern political leadership. General elections nowadays enable the top candidates to continue or to take over the position of the chief government official. Irrespective of their different constitutions parliamentary and presidential democracies are approximating. Elections become 'presidential', while the individual parliamentary candidates are moving into the background.

# Notes

1 See also Wolfgang Rudzio in this volume.
2 See Ferdinand Müller-Rommel, 'The Chancellor and his Staff', in Stephen Padgett (ed.), *Adenauer to Kohl: The Development of the German Chancellorship* (London: Hurst & Company, 1994), pp. 106–26.
3 See Robert Elgie, *Political Leadership in Liberal Democracies* (London: Macmillan, 1995), pp. 36–7.
4 See Alistair Cole, 'Political Leadership in Western Europe: Helmut Kohl in Comparative Context', *German Politics*, 7 (1998), p. 139; R. Elgie (note 3), pp. 78–105.
5 See David Southern, 'The Chancellor and the Constitution', in S. Padgett (note 2), p. 34.
6 However, when the two concerned cabinet members Hans-Joachim Merkatz and Hans-Christoph Seebohm changed their party affiliation and became members of the CDU in 1960, the coalition government was silently transformed into a single-party government.
7 See Karlheinz Niclauss, 'Le Gouvernement fédéral', *Pouvoirs*, No. 66 (1993), pp. 102–4.
8 See Frank Elbe and Richard Kiessler, *A Round Table with Sharp Corners: The Diplomatic Path to German Unity* (Baden-Baden: Nomos, 1996).
9 See Volker Hentschel, *Ludwig Erhard: Ein Politikerleben* (Munich: Olzog, 1996), pp. 592–8.
10 See Karlheinz Niclauss, *Kanzlerdemokratie – Bonner Regierungspraxis von Konrad Adenauer bis Helmut Kohl* (Stuttgart: Kohlhammer, 1988), pp. 190–204.
11 See V. Hentschel (note 9), pp. 138–46 and 154–9.
12 See Wolfgang Rudzio, 'Informelle Entscheidungsmuster in Bonner Koalitionsregierungen', in Hans-Hermann Hartwich and Göttrik Wewer (eds), *Regieren in der Bundesrepublik II* (Opladen: Leske & Budrich, 1991), pp. 125–41.
13 See Waldemar Schreckenberger, 'Informelle Verfahren der Entscheidungsvorbereitung zwischen Bundesregierung und Meherheitsfraktionen', *Zeitschrift für Parlamentfragen*, 25 (1994), pp. 329–46.
14 See D. Southern (note 5), pp. 36–7; Ludger Helms, 'Das Amt des deutschen Bundeskanzlers in historisch und international vergleichender Perspektive', *Zeitschrift für Parlamentsfragen* 27 (1996), p. 704.
15 See Rupert Scholz, 'Die Befugnisse des Kanzlers haben an Substanz verloren', *Die Welt*, 5 April 1989.
16 See Stephen Padgett, 'The Chancellor and his Party', in S. Padgett (note 2), p. 75.
17 See K. Niclauss (note 10), pp. 66–9
18 See William E. Paterson, 'Helmut Kohl, the Vision Thing and Escaping the Semi-Sovereignty Trap', *German Politics*, 7 (1998), pp. 25–7.
19 See Jacques Ellul, 'Propagande et personnalisation du pouvoir', in Léo Hamon and Albert Mabileau (eds), *La Personnalisation du pouvoir* (Paris: Presses Universitaires de France, 1964), pp. 331–41.
20 See Jacques Ellul, *Propagandes* (Paris: Armand Colin, 1962), p. 196.
21 Maurice Duverger, *La Monarchie Républicaine* (Paris: Robert Laffont, 1974), pp. 30–3.

22 *Ibid.*, pp. 33–5.
23 See Alfred Grosser, 'Les Elections allemandes. Le Plébiscite du 15$^e$ Septembre 1957', *Revue française de science politique,* 7 (1957), pp. 838–64; Jean Amphoux, *Le Chancellier Fédéral dans le Régime Constitutionnel de la République Féderal d'Allemagne* (Paris: Pichon, 1962), pp. 378–86.
24 See Jean-Claude Colliard, *Les Régimes parlementaires contemporaines* (Paris: Fondation National des Sciences Politiques, 1978), p. 76.
25 See Karlheinz Niclauss, *Der Weg zum Grundgesetz – Demokratiegründung in Westdeutschland 1945–1949* (Paderborn: Schöningh, 1998), pp. 73–108.
26 R. Elgie (note 3), pp. 104–5.

# 5

# The Federal Constitutional Court: Institutionalising Judicial Review in a Semisovereign Democracy

*Ludger Helms*

## Introduction

Among the political institutions created by the Basic Law, the Federal Constitutional Court represented a genuine institutional innovation. As one scholar has put it, it 'came to the German legal system as a late realisation of a liberal nineteenth-century dream'.[1] In the German Confederation (1815–66) the setting up of such an institution failed mainly due to the opposition from the Southern German states. While the 1849 Constitution (the so-called *'Paulskirchenverfassung'*), provided for the first genuine constitutional court in Europe,[2] the political circumstances in Germany until the end of the Weimar Republic remained altogether hostile to an institutionalisation of the principles of judicial and constitutional review. During the Empire the opinion prevailed that questions regarding the political order were to be solved by political, not judicial means. Consequently, disputes between members of the federation were decided upon by the Bundesrat.[3] Also the area of competence of the Weimar State Court (*Staatsgerichtshof*) remained rather restricted with the authority to decide on cases of judicial referral resting with the Imperial Court (*Reichsgericht*).[4]

In creating the Federal Constitutional Court the framers of the Basic Law were inspired by different foreign traditions. While the 'Austrian model' of 1920 – marked by a concentration of the right to scrutinise the constitutionality of laws and administrative actions in a single supreme body – became the dominant source of influence, the 'American model' inspired a number of minor institutional features, such as the reservation of the right to carry out judicial review to the Court as a whole.[5] The creation of a Constitutional Court fitted with more powers than any of its counterparts in the Western world was strongly influenced by the experiences which the founding fathers of the Basic Law had with the undemocratic Nazi regime in Germany's most recent historical past.

Despite the recurring waves of criticism which have accompanied the Court's work from the very beginning, the Constitutional Court has regularly topped the list of German institutions in terms of public esteem and credibility[6] – a positive judgement which was also reflected in the assessments of the overwhelming majority of scholars. This remarkable position became less secure in the 1990s following a number of highly contentious decisions, leaving unqualified positive judgements about the Court's performance almost exclusively to foreign scholars who became less infected with the highly emotional thrust of arguments.[7] Together with the Bundesrat, the Constitutional Court stands out as the most intensively and heatedly debated German constitutional organ of the 1990s.

Starting with an assessment of the institutional profile and development of the Constitutional Court, this chapter addresses four different aspects on which the more recent discussion of the Court's role within the German polity has focused. The first set of arguments to be dealt with relates to the much-discussed subject of 'judicialisation' of politics, that is the Court's growing importance in the process of settling political and societal conflicts. The second one focuses on the question as to whether the Court can be rightly judged as a 'counter-government' within the German polity. A third aspect, raised more recently, is the question as to whether there are signs that the Court has lost touch with the dominant values in German society, the so-called '*Zeitgeist*', thereby possibly reducing the public acceptance of its decisions. The fourth aspect well worth being discussed is the Court's ever-growing work overload and the institutional reform proposals that have been put forward to tackle this problem.

## The institutional profile of the Federal Constitutional Court

While the framers of the Basic Law set out the different areas of the Court's jurisdiction, it left the task of regulating the Court's organisation and procedure to parliament. The Federal Constitutional Court Act (FCCA, *Bundesverfassungsgerichtsgesetz*), passed in 1951, includes the general and special provisions governing each category of jurisdiction, the Court's organisation and its general procedures.[8] In 1975, following numerous disputes between the Court's president and its individual judges, parliament also enacted a set of standing rules of procedure (*Geschäftsordnung des Bundesverfassungsgerichts*), regulating the Court's internal administration and operations, such as the manner in which decisions are made and announced or the conditions under which a judge may be excluded from a case.

The two-senate structure probably represents the most remarkable structural feature of the Constitutional Court. The Court consists of two senates with mutually exclusive jurisdiction and personnel. Some observers have argued that this 'bifurcation was the institutional expression of the old debate between those who viewed the Court in conventional legal terms and those who saw it in political terms'.[9] According to the initial division of labour, the First Senate's term of reference was to deal with 'non-political' issues, such as the review of the constitutionality of laws and the resolution of constitutional doubts arising out of ordinary litigation, while the Second Senate would decide on the more 'political issues', such as disputes between branches and levels of government or abstract questions of constitutional law. This soon led to a significant work overload of the First Senate.

Thus, as early as 1956, the FCCA was amended redistributing the highly unequal caseload of the original system. Through this reorganisation much of the First Senate's work was transferred to the Second Senate, which was entrusted with dealing with all constitutional complaints and concrete judicial review cases concerning issues of civil and criminal procedure. The Plenum, made up of the members of the First and Second Senate, was authorised to reallocate jurisdiction if necessary as an attempt to ensure relatively equal caseloads between the two senates. Moreover, to accelerate the Court's decision-making process, the internal structure of the two senates was changed by authorising each one to set up three or more preliminary examining committees to filter out frivolous constitutional complaints. Thirty years later the powers of the three-judge committees, henceforth referred to as chambers (*Kammern*), were significantly enhanced. The chambers have since been empowered to rule on the merits of a constitutional complaint if all three justices agree unanimously, and the decision clearly lies within standards already laid down in a case decided by the full senate. Following a further reform the chambers have been authorised to reject referrals concerning concrete review from other courts as 'inadmissible' (excluding those referrals originating in a state constitutional court or one of the high federal courts).

As Kommers points out, 'the chamber system has been the subject of several constitutional challenges, the complainant having argued in each case that a chamber's dismissal of his complaint denied him the right to "the jurisdiction of his lawful judge" under Article 101 of the Basic Law. Complainants have argued that, as the Basic Law provides for one Constitutional Court, the full senate is constitutionally required to decide every case'.[10] However, the Court has rejected each of the complaints, firmly establishing the finality of committee decisions unanimously rejecting complaints. Interestingly, the introduction of chambers seems not only to have eased the work pressure on the senates but also to have made the Court more active. Never before have so many constitutional complaints been accepted as in the 1990s.[11]

There have been a number of other institutional changes over recent decades, the most important of which will be outlined in the following paragraphs. A first complex of reform measures (and unrealised proposals) has concerned the election of judges, their number as well as their term limits. The formal procedure for selecting judges, involving the Judicial Selection Committee (*Wahlmännerausschuß*) of the Bundestag and the Bundesrat, which each elects half of the judges with a two-thirds majority,[12] has only marginally been altered since its first application in 1951.[13] Still, the issue has proved to be of continuous political relevance with most proposals centring on the introduction of an election modus which would transfer nominating powers from the Bundestag's election committee to the plenary assembly.[14] The number of judges serving on each senate was reduced twice, from 12 to 10 in 1956, and 6 years later to eight due to considerations of efficiency. Lifetime terms for Constitutional Court judges nominated from the group of judges at high federal courts were abolished in 1961; following a number of other minor changes in this field, the term for all members of the Constitutional Court was finally set at 12 years (without re-election) with a compulsory retiring age of 68.

The actual recruitment patterns and the social composition of judges can be seen as another important aspect of the Court's institutional profile. There are at least three features worth mentioning in this context. First of all, almost from the very beginning there has been a strong attempt of the CDU/CSU and SPD at establishing a consociational system of nominating judges to the Court. The bulk of members of the Constitutional Court have been formal members of one of the two major parties. Even if there was no formal party affiliation of candidates in a number of cases it was still the parties that served as the 'gatekeepers' to positions at the Court. While on very rare occasions formal members of the small FDP were nominated, the Greens (as well as the PDS) so far have been denied all access to the established system of nominating judges.[15]

The decisions of the Bundesrat and the Bundestag's Judicial Selection Committee are prepared by informal bodies. According to Pieper, the decisions by the Bundesrat are prepared by a specific *ad-hoc* commission laid down in §15 of the Bundesrat's standing orders, while agreement over candidates to be elected by the Judicial Selection Committee is sought through informal channels determined by party political bodies.[16] More recent reports from the media suggest, however, that the nomination process in the Bundesrat is prepared by special 'finding commissions' (*Findungskommissionen*), led by senior representatives of the two major parties. As was revealed during the lengthy debate over the successor to Judge Helga Seibert in 1998, the latest bipartisan 'finding commission' included the Minister-President of Thuringia Vogel, the Minister of Justice of the Saarland Walter and, until his resignation, former Minister-President of North Rhine-Westphalia Rau.[17]

Secondly, it is possible to discern a marked tendency of change with regard to the professional background of judges.[18] Compared to the 'first generation of judges' nominated in the early 1950s the number of judges with professional experience in politics and economics seems to have declined significantly, while the number of judges with a career background in administration, the judiciary or academia has increased. Among the 16 judges serving in early 1999 only one (Kühling) had some former business experience, and three others (Limbach, Jentsch, and Hohmann-Dennhardt) had left genuinely political careers to join the Court. All others had a career background in the judiciary, higher administration or in the academic world.[19] Some scholars tend to see the former professional experiences of judges as being of even greater importance in terms of judicial outcomes than the party affiliation of members of the Constitutional Court. In this context it has been maintained that the strong representation of professors and candidates with careers in the judiciary may lead to a neglect of social factors in judicial review.[20]

The third feature relates to the representation of male and female judges at the Court. With the nomination of only 10 female judges against 72 male judges nominated in the period of 1951–98 the overall representation of females among Court members has been rather modest. However, the more recent tendency has clearly been to increase the share of female judges. Of the total of 23 judges nominated since the second half of the 1980s no less than seven have been women. Half of the total of female judges since 1951 have been nominated within the past decade. In September 1994 the first female president in the Court's history was inaugurated. Moreover, the representation of female judges at the Court has been distributed very unevenly among the two senates. Eight of the 10 female judges have been members of the First Senate. While the first female judge of the First Senate (Judge Erna Scheffler) started her work in 1951, one had to wait 35 years to see the first female member of the Second Senate (Judge Karin Graßhoff, appointed in 1986). A final noteworthy aspect relates to the preferences of the two electoral bodies, the Bundesrat and the Judicial Selection Committee of the Bundestag. Until the mid-1980s all female judges owed their nomination to the Bundesrat; Judge Karin Graßhoff was the first female member of the Court to be elected by the Bundestag's Judicial Selection Committee.

There have been other important institutional changes in the Court's history. In 1971 the Court was given the right to publish signed dissenting opinions of its members as enclosure to its majority decisions. While this aspect had played no role in the debate over the Constitutional Court in the Parliamentary Council, the introduction of dissenting votes was strongly advocated by the SPD during the deliberations of the FCCA. It then found no backing among the conservative parties which feared that the publication of split votes and minority opinions would damage the Court's authority.[21] As some observers have maintained, it was hardly a coincidence that the introduction of 'dissenting opinions' was accompanied by a revision of the rules regarding the period of office of members of the Court (a maximum 12-year term of office with no possibility of re-election).[22] The latter was designed to reinforce the principle of judicial independence to counter a possible shift towards a greater exposure of individual judges which was expected to develop from their new powers to deliver dissenting opinions.

An empirical evaluation of all decisions made since 1971 reveals that older assessments suggesting a steady decrease of dissenting opinions since the 1980s[23] have to be revised. The share of decisions published with a dissenting opinion of one or more judges was highest between 1970 and 1980 (11.6 per cent on average). It then fell to an average of 6.4 per cent in the period 1980–87. However, the decade between 1988 and 1997 was marked by a slight increase of dissenting opinions with a long-term average of 6.6 per cent. The share of dissenting opinions was extremely high in 1995 when every fifth decision of the Court (seven out of 35) had enclosed a dissenting opinion of one or more judges.[24] To be sure, these figures are hardly impressive when compared to the share of 'separate votes' issued by the United States Supreme Court. In 1995, for instance, only 37 per cent of all Supreme Court decisions had the full backing of all judges.[25] These big differences reflect the very different judicial traditions of the two countries. In Germany judicial decision-making has always been understood mainly as a co-operative process. Thus, the comparatively modest number of dissenting opinions has much to do with a widely shared 'sense of institutional loyalty'.[26]

While the rules of recruitment for judges and the internal decision-making structure of the Court have been subject to considerable reform, its area of competence, as set out in the Basic Law and the FCCA, has remained remarkably stable.[27] The legislator has been extremely careful not to restrict the Court's broad area of responsibility, despite various proposals from individual politicians and academics to abolish some of the types of cases listed in Article 13 of the FCCA. The only reform of restrictive nature dates back to the early 1950s when the Court's right to produce official reports requested by the federal government, the Bundestag or the federal president was abolished (in accordance with the Court's own recommendations). Also, the direct effects and implications of German unification for the Court have remained very limited. The most important reform was a slight revision of the professional qualification profile of potential judges designed to account for the different education systems in the former German Democratic Republic (GDR).[28]

## Governing by judicial means?

The bulk of scholars have long accepted the fact that for an institution such as the Federal Constitutional Court it is impossible to remain completely above or beyond the sphere of politics, at least in the sense that judicial decisions sometimes have considerable political implications.[29] As one observer has put it, 'in fact much of the political history of the Federal Republic, both in domestic and international affairs, and many important chapters of its social and economic history can be written through the Court judgements'.[30] The thesis of a growing tendency towards 'judicialisation' of politics, however, reaches somewhat further. Its proponents argue that the Constitutional Court – despite its comparatively limited democratic legitimacy – has come some way to take on the role assigned by the constitution to parliament, thereby reducing the political alternatives of future generations.[31]

While it is important to remember that the Constitutional Court can decide on an issue only after being invoked by the other political players, there are a number of ways for the Court to take part in policy-making. First of all, the Court has the authority to declare laws invalid or incompatible with the constitution.[32] There are, however, two other possible forms of decisions by which the Court can more or less directly influence the political fate of a specific law while acknowledging that the measure is still within the boundaries of the constitution. The Court may, first, deliver a so-called 'appeal decision' (*Appellentscheidung*) by which the legislator is required to revise the law concerned in order to prevent it from becoming unconstitutional. Alternatively the Court may determine the manner in which an act is interpreted by issuing a *verfassungskonforme Interpretation*, which sets out a single form by which the act can be deemed to conform with the constitution. Quite often these declarations include precise prescriptions for the implementation of a legal measure which clearly restrict the scope of action of parliament. A spectacular example of this judicial practice was given in the case of the decision on the Federal Republic's so-called 'Basic Treaty' (*Grundlagenvertrag*) with the GDR (BVerfGE 36, 1) when the Court claimed for the first time that any single phrase of its judgement was judicially binding for the government. An important more recent example may be seen in the Court's decision on abortion in 1993 (BVerfGE 88, 203).

The available figures seem largely to justify those critics who point to the danger of an increasing 'judicialisation of politics' in Germany. If the phenomenon is measured exclusively in terms of the total number of cases in which opposition parties have invoked the Court with a view of challenging a legislative majority decision, there may be little need to worry.[33] However, if additional indicators are taken into account a different picture emerges. Calculations by Landfried suggest that about 5 per cent of all federal laws have been invalidated since the early 1950s, with the largest number of cases belonging to the field of social policy, fiscal and financial policy and legal policy.[34] Among legislative 'key decisions' the share of cases which underwent judicial review was significantly above average, however. According to von Beyme, about 40 per cent of all 'key decisions' of the Bundestag passed in the period 1949–94 were dealt with by the Constitutional Court.[35] Generally, it can be argued that the Court's potential for controlling the legislator varies according to the precision with which individual issues are regulated in the Basic Law. The intensity of judicial review has been greatest in cases touching the material core of the Basic Law, such as individual basic rights (*Grundrechte*) and the fundamental organisational principles of the constitution.[36]

A judgement on the degree of 'judicialisation' of politics observable in Germany, of course, remains dependent on normative considerations on the nature of democratic policy-making.[37] As for the empirical dimension, a considerable degree of involvement of the Constitutional Court in the policy-making process seems hard to deny. This cannot really be blamed on the judges, although some observers have called for a more guarded behaviour of the Court's members in the public political debate.[38] The silent transformation of judicial review in Germany into what could be called 'governing by judicial means' was favoured significantly by at least two other factors. First of all, the strongly legalistic political culture which tends to accept judicial decisions more easily than parliamentary majority decisions as the final say in highly politicised matters played an important role in setting the parameters of judicial review in Germany, although there have been signs in the 1990s that this background variable has started losing its formerly dominant influence (see below). Secondly, and perhaps even more important, a powerful position of the Court is fostered by the inclination among the political elite to wait for the Court's guidance rather than to set the course if this is deemed politically expedient.[39] In this sense the Constitutional Court sometimes represents an institution of last resort not only for the opposition, but also for a government fearful of the political consequences of unattractive legislative measures. The combination of this tendency with the above-mentioned attempt of the major political parties to keep a firm grip on the nomination process of judges has been judged as 'arguably the most dangerous institutional development of recent years'.[40]

## The Constitutional Court as a counter-government?

The argument of a growing involvement of the Constitutional Court in the policy-making process does not normally include any specific assumptions about the political direction of the Court's activities. However, the suspicion that the Court could take the position of a 'counter-weight' to the government of the day has figured large since the early days of the Federal Republic, among politicians and scholars alike.[41]

The debate on the Court's attitude towards parliamentary majority decisions has traditionally centred on the institutional device of abstract norm review which may be initiated by the federal government, a Land government, or one-third of the members of the Bundestag in case of doubts about the compatibility between a federal and Land law or between these laws and the constitution. Although it is constitutional complaints rather than abstract judicial review procedures that have often resulted in judicial 'key decisions',[42] most observers see the latter as the type of cases in which 'the Constitutional Court is most politically exposed'.[43]

The threat to invoke the Constitutional Court has come to be seen as one of the most forceful components of the institutional opportunity structure of the opposition in the Bundestag.[44] More recent research into the use of different types of cases has revealed that abstract judicial review, as well as disputes between institutions in the federation and federation–Länder disputes, are most often initiated by the parliamentary opposition or groups with a close party affiliation to the former.[45] Apart from a bipartisan initiative of the early 1960s, the first abstract judicial review procedure initiated by the majority parties in the Bundestag dates back only to the mid-1980s. Of the total number of abstract judicial review procedures initiated by the state governments in the period 1951–96, 64 per cent stemmed from governments which had close party political affiliations with the opposition in the Bundestag. Even in the field of disputes between institutions in the federation and federation–Länder disputes, 60 per cent of cases were initiated by the parliamentary opposition. Within the category of disputes between the federation and the Länder, no less than 78 per cent of the total number of cases initiated by a Land government originated from those close to the opposition parties in the Bundestag.

While the frequency with which the Constitutional Court is invoked by different political players shows a clear dividing line between government and opposition, with the latter being in a clearly dominant position when it comes to carrying legislative measures to Karlsruhe, the results of initiated proceedings have provoked much debate. Although individual cases – such as the Court's highly contentious ruling on abortion in 1993 which clearly challenged the decision of the parliamentary majority – are easily exploited by proponents of the counter-government thesis, more general empirical evidence supporting the thesis of a judicial 'counter-government' remains rather patchy. According to a study by Wewer, rather the opposite thesis, which emphasises the Constitutional Court's inclination to support the general political line set out by the ruling majority, seems to be true[46] – a finding which is explained with the Court's limited potential as a counter-government and the need to maintain public acceptance by smoothly integrating itself into the larger social and political order. In this context the Court's quite obvious opposition to the Social–Liberal reform policies in the 1970s is explained by the government's extremely narrow majority in the Bundestag and the permanent dominance of the conservative opposition in the Bundesrat, both reflecting the rather modest electoral mandate for Social–Liberal reform. As Kutscha has argued, also more recent decisions of the Constitutional Court also suggest one should avoid drawing hasty conclusions with regard to the counter-government thesis.[47] Taking into account the strong position of the Court within the German polity *and* its general inclination to support the legislator's views rather than to challenge them it may be adequate to consider the Constitutional Court as somewhat of a 'parallel government'.

## The Constitutional Court and the changing *'Zeitgeist'*

The difficulties of forming a more general hypothesis from a number of spectacular cases, however, should not blind us to the significantly increased amount of public criticism directed to the Court during the 1990s. Many observers judged the public criticism formulated in response to some more recent Court decisions as being of a completely new quality. Indeed, never before have members of a Land government tried to mobilise public disobedience to Court decisions, as happened in the aftermath of the *'Kruzifix'*-decision which ruled compulsory display of crosses in classrooms of Bavarian primary schools unconstitutional (BVerfGE 93, 1). Another case which stirred up considerable public opposition was the so-called 'Soldiers'-decision (BVerfGE 93, 266), in which the Court defended the basic right of freedom of speech against the complainant's accusation of slander.

What these and a number of other recent decisions, such as the 'sit in'-decision (BVerfGE 92, 1), have in common, is the great importance the Court attached to the principle of individual freedom. As Wassermann has argued, this general line of judicial interpretation of cases must be seen as a confirmation of the Court's traditional jurisdiction rather than a break with the past.[48] Indeed, the Court's strong defence of the freedom of opinion can be traced back to an early precedent of the 1950s, the so-called 'Lüth-judgement' (BVerfGE 7, 198). The interesting aspect behind this remarkable amount of judicial continuity – and a possible explanation for the quite unusual amount of public criticism that has plagued the Court in the 1990s – is the fact that the canon of political values supported by the Constitutional

Court no longer seems to correspond with the dominant values in society.[49] According to Bull, there are other examples of cases to be found in which the Court has tended to stick to its traditional normative codex (especially its understanding of 'democracy'), thereby opening a gap between the Court's line of arguing and the '*Zeitgeist*'.[50] While the dominant developmental tendency in state organisation and public policy-making has been towards deregulation, co-operation, negotiation and self-government, the Court has used a number of more recent cases, such as its judgement on the Schleswig-Holstein co-determination law (*Mitbestimmungsgesetz*), to defend the principle of hierarchy as the dominant organisational principle for the modern state and public administration.

The significance of a changing relationship between the '*Zeitgeist*' and the set of values represented by the Constitutional Court should not be underestimated. While a strong formal position of the Court towards the other constitutional organs is guaranteed by the Basic Law, the Court's capacity to perform an integrative function for the political system as a whole is conditioned on its normative acceptance by the citizens. In the mid-1990s the number of citizens who believed that their political basic values corresponded with those represented by the Constitutional Court decreased dramatically. According to Schäuble, about two-thirds of all German citizens found their set of basic values did not correspond with those maintained by the Court.[51] Although the crisis of the mid-1990s does not seem to have irreparably damaged the relationship between the Court and the public, seeking a flexible balance between judicial integrity and (changing) societal expectations remains a major task of the German constitutional democracy. Nevertheless, it would be misleading to evaluate the Court's future performance only on the basis of the amount of spontaneous public support for, or opposition against, individual decisions. In addition, a less hostile attitude to political conflicts in general, which has separated Germany's political culture from the Anglo-Saxon tradition for so long, seems necessary to give political institutions a chance to perform their duties in an ever-more fragmented modern society.[52]

## Overload

Permanent work overload has been one of the main characteristics of the Constitutional Court virtually since its very creation. To a certain extent the large number of cases brought before the Court does underline its centrality and importance for the German political system, and could be seen as a positive confirmation of its far-reaching acceptance among individual political players and the public alike. However, in the 1990s the work pressure on the Court reached unprecedented levels. In 1997 the Federal Constitutional Court was admonished by the European Court of Human Rights, which considered the long duration of procedures in Karlsruhe as a violation of the European Convention of Human Rights.[53] As early as mid-1996 a highly specialised reform commission was set up by the Minister of Justice, which reported in December 1997.[54]

In most categories of cases there has been a considerable increase in cases brought before the Court in the aftermath of German unification, though it is difficult to assess the exact impact of unification on this tendency in the individual fields of cases.[55] For instance, of all the 117 cases concerning evaluations of electoral rules brought before the Court between 1951 and 1996, more than 40 per cent were initiated in the period 1991–96. The same holds true for cases concerning disputes between institutions in the federation, where 46 of a total of 114 cases since the early 1950s were initiated between 1990 and 1996. However, most dramatic was the increase of cases within the category of constitutional complaints, at least if absolute figures are considered. In the three decades between the early 1950s and 1982 the Court received about 51 000 constitutional complaints; the number of constitutional complaints put before the Court in the period 1983–96 exceeded 56 000. Still, contrary to widely held beliefs, the increase in constitutional complaints in the 1990s cannot primarily be explained by the considerable increase in the German population through the integration of the former GDR. As Blankenburg has emphasised, the total share of constitutional complaints stemming from citizens in the new eastern Länder is proportionally lower than that of their compatriots in the Western parts of Germany.[56]

Acknowledging the fact that the traditionally high degree of the Court's public acceptance has much to do with its very wide area of competence,[57] the reform commission stuck to the general line of reforming the Court's working procedures without narrowing its wide area of competence. At the centre of reform proposals was a plan to make the Court's dealings with constitutional complaints more efficient by granting the Second Senate the authority to decide as to whether a complaint should be accepted or not. A reform in this direction, clearly inspired by the American Supreme Court's 'writ of certiorari' procedure, was considered by the Court itself as early as 1954.[58] A realisation of this proposal would mean abolishing the system of scrutinising complaints on their chances of success by the chambers. Other proposals of structural reform, such as the increase in the number of judges, the creation of a Third Senate or the introduction of a 'political question' doctrine, were not recommended by the commission.

## Conclusions

All in all, the Federal Constitutional Court can be seen as one of the most successful political institutions of the German polity. Public criticism has waxed and waned over recent decades but at the close of the 20th century the strong public support for this most innovative of all institutional creations by the Basic Law seems virtually unbroken.

The place of the Constitutional Court within the German political system is, however, less easily described than one would expect judging by the framers' clear intentions to construct the Court as a *'pouvoir neutre'*, a position the Weimar Constitution assigned to the head of state, the *Reichspräsident*.[59] The Court has come to be an important pillar of what Katzenstein has called the German 'semisovereign democracy', a highly checked and balanced type of Western democracy which makes compromising an indispensable qualification for successful political players.[60] Not only has the Court influenced the political history of post-war Germany by its numerous decisions in virtually every important policy field. Accounting for the possible reactions of the Constitutional Court has come to be part of the usual strategic considerations of government and opposition alike.

Recurring temptations of governing majorities to cut the Court's role as a crucial institutional device of the political opposition have been eased by the reasonable chance of alternation between government and opposition and the ensuing reallocation of the opportunity structure of competing political players. For a long time Germany's strongly legalistic political culture served as an additional safeguard against attacks upon the Court's far-reaching judicial responsibilities through sweeping institutional reforms. Any attempt to seriously weaken the Court's power in pursuing short-lived political gains seemed bound to incur incalculable political costs to the proponents of radical reform. However, the more recent developments seem to indicate that the social foundations of the Court's central position within the German polity are changing. At the height of the crisis of the 1990s, politicians could draw considerable public support for criticising the Court's strong position in the political decision-making arena. It remains to be seen if the whole construction of judicial review in the Federal

Republic is about to be overcome by a changing political culture, as some observers have argued recently.[61]

Despite the rather modest reforms of the Court's institutional profile, it is important to see that the overall position of the Constitutional Court within the German polity has not been immune to change. In the recent past there seem to have been two different tendencies at work. On the one hand, German unification produced a number of background conditions favouring an up-grading of the Court's role in the German political system, such as the significant increase in the number of citizens able to put forward a constitutional complaint or the creation of an enlarged and more complicated federal system including many unsolved legal issues.[62] Also some of the older factors responsible for the traditionally strong position of the Court, such as the highly legalistic tradition of the German political culture, seem to have survived the more recent waves of social and cultural modernisation. Finally, some authors see an important additional source of increasing power of the Constitutional Court in the declining public trust in political parties and the 'political class' as a whole.[63]

However, at the same time it is possible to discern an opposite developmental tendency towards a reduced weight of the Court within the German political system. Among the factors restricting the Court's parameters in the political decision-making process, the growing importance of European integration with an ensuing up-grading of the European Court of Justice has rightly been highlighted as a core variable.[64] As the role of the Basic Law in German politics decreases due to the increasing importance of EU-wide regulations, the position of the 'guardian of the constitution' can hardly remain untouched.

The growing significance of EU regulations is, however, not the only factor worth mentioning in this context. The Federal Constitutional Court's position within the German polity is diminishing also as a result of the growing weight of the Land constitutional courts. Before unification, only three of the existing constitutional courts in the Länder were authorised to tackle constitutional complaints. After unification the number of state constitutional courts increased to 15, with 10 of them having the right to decide on constitutional complaints.[65] As a result the Federal Constitutional Court will much less frequently become involved in cases originating in the Länder – a tendency that could further be strengthened by a more offensive interpretation of the Land constitutional courts' area of responsibility in other fields.[66]

While the Constitutional Court is to a very large extent dependent on external factors influencing its weight and position in the German polity, it is necessary to emphasise the Court's own responsibility for defining its position in a changing political environment. This seems to be particularly true with regard to the Court's position in European matters. Of the three conceivable strategies the Court has at its disposal – acquiescence, reassertion or co-operation – only the latter seems to hold some positive implications for the future. As Goetz has put it, 'in order to continue to contribute positively to the stability and vitality of the German political system, the Court will have to take full account of the need for co-operation. This does not equal conflict avoidance; rather it requires an appreciation of the functional limitations of constitutional legislation and review in a Europeanised democratic nation state and of the political and societal underpinnings of constitutional interpretation.'[67] The Court's stance formulated in the 1993 Maastricht decision (BVerfGE 89, 155) could be seen as an important first step towards applying a co-operative strategy as a future guiding principle in European matters.[68] Another more recent example of the Court's co-operative stance was the handling of the dispute surrounding the European Monetary Union.[69] Also at the domestic front, the Court has tried to redefine its position in a changing systemic context as smoothly as possible. In October 1998 it further strengthened the role of the constitutional courts of the Länder by ruling that certain forms of violations of the basic constitutional principles regarding elections are no longer to be taken to Karlsruhe if these violations relate to Land or local elections.[70]

The challenges that the Federal Constitutional Court is going to meet beyond the turn of the century are manifold: Europeanisation and a tendency towards functional and territorial differentiation of judicial review within the German polity are among the most simple ones to identify. These will be accompanied by much less tangible developments in the area of political culture which tend to question some of the social preconditions of strong judicial review in the Federal Republic.

## Notes

1  Erhard Blankenburg, 'Changes in Political Regimes and Continuity of the Rule of Law in Germany', in Herbert Jacob (ed.), *Courts, Law, and Politics in Comparative Perspective* (New Haven/London: Yale University Press, 1996), p. 308.
2  Article 126 of the 1849 Constitution already provided for the institutionalisation of constitutional complaints but did not establish the principle of judicial referral.

3  See Helmut Simon, 'Verfassungsgerichtsbarkeit', in Ernst Benda, Werner Maihofer and Hans-Jochen Vogel (eds), *Handbuch des Verfassungsrechts der Bundesrepublik Deutschland*, 2nd edn (Berlin/New York: de Gruyter, 1994), pp. 1640–1.

4  See Wolfgang Wehler, 'Der Staatsgerichtshof für das Deutsche Reich: Die politische Rolle der Verfassungsgerichtsbarkeit in der Zeit der Weimarer Republik', PhD dissertation, University of Bonn (1979).

5  See Klaus von Beyme, 'The Genesis of Constitutional Review in Parliamentary Systems', in Christine Landfried (ed.), *Constitutional Review and Legislation: An International Comparison* (Baden-Baden: Nomos, 1988), p. 34.

6  See the figures compiled by Hans-Ulrich Derlien, 'Institutionalising Democracy in Germany: From Weimar to Bonn and Berlin', in Metin Heper, Ali Kazancigil and Bert A. Rockman (eds), *Institutions and Democratic Statecraft* (Boulder, Col.: Westview Press, 1997), pp. 158–9.

7  See Gian Enrico Rusconi, 'Quale "democrazia costituzionale"? La corte federale nella politica tedesca e il problema della costituzione europea', *Rivista Italiana di Scienza Politica*, 27 (1997), pp. 272–306; Donald P. Kommers, *The Constitutional Jurisprudence of the Federal Republic of Germany*, 2nd edn (Durham/London: Duke University Press, 1997). However, as a review of the literature suggests, foreign judgements of the Court seem to have always been somewhat more favourable than the majority of assessments by German scholars. See Heinz Laufer, 'Verfassungsordnung und Verfassungsentwicklung', in Franz Schneider (ed.), *Der Weg der Bundesrepublik von 1945 bis zur Gegenwart* (Munich: Beck, 1985), p. 163.

8  For a detailed analysis of the FCCA's genesis see Willi Geiger, *Gesetz über das Bundesverfassungsgericht* (Berlin: Franz Vahlen, 1951), and Hans J. Lietzmann, *Das Bundesverfassungsgericht. Eine sozialwissenschaftliche Studie* (Baden-Baden: Nomos, 1985), pp. 30–59. Some very important aspects of the Court's self-conception as a supreme constitutional organ and its full budgetary and organisational independence from any other institution were formulated in a memorandum drafted by Judge Gerhard Leibholz, published in June 1951 on behalf of the Court.

9  D. Kommers (note 7), p. 17.

10  *Ibid.*, pp. 19–20.

11  See Erhard Blankenburg, 'Die Verfassungsbeschwerde – Die Nebenbühne der Politik und Klagemauer von Bürgern', *Kritische Justiz*, 31 (1998), p. 212.

12  Until 1956 a successful nomination by the Judicial Selection Committee was conditioned on the support of at least 9 of its members which meant a three-quarters-majority quorum. See Richard Ley, 'Die Wahl der Mitglieder des Bundesverfassungsgerichtes: Eine Dokumentation anläßlich des 40 jährigen Bestehens', *Zeitschrift für Parlamentsfragen*, 22 (1991), pp. 435–6.

13  See Christian Pestalozza, *Verfassungsprozeßrecht: Die Verfassungsgerichtsbarkeit des Bundes und der Länder mit einem Anhang zum Internationalen Rechtsschutz*, 3rd edn (Munich: Beck, 1991), pp. 43–5.

14  Sybille Koch, 'Die Wahl der Richter des BVerfG', *Zeitschrift für Rechtspolitik*, 29 (1996), pp. 41–4.

15 Still, most observers maintain that the party political affiliation of individual judges has no decisive impact on Court judgements; see Peter Häberle, 'Die Verfassungsbeschwerde im System der bundesdeutschen Verfassungsgerichtsbarkeit', *Jahrbuch des öffentlichen Rechts*, 45 (1997), p. 93. For a number of important decisions where party affiliation seemed to play a role see Christine Landfried, 'Constitutional Review and Legislation in the Federal Republic of Germany', in C. Landfried (note 5), p. 148.

16 See Stefan Ulrich Pieper, *Verfassungsrichterwahlen* (Berlin: Duncker & Humblot, 1998), pp. 27–8.

17 See *Frankfurter Allgemeine Zeitung*, 3 December 1998, p. 6.

18 See C. Landfried (note 15), p. 149.

19 Figures calculated by the author on the basis of data provided by the public relations office of the Federal Constitutional Court.

20 See C. Landfried (note 15), p. 164.

21 See H. Lietzmann (note 8), pp. 53–5.

22 See Christian Rau, *Selbst entwickelte Grenzen in der Rechtsprechung des United States Supreme Court und des Bundesverfassungsgerichts* (Berlin: Duncker & Humblot, 1996), pp. 155–6.

23 See Klaus Schlaich, *Das Bundesverfassungsgericht: Stellung, Verfahren, Entscheidungen*, 4th edn (Munich: Beck, 1997), p. 41.

24 The figures for the period between 1971–80 and 1980–87 are taken from Ernst Gottfried Mahrenholz, 'Das richterliche Sondervotum', in Werner Hoppe, Werner Krawietz and Martin Schulte (eds), *Rechtsprechungslehre – 2: Internationales Symposium Münster 1988* (Köln: Carl Heymanns, 1992), p. 168. The figures for the last decade until November 1997 have been calculated by the author.

25 See Lawrence Baum, *The Supreme Court*, 6th edn (Washington, DC: Congressional Quarterly Press, 1998), p. 139.

26 D. Kommers (note 7), p. 26.

27 Of the 15 principal types of cases laid down in the FCCA, the following five have proved to be of particular importance with regard to their political impact: disputes between institutions in the federation, disputes between the federation and the Länder, concrete norm review (judicial referral), abstract norm review, and constitutional complaints. See Klaus H. Goetz, 'The Federal Constitutional Court', in Gordon Smith, William Paterson and Stephen Padgett (eds), *Developments in German Politics 2* (London: Macmillan, 1996), pp. 97–8. In contrast to all other listed types of cases, constitutional complaints were not originally provided for by the framers of the Basic Law but only introduced in the FCCA in 1951 and embodied in the Basic Law in 1969.

28 See Friedrich Karl Fromme, 'Bundesverfassungsgericht', in Werner Weidenfeld and Karl-Rudolf Korte (eds), *Handbuch zur deutschen Einheit* (Bonn: Bundeszentrale für politische Bildung, 1996), pp. 84–5; see also Nevil Johnson, 'The Federal Constitutional Court: Facing up to the Strains of Law and Politics in the New Germany', *German Politics*, 3 (1994), pp. 137–8.

29 See Michael Piazzolo (ed.), *Das Bundesverfassungsgericht: Ein Gericht im Schnittpunkt von Recht und Politik* (Mainz/Munich: v. Hase & Koehler, 1996).

30 K. Goetz (note 27), p. 102.

31  See Christine Landfried, 'The Judicialisation of Politics in Germany', *International Political Science Review*, 15 (1994), p. 119, and Walter Schmitt Glaeser, 'Das Bundesverfassungsgericht als "Gegengewalt" zum verfassungsändernden Gesetzgeber? – Lehren aus dem Diäten-Streit 1995', in Joachim Burmeister (ed.), *Verfassungsstaatlichkeit. Festschrift für Klaus Stern zum 65. Geburtstag* (Munich: Beck, 1997), p. 1198. It is also possible, however, to identify a minority opinion among German scholars in which the Court is positively assigned the role of a 'substitution legislator' (*Ersatzgesetzgeber*) which should provide parliament with suggestions for its legislative activity; see, for example, Alexander von Brünneck, *Verfassungsgerichtsbarkeit in den westlichen Demokratien* (Baden-Baden: Nomos, 1992), p. 177; Bernd Guggenberger, 'Die Rechtsprechung des Bundesverfassungsgerichts und die institutionelle Balance des demokratischen Verfassungsstaates', in Bernd Guggenberger and Thomas Würtenberger (eds), *Das Bundesverfassungsgericht im Widerstreit* (Baden-Baden, Nomos, 1998), pp. 209–12.

32  Until the reform of the FCCA in 1970, this was the Court's only formal alternative to declaring a legislative measure unconstitutional with the Basic Law. See Martin Schulte, 'Appellentscheidungen des Bundesverfassungsgerichts', in W. Hoppe, W. Krawietz and M. Schulte (note 24), p. 180.

33  See Klaus Stüwe, 'Der "Gang nach Karlsruhe". Die Opposition im Bundestag als Antragsstellerin vor dem Bundesverfassungsgericht', *Zeitschrift für Parlamentsfragen*, 28 (1997), p. 557.

34  See C. Landfried (note 31), p. 114.

35  Klaus von Beyme, *The Legislator: German Parliament as a Centre of Decision-Making* (Aldershot: Ashgate, 1998), p. 108.

36  See Horst Säcker, 'Gesetzgebung durch das Bundesverfassungsgericht? Das Bundesverfassungsgericht und die Legislative', in M. Piazzolo (note 29), p. 207.

37  See Torbjörn Vallinder, 'The Judicialization of Politics – a World-wide Phenomenon: Introduction', *International Political Science Review*, 15 (1994), pp. 91–9.

38  See Otfried Höffe, *Vernunft und Recht. Bausteine zu einem interkulturellen Rechtsdiskurs* (Frankfurt a.M.: Suhrkamp, 1996), pp. 266–9.

39  See Wolfgang Knies, 'Auf dem Weg in den "verfassungsgerichtlichen Jurisdiktionsstaat"? Das Bundesverfassungsgericht und die gewaltenteilende Kompetenzordnung des Grundgesetzes', in J. Burmeister (note 31), p. 1179; C. Landfried (note 31), pp. 116–18.

40  Werner Patzelt, 'Deutsche Politik unter Reformdruck', in Robert Hettlage and Karl Lenz (eds), *Deutschland nach der Wende: Eine Zwischenbilanz* (Munich: Beck, 1995), p. 82.

41  See Michael Reissenberger, 'Wer bewacht die Wächter? Zur Diskussion um die Rolle des Verfassungsgerichts', *Aus Politik und Zeitgeschichte*, B 15/1997, p. 12; Richard Häußler, *Der Konflikt zwischen Bundesverfassungsgericht und politischer Führung: Ein Beitrag zur Geschichte und Rechtsstellung des Bundesverfassungsgerichts* (Berlin: Duncker & Humblot, 1994), pp. 22–74.

42  The Court's decision on the rules for admission to university courses, the so-called 'Numerus Clausus' decision (BVerfGE 33, 303), provides a case in point.

43 D. Kommers (note 7), p. 28.
44 See Ludger Helms, *Wettbewerb und Kooperation. Zum Verhältnis von Regierungsmehrheit und Opposition im parlamentarischen Gesetzgebungsverfahren in der Bundesrepublik Deutschland, Großbritannien und Österreich* (Opladen: Westdeutscher Verlag, 1997), pp. 59–60.
45 See K. Stüwe (note 33).
46 Göttrik Wewer, 'Das Bundesverfassungsgericht – eine Gegenregierung? Argumente zur Revision einer überkommen Denkfigur', in Bernhard Blanke and Hellmut Wollmann (eds), *Die alte Bundesrepublik: Kontinuität und Wandel* (Leviathan Sonderheft 12/1991) (Opladen: Westdeutscher Verlag, 1991), pp. 310–35.
47 Martin Kutscha, 'Das Bundesverfassungsgericht und der Zeitgeist', *Neue Justiz*, 50 (1996), pp. 171–5.
48 Rudolf Wassermann, 'Zur gegenwärtigen Krise des Bundesverfassungsgerichts', *Recht und Politik*, 32 (1996), p. 62.
49 See also Rainer Wahl, 'Quo Vadis – Bundesverfassungsgericht? Zur Lage von Verfassungsgerichtsbarkeit, Verfassung und Staatsdenken', in B. Guggenberger and Th. Würtenberger (note 31), p. 90.
50 Hans Peter Bull, 'Hierarchie als Verfassungsgebot? Zur Demokratietheorie des Bundesverfassungsgerichts', in Michael Thomas Greven, Herfried Münkler and Rainer Schmalz-Bruns (eds), *Bürgersinn und Kritik: Festschrift für Udo Bermbach zum 60. Geburtstag* (Baden-Baden: Nomos, 1998), pp. 241–56.
51 Thomas Schäuble, 'Gewaltenteilung und Bundesverfassungsgericht', in: *Recht und Politik*, 32 (1996), p. 67.
52 See also Helmuth Schulze-Fielitz, 'Das Bundesverfassungsgericht in der Krise des Zeitgeists. Zur Metadogmatik der Verfassungsinterpretation', *Archiv des öffentlichen Rechts*, 122 (1997), p. 31.
53 *Frankfurter Allgemeine Zeitung*, 30 June 1997, p. 5.
54 However, at the time of writing no concrete legislative measure was in sight to answer the commission's requests centring on making the procedure of dealing with constitutional complaints less time-consuming for the Court.
55 All figures presented in this paragraph are drawn from Bundesministerium der Justiz (ed.), *Entlastung des Bundesverfassungsgerichts: Bericht der Kommission* (Bonn, 1998), p. 153.
56 E. Blankenburg (note 11), p. 212.
57 See Rainer Faupel, 'Das Bundesverfassungsgericht in Nöten. Die Vorschläge der Kommission zur Entlastung des BVerfG', *Neue Justiz*, 52 (1998), p. 58.
58 See Hans-Justus Rinck, 'Die Vorprüfung der Verfassungsbeschwerde', *Neue Jursitische Wochenschrift*, 12 (1959), p. 170.
59 Indeed, as some scholars have suggested, the abolition of the Constitutional Court would entail a significant strengthening of the position of the federal president within the German polity; see H. Säcker (note 36), p. 223. However, as the main principle of constitutional policy in post-war Germany towards the office of the federal president could be described as 'keeping Weimar at bay', this position remains a highly hypothetical assumption with practically no bases of political support.
60 Peter Katzenstein, *Policy and Politics in West Germany: The Growth of a Semisovereign State* (Philadelphia: Temple University Press, 1987).

61 See for instance Hans J. Lietzmann, '"Reflexiver Konstitutionalismus" und Demokratie. Die moderne Gesellschaft überholt die Verfassungsrechtsprechung', in B. Guggenberger and Th. Würtenberger (note 31), p. 259.

62 See Matthias Hartwig, 'Die zukünftige Position des Bundesverfassungsgerichts im staatsrechtlichen Gefüge der Bundesrepublik Deutschland', in M. Piazzolo (note 29), p. 166. Indeed, the Court's involvement in the handling of the internal unification process was quite remarkable, including crucial decisions in fields as different as the electoral system, land reform or prosecution of former GDR officials. See F. K. Fromme (note 28).

63 See Hans Herbert von Arnim, 'Reformblockade der Politik? Ist unser Staat noch handlungsfähig', *Zeitschrift für Rechtspolitik*, 31 (1998), p. 145.

64 See K. Schlaich (note 23), pp. 237–52; Hans Heinrich Rupp, 'Ausschaltung des Bundesverfassungsgerichts durch den Amsterdamer Vertrag?', *Juristen Zeitung*, 53 (1998), pp. 213–7; Hans-Peter Folz, *Demokratie und Integration: Der Konflikt zwischen Bundesverfassungsgericht und Europäischen Gerichtshof über die Kontrolle der Gemeinschaftskompetenzen* (Berlin: Springer, 1999).

65 See Kai Danter, 'Entlastung des Bundesverfassungsgerichts durch Regionalisierung von Kompetenzen zu den Landesverfassungsgerichten', *Die Öffentliche Verwaltung*, 51 (1998), p. 240.

66 See Konrad Hesse, 'Verfassungsrechtsprechung im geschichtlichen Wandel', *Juristen Zeitung*, 50 (1995), p. 269.

67 K. Goetz (note 27), p. 115.

68 See Ralf Wittkowski, 'Das Maastricht-Urteil des Bundesverfassungsgerichts vom 12.10.1993 als "Solange III"-Entscheidung?', *Bayerische Verwaltungsblätter*, 40 (1994), pp. 359–63; Konrad Hesse, 'Stufen der Entwicklung der deutschen Verfassungsgerichtsbarkeit', *Jahrbuch des öffentlichen Rechts*, 46 (1998), p. 21.

69 See Rainer Arnold, 'L'union monétaire européenne et la Constitution allemande', *Revue du droit public et de la science politique en France et a étranger*, 3 (1998), pp. 654–7.

70 *Frankfurter Allgemeine Zeitung*, 7 October 1998, p. 6.

# 6

# The Federal System: Breaking through the Barriers of Interlocking Federalism?

*Roland Sturm*

## Introduction: 'the end of federalism as we know it?'

Federalism in Germany today attracts more public attention than it ever has since its ground rules were determined by the Parliamentary Council (*Parlamentarischer Rat*) who wrote Germany's constitution in 1948. Politicians of all parties suggest a wide range of measures for a reform of federalism. Some want to reduce the number of Länder, others stress the need for reconsidering the way the Länder are financed. Those discontent with the *status quo* also believe that it is essential to legislate a new division of responsibilities between the federal government and the Länder, or they want to improve the role of the Länder in the decision-making process of the European Union (EU). Even the Organisation for Economic Co-operation and Development (OECD) in its 1998 economic survey of Germany has criticised the fact that the German federal system makes no use of the economic advantages which federal financial autonomy and flexibility could secure.[1]

Does this imply that a major constitutional reform in Germany is about to be made part of this country's political agenda? Yes and No. Yes, because the crisis of the German federal system seems to demand political initiatives to solve its major problems. No, because it is difficult to envisage the two-thirds majorities required for constitutional reform both in the Bundestag and the Bundesrat.

Further clarification is necessary to better understand this dilemma. This contribution will therefore look at the most important and currently most controversial aspects of German federalism in order to give the reader information and orientation which helps him or her to understand the ongoing political debate. The first question which will be asked here is what is the political role of federalism today and how has the underlying philosophy of German federalism changed over time? This leads us to the analysis of some institutional aspects of federalism. When we look at the way federalism works in practice, we first notice the number of actors on the sub-national level. Why are there 16 Länder, and could it not be less? Another institutional feature of German federalism is the division of competences in the German political system between the federal government (*Bund*) and the Land level. The Länder have an important role in federal legislation which they exercise via the Bundesrat. Länder politics need to be financed and there is a highly complex set of rules to determine Länder income, which also requires some explanation. Finally, there is the European context for the Länder, in which the Länder – in their perspective – if they are successful become a more important part of political life as major actors in a 'Europe of the Regions', or if they fail are reduced to second-class political status as insignificant administrative entities of the German nation-state. In conclusion this contribution will bring together the different aspects which characterise today's federalism in Germany and the different arguments made for its reform. It has to be left to the reader, however, to judge how radical a reform of German federalism needs to be to rescue its substance. One of the problems of a reform of German federalism seems to be that there is a lack of consensus on the question of what still counts or can be defined as an essential element of 'true' federalism? The heated debate, we observe today, mixes arguments and political interests. Still, its bottom line is a consensus that German federalism 'looks cumbersome and flawed'.[2]

## Concepts of federalism

Before statehood was re-created in post-war West Germany , i.e. before 1949, the Länder were already established as political actors. Because of this fact, but also because of a certain historical tradition of federalism in Germany, and last but not least because of the strong support for federalism by the Western Allied Powers, the unitary state was no realistic option for West Germany. Even in East Germany, where the Soviet Union established a centralised political system, it took until 1952 to abolish the five East German Länder and to introduce 14 administrative regions (*Bezirke*).

## Dual or cooperative federalism?

West Germany's federalism was from the start a watered-down version of federalism. This is at least what early[3] and certainly more recent critics have argued. They compare it to an ideal type of federalism which is modelled on the idea of dual federalism for which we find the best examples in the history of Switzerland and the United States.[4] Dual federalism refers to more than a clear separation of responsibilities between different levels of government and the existence of a full set of political institutions on both the national and the sub-national level of government. It also incorporates the belief that in a nation-state the citizens' priority of allegiance is local and regional. This belief is deeply rooted in a nation's political culture. Such a federal state 'tolerates' national politics, but it does not rely on them for its social and economic development. In this context it is of only secondary importance to ask how much unity and how much diversity is needed for a well-functioning federal order. Diversity is the rule, and every political initiative which aims at a reduction of diversity needs justification.

In post-war Germany federalism never aspired to become such a kind of dual federalism. It lacked all prerequisites. How could it be built on regional loyalties when most of the newly founded Länder were artificially created territorial entities with completely new boundaries. And how could separate decision-making processes on the national and the sub-national level develop diversity when a great deal of co-operation between these two levels of government was required by law to make the new constitution work. Public administration, also of national laws, for example, was mostly made a responsibility of Land administrations. A 'functional' interpretation of federalism seemed to expect that the task of policy-making was to be performed mostly on the federal level. The laws made here were to be implemented by the Länder. The Bundesrat, a federal institution, provided access for the Länder to federal decision-making and to shared control over federal power. The Länder were given here a voice in federal legislation and even a right to veto this legislation. So, the Basic Law provided amble room for co-operation and collaboration.

But also where the Länder were not forced to co-ordinate their politics with the federal government they preferred co-operation to a diversity of Länder policies. As early as 1948 the Länder began to co-ordinate their education policies, for example. Meanwhile, more than 1000 task forces exist in which the Länder co-ordinate in many cases even minute details of their policies.

If neither a diversity of Länder policies, nor the protection of regional cultures was expected from federalism, what then was the role it should play in post-war Germany? The answer is: to help secure democracy after the experience of the Nazi dictatorship which had used a unitary state structure to strengthen its grip on society. In post-war Germany federalism was seen as a principle to organise the state, not society. In addition to the traditional separation of powers in the tradition of Montesquieu, federalism introduced with sub-national government a new level of separate political power. From the point of view of dual federalism there are two problems with this interpretation of federalism. One is that it does not see sub-national government as the level of government which has or at least should be given political priority, but as an instrument to check and balance national government. And, in addition, once democracy in Germany was firmly established there was a danger that the need for such checks, and by implication the need for a meaningful degree of autonomy of the sub-national level, might be forgotten.

And this is exactly what happened. This observation is not meant as criticism. Who would object to the fact that in post-war Germany democracy was not seriously under threat. However, though this observation is only one factor which explains the development of German federalism, the marginalisation of the 'control of federal power' argument may help us understand why there was so little resistance to the strengthening of joint decision-making by the Länder and federal government which the Grand Coalition government of the late 1960s initiated. At that time when, with the Keynesian reform of West Germany's economic constitution, the tendency to an ever-greater uniformity of living conditions in Germany was accelerated, one looked in vain for the defenders of sub-national political autonomy. Already in the first two decades of the Federal Republic the federal government had claimed responsibility in many of the policy fields which the Basic Law in its Article 72 had reserved for the Länder, as long as the federal level did not justify its intervention by the need to secure a uniformity of living conditions in Germany or the uniformity of economic and legal provisions. The centralisation of federalism had been seen as a quasi-'natural' development. In the late 1960s it was declared to be a virtue.

## The crisis of interlocking federalism

With the constitutional changes of the late 1960s and a number of laws which accompanied these changes joint decision-making of the national and the federal level became the rule in German politics. Interlocking federalism (*Politikverflechtung*[5]) institutionalised federalism as a method of decision-making. The spotlight was now firmly on those political actors – the national and regional governments – who became masters of the 'federalism game' and on their bargaining skills.

Interlocking federalism was successfully established because of both the need to create the tools for Keynesian economic intervention into the economy, for example joint economic and financial planning of the federal government and the Länder, and the political decision in favour of the expansion of the welfare state. In the logic of the latter, equality of benefits for individual citizens was of central importance. Federalism was at best seen as a negative influence which might distort equality and which therefore had to be controlled, or it was simply ignored when legislation was passed.

The success of a greater centralisation of federalism was also facilitated because of the way in which political parties acted as important agents of change. The little that was left of the opposition of one or the other Land to greater uniformity of Germany's political system could not withstand party political pressures. Land party organisations in Germany do not display significant programmatic independence from their national party organisation. As a consequence, Land governments at least until the 1990s mostly tended to define their policies with reference to the national role of their party in Bonn. Land elections were often regarded as popularity tests for the national parties. Land interests were relegated to second-order problems. To overcome the dominance of party political interests over Land interests in Land electoral contests and in the politics of Land governments, the somewhat strange suggestion has been made to rewrite the Basic Law in order to force the Länder parties to form all-party coalition governments. All-party coalitions, it is argued, would not be able to support special party political interests and would therefore automatically better represent Länder interests.[6]

This suggestion by a political scientist was not taken up in the political discourse. The only reform of federalism which ignored party political dividing lines was brought about by the legislation of the Grand Coalition government of 1966–69. As in this case the big parties had agreed on the need for an institutional reform of federalism, this did not leave much room for any party politician representing a Land government to voice opposition. This reform aimed, however, at a greater efficiency of policy outcomes. It strengthened the power of the federal government and increased centralisation.

The development of interlocking federalism was also 'rational' in the eyes of the decision-makers in the Länder. This is a factor one should not underestimate. If we look more closely at the results of the federalism reform of the late 1960s, we can see that it would be wrong to identify in this context only losers on the Land level and no winners. Those who lost because of these reforms were the Land parliaments. Their responsibilities were reduced and their autonomy shrank. The Baden-Württemberg Economics Minister Walter Döring[7] sees the Land parliaments reduced to 'administrative units' with the quality of 'county councils' (*Landkreisqualität*). At the same time, however, the Land governments who had to give their consent to constitutional change, for which a two-thirds majority in the Bundesrat was needed, were among the winners. Their influence grew due to the loss of regional autonomy. They were compensated by a greater say in federal affairs via the instrument of the Bundesrat who is involved in every piece of federal legislation.

Interlocking federalism strengthened political executives on all levels of government. Most decisions now have to be made jointly between the Länder and the federal government behind closed doors in negotiations and are mostly prepared and often also made by civil servants. Political compromises found here have several advantages for decision-makers. Criticism can easily be deflected to other partners of the negotiation process. Responsibility for popular policies, however, can be claimed no matter what role a specific person or Land had really played behind the scenes. And parliaments on all levels can be tamed with the argument that the complicated compromise found in negotiations with so many partners should not be vetoed or modified, because any modification asked for by one parliament might restart the time-consuming negotiation process with unknown consequences.

It is debatable whether one can argue that the kind of negotiated democracy which is the result of the ever-present need for German federalism to organise co-operation is something one should really criticise. Defenders of the *status quo* have argued that for Germany's consensus-seeking democracy this is the logical and adequate way to moderate conflict and to solve political problems. After all, has Germany's low-conflict society not become an internationally admired success? Those who hold these views think that it is completely unjustified to take the examples of the United States or Switzerland as a yardstick and to criticise German federalism for its low degree of regional diversity and autonomy.[8] They believe that improvements with regard to the instruments and techniques of decision-making are the key for an increased efficiency of interlocking federalism to which there is no realistic alternative.

The problem with this position is, however, that it forgets to reflect on the preconditions for the success of the German kind of negotiated federal decision-making. This success had at least three preconditions which in the 1990s have continuously lost political importance. It is therefore not surprising that for many observers and politicians today the formerly cherished *status quo* of interlocking federalism is no longer an option. These three preconditions are:

- *Economic success*. Only economic success can provide the resources needed to facilitate success in political negotiation processes, including those between the relevant political actors in a federal system. Here, as elsewhere, negotiations are about the distribution of public goods and private benefits. As long as in such negotiations every participant can improve his position, even if it is by less than the gain of other participants, compromise is highly probable. If economic success or public borrowing can no longer provide the necessary resources to finance gains for everybody, political compromises become more difficult. When the definition of net winners and losers in negotiation processes is unavoidable, the richer Länder are tempted to ask for greater autonomy, because they are not so much in need of help from either the other Länder or the federal government. This demand for greater autonomy may find an echo on the federal level, because in a situation of a shortage of resources the federal government wants to get rid of costly responsibilities for policies and would be more than happy to transfer them back to the Länder. So it is not, as the supporters of the *status quo* assume, the attempt to introduce into the German debate an inadequate model for German federalism which focuses the current discussion on the demand for greater autonomy of the Länder, but a kind of reasoning quite compatible with the earlier preference of the same decision-makers for consensus-based negotiations.
- *An important economic role for national markets*. The preference for greater regional autonomy, especially of the richer Länder, is re-enforced by the fact that in the Single European Market with the Euro as common currency in economic terms national boundaries have become meaningless. National negotiations with other German Länder governments and the federal government no longer define the economic future of a Land. Competition in the Single Market is a challenge for every Land. In the European context it is

therefore more important for Land governments to make, at least in economic terms, the most of the potential of their Land. The way this can be done is not by negotiations with other Länder, but by a strategy which is based on regional autonomy. At least some degree of regional autonomy is the logical precondition for economic competition.

German federalism will in future also be challenged by the need for budgetary discipline in Europe. The question will have to be answered, how individual Länder control their budgets, or in other words what their responsibility for the national budget deficit should be, when Germany as a whole tries to meet the Maastricht criteria. In this context regional autonomy has the definite advantage for every Land not to be made responsible for budget overdrafts of others.

- *Relative social and economic homogeneity.* In the 1980s and 1990s the three traditional German parties (Christian Democrats, Social Democrats, Liberals) to a great extent lost their monopoly control over federal negotiation processes. Conflicts to be solved are now to a much smaller degree a result of party political confrontations which follow the government–opposition pattern of national politics. The rise of new parties has at least to some degree broken up this kind of party political discipline. Land interests have gained much more importance, be it with regard to differences of interest between the German Länder in the East and the German Länder in the West, be it with regard to differences of interest between a coalition of the poorer Länder and the federal government on the one hand and the richer Länder on the other, or be it with regard to the reduced relevance of the coalition pattern at the federal level for party political co-operation in the Länder.[9]

Because of the new social and political environment in which German federalism operates, strong forces in German society today see competition between the Länder as the most appropriate driving force behind a process which leads to the modernisation of federalism. From a theoretical and a comparative point of view the idea of 'the states as laboratories'[10] is not new. It would be apolitical to deny that it is above all in the short-term interest of the more successful Länder to become strong autonomous competitors, though one can also make the case that, as we will see later, reform is important for all the Länder, because German federalism will hardly be able to overcome its problems of efficiency if it does not escape the 'joint-decision trap'[11] of interlocking federalism.

## Competition-based federalism as alternative?

The mixture of arguments brought forward to justify more competition in federalism is still breathtaking. First of all, there are all the ideas borrowed from economics, such as the general assumption that competition is the best principle for organising a state and for provoking the Länder into finding innovative solutions for their problems, or the principle of 'fiscal equivalence',[12] which is interpreted as the need for a close correspondence of regional tax burdens and regional expenditures. The aim of the latter is to improve the democratic accountability of regional governments and to give the voters at regional elections a better chance to react to a government's track record.

Second, there is a revival of Catholic social thought embodied in the subsidiarity principle (though the connected principle of solidarity is in these arguments to some extent ignored). Subsidiarity is understood to mean that social problems should be solved by the smallest political entity available. Upper levels of government should get involved only if the lower level cannot cope with the problems with which it is confronted, and asks for help. The role of regions as the relevant level for political decision-making in many respects was recently strengthened by the efforts of the Commission of the European Union to improve the efficiency of her regional and structural policies with the help of information gained by the direct contact of the EU with the European regions.

Third, the old argument of the greater democratic quality of a polity which balances national political power by a multitude of regional power centres has been revived. Federalism in this respect is seen as a remedy for the problem of '*Politikverdrossenheit*' (being fed up with politics), because Land parliaments and governments are seen as a political level close to the citizens. Here, participation is said to be much easier and much more promising, and has more concrete results for the individual citizen than his or her influence on the national level could ever yield.

German federalism today has discovered competition-based federalism as the best alternative to interlocking federalism. Still, political reform is slow and it is difficult to find majorities among the Länder for reform with 11 Länder profiting from the *status quo* and five better-off ones (Baden-Württemberg, Bavaria, Hamburg, Hesse and North Rhine-Westphalia) with governments who have their heads full of new ideas. What makes reform so complicated is that a radical remodelling of federalism is necessary to make it fit for competition.

To change the current system of federalism from a procedural device which gives ever-greater power to Land governments in federal affairs (*Beteiligungsföderalismus*), which is, as mentioned above, the result of interlocking federalism, to a competitive environment for regions with enough autonomy to be able to determine the outcome of important policies (*Gestaltungsföderalismus*) it is unavoidable that:

- The size and shape of many Länder is changed and the number of Länder is reduced.
- The current system of financial equalisation is changed in order to re-establish the responsibility of a Land government for its expenditure policies.
- Joint decision-making is reduced to a minimum, and instead of being ever-present in policy-making is restricted more to the necessary co-ordination of the implementation of policies.
- The Länder rethink their role in the Bundesrat, i.e. in federal legislation, and use the Bunderat less than they have traditionally done as a party political arena.

All these demands for institutional change are logically connected. Their political importance has grown in the past few years.[13] To provide the full picture of what is on the agenda we will now look at the major reform proposals in greater detail.

## The redrawing of Länder boundaries

After unification Germany has 16 Länder. Only half of them have always had their present shape since 1949. In 1952 a successful merger of three post-war Länder (Württemberg-Hohenzollern, Baden and Württemberg-Baden) created the new Land of Baden-Württemberg. The Saarland did not join West Germany until 1957 and it was not until 1990 that in the course of German unification five East German Länder were re-established and then joined the Federal Republic, and that the special status of Berlin (under formal control of the four Allied Powers of the Second World War) ended and Berlin became a Land with full constitutional rights. A constitutional amendment of 1994 (Article 118a) permitted a fast-track procedure for a merger of Berlin and the Land Brandenburg. Although two-thirds majorities in the parliaments of both states supported the merger, it was rejected in the necessary referendum by a majority of voters in Brandenburg (62.7 per cent) in May 1996. Whatever the reasons for this negative result were (many commentators have argued that it had less to do with federalism than with the problems of German unification), its political consequence was to prevent a possible bandwagon effect for a territorial reform in Germany with the aim of creating fewer, but more efficient, Länder.

The formation of Länder large enough, with a population of about 10 million or even more, and sufficient economic weight, which can compete with other Länder in Germany and other European regions is, however, the precondition for making the idea of a competition-based federalism work. In Germany there have always been two approaches to the redrawing of the Länder boundaries. One of them is the 'technocratic' approach which wants to use a kind of 'social engineering' to model society. The most important intellectual effort to find, in this spirit, 'rational' criteria for the redrawing of the Länder boundaries was made in 1973. A government commission on federalism reform (the so-called '*Ernst-Kommission*') referred to Article 29 of the Basic Law and suggested the following criteria for reform: (a) no new boundary should divide agglomerations or regions with strong internal economic ties; (b) all the Länder should be big enough and rich enough to cope with their responsibilities; (c) new boundaries should not change political majorities at elections, and (d) a reduction by half of the necessary financial equalisation payments of the richer Länder to help the poorer ones should at least be achieved.

Reform was stopped, however, by another kind of political logic which has also to be taken into account, when we consider the redrawing of Länder boundaries. It may be fairly easy for politicians to agree on the above-mentioned criteria for reform. It is, however, often unlikely that politicians and state bureaucracies are willing to vote for their own elimination. That this was the case in Berlin and Brandenburg was truly remarkable. One could hope that in the North of Germany this would be possible, too. Here there has long been a debate on a '*Nordstaat*', and the Northern Länder co-operate in many respects[14] – a model which is now used for the post-referendum co-operation of Berlin and Brandenburg. But what about the Saarland (with a population of 1 million inhabitants), for example, home state of the former chairman of the Social Democrats, Oscar Lafontaine, or the five new East German Länder (population of the smallest: 1.9 and of the biggest: 4.9 million) whose politicians and bureaucrats have very recently begun to enjoy the spoils of statehood?

Even if the redrawing of Länder boundaries were to find the full-hearted support of politicians, it would still need to be the preferred solution in a referendum to be held in all territories affected by reform. This may sound perhaps surprising; but for the artificial Länder created after the Second World War, and also already for the new Länder in East Germany, the population has developed a sense of identity. In East Germany the five new Länder are all that remained of the separate East German statehood. In West Germany the pride of place has evolved over time and can today be made the subject of Land image campaigns (e.g. 'we in North Rhine-Westphalia'). The outcome of referenda to merge some of the existing Länder is therefore difficult to predict and at the moment majorities for the *status quo* seem very likely.

A Land politician of the FDP has suggested that a necessary referendum on territorial reform be held nation-wide,[15] but this would have a prior revision of Article 29 of the Basic Law as its precondition. It may be more realistic to put the redrawing of Länder boundaries on the agenda together with another reform of federalism, namely the reform of the financing of Länder budgets. In a scenario in which every Land has to live without any transfers either from the federal government or the other Länder the poorer (i.e. mostly smaller) Länder will need less convincing that it is profitable for them to merge with some of their neighbours. But will it be so easy to change the systems of financial equalisation between the Länder and between them and the federal government?

## Who should finance the Länder?

To an outside observer the obvious answer might be that the Länder should themselves secure their financial base. This is, however, technically impossible, because two-thirds of the German tax income is tax income by joint taxes of the Länder and the federal government (VAT, individual and corporation income tax). The Länder receive 50 per cent of the income tax yield and currently 49.5 per cent of VAT. It is under debate whether a system with a clear separation of tax incomes on the federal and the Land level would not be more adequate if the aim is to increase Land autonomy and democratic accountability. The example of Switzerland is often cited here. The argument is made, for example, that in a situation in which the Land citizens are charged with higher taxes whenever their government overspends, the pressure will grow on the government to act in the interest of the respective Land. Bavaria and Baden-Württemberg have argued that one could consider at least separate Land income taxes, or alternatively could allow the Länder a certain variation in income tax rates.[16]

Of greater practical consequence at the moment, however, is a debate on a smaller scale, namely with regard to the financial equalisation payments the richer Länder have to make to the poorer ones. The current rules force the richer Länder to transfer above their Länder average income to the poorer ones until the income of the poorer Länder reaches at least 95 per cent of the Länder average. This can mean a considerable drain on resources. About 67 per cent of the Bavarian above-average Länder income, for example, has to be transferred.

This in itself may be annoying; but what annoys the richer Länder even more is that, because of a number of additional financial transfers from the federal government to the poorer ones, in the end the poorer Länder are financially better off than the richer. In recent years at the end of the process of financial redistribution the 'poorest' Land has been Hesse, followed by Baden-Württemberg and Bavaria. It is not surprising that the five richer Länder demand a reform of Germany's system of financial equalisation payments, whereas the poorer ones do not see the need for it. The finance ministers of the latter were not even ready to discuss these problems with their colleagues. The East German Finance Ministers and Berlin's Finance Senator interpreted initiatives for reform as a strategy to undermine financial transfers to East Germany. Bavaria and Baden-Württemberg offered a compromise: a long-term reduction of the percentage of the rich Länder surpluses which have to be transferred. But as the majority of the Länder are profiting from the current system there was gridlock. In 1998 Bavaria and Baden-Württemberg jointly, and Hesse separately, have asked for a judgement of the Constitutional Court as to whether or not the current rules for financial equalisation are unconstitutional.

There is, of course, the suspicion among the poorer Länder that the richer ones are less interested in a reform of federalism than in securing for themselves more financial resources. The federal government could perhaps live with more financial asymmetry in German federalism, but not at the price of transferring to the poorer Länder an additional amount of money to make up for the reduction of transfers from the richer ones. From an economic point of view the current financial equalisation arrangements definitely give the wrong kind of incentives. Why should a poor Land be careful with its resources, or why should it make efforts to improve its economic strength when it only loses in transfers from the richer Länder by doing so. And why should the richer Länder be thrifty and outperform others when the additional money earned disappears to a large extent into the budgets of the poorer Länder?

But maybe this discussion is, anyway, putting the cart before the horse. One can argue that it makes greater sense first to discuss a rearrangement of responsibilities between the Länder and the federal government in order to determine the budgetary needs of every Land and the federal government respectively, before the abstract question of the redistribution of income for different levels of government is solved.

## A case for the re-federalisation of Germany?

Re-federalisation, i.e. the more rigid separation of responsibilities between the Länder and the federal government, has been discussed since the early 1980s.[17] In the context of interlocking federalism this meant above all a criticism of joint decision-making of the Länder and the federal government. Joint decision-making reduced Länder autonomy to the fields of public administration, regional development policies, police, education and culture, and the media. This development implied a political marginalisation of the Länder parliaments. The reduced Länder autonomy has come under additional threat by decision-making on the level of the European Union.

To secure more autonomy for the Länder in policy-making the Basic Law would have to be changed. There needed to be an end to the co-financing of policies, such as the joint tasks of the federal government and the Länder (Article 91a, b or 104a). One could also argue that federal framework legislation which defines some degree of uniformity for Länder legislation (Article 75) should be abolished and that some other competences which the federal government has should be returned to the Länder. Whatever the details may be, what would be needed would be a constitutional arrangement which does away with the idea that there is a broad area of policies for which the federal government can fairly easily claim responsibility, though originally it did not have the competence for these policies. In the process of constitutional reform which accompanied unification the Länder were successful in raising the hurdles for the federal government in this respect. Article 72 no longer allows the federal government to intervene in order to secure the uniformity (*Einheitlichkeit*) of living conditions in Germany. It now suffices for the federal government to secure comparability (*Gleichwertigkeit*). Intervention is also no longer justifiable only because there may be a need for it (*Bedürfnis*), now intervention has to be essential (*Erfordernis*) to achieve the comparability of living conditions.

Still, the language of the Basic Law leaves much room for interpretation, and is certainly not the tool the Länder need to restrict federal intervention. In the European context the Länder have time and again asked for the introduction of so-called 'subsidiarity lists' which would clearly define the responsibilities of each level of government (be it European, national or regional).[18] Something like that would probably have to be included in the Basic Law. The radical solution would, of course, be only to list federal responsibilities in the Basic Law, to exclude the possibility that the federal level extends its responsibilities and to reserve every responsibility not mentioned for the Länder.

A clear separation of responsibilities between the federal level and the Land level would also help to solve the structural problems of the Bundesrat. The Bundesrat is involved in federal legislation as the voice of the Länder. Originally the Basic Law had 13 provisions for which the consent of the Länder was needed. Their number has more than trebled today. Almost two-thirds of federal legislation need the consent of a majority of the Bundesrat, because Länder responsibilities are affected.[19] Most of the time this is only the case because of joint responsibilities, or because the Länder are responsible for the administration of laws. The Constitutional Court has ruled that, even if a bill has only one clause which needs the consent of the Bundesrat, the whole bill needs this consent to become an act of parliament.

A reform which would separate responsibilities of the different levels of government and also separate the decision on the administration of laws and other legal instruments from the substance of policies would reduce the number of times on which a Bundesrat majority can stop federal legislation. This would make central government more efficient and would speed up the decision-making process. It would also make the federal government more accountable for its decisions, because it would avoid the need for informal grand coalitions in a Bundesrat with a majority of the opposition parties.

Finally, it would also help to solve another long-standing problem of German federalism.[20] When majorities in the Bundesrat were used to stop legislation this has in the past in most cases not been done, because Länder interests needed protection. The motivation behind the Länder veto was above all party political, as can be easily shown by the fact that the number of vetoes increases whenever there are different party political majorities in parliament and in the Bundesrat. A further proof is the inclusion of Bundesrat 'clauses' in coalition treaties on the Land level in order to avoid party political conflict over a Land coalition's voting behaviour.[21] A clear separation of responsibilities between the Land level and the federal government could end the ongoing German debate about the Bundesrat being misused as a political instrument of the parliamentary opposition parties.

Such advice, which sounds plausible in theory, is, however, much more complicated to implement. Only two problems will be mentioned here. The first has to do with what has already been discussed above in the context of interlocking federalism, namely the fact that interlocking federalism is also executive federalism. The executives of the Länder gained political power by the extension of joint decision-making, because their role in the Bundesrat became more important. Will they be willing to give up this power? Furthermore, this problem has acquired a new dimension with European integration. The pattern of increased executive power of the Länder governments in exchange for the loss of Länder competences is repeated in this context. When European law forces the Länder to accept restrictions with regard to policy-making their governments demand greater access to the European policy-making process. The new Article 23 of the Basic Law has increased the role of the Bundesrat and its representatives in European decision-making even to the extent that whenever Länder interests are affected a Bundesrat member may represent Germany in Brussels. The complicated bargaining process in interlocking federalism between the federal and the Land level has in this way been extended to the European level, and the Länder even demand more of that kind of influence, for example access to the Committee of Permanent Representatives of the national governments (COREPER).[22] This, of course, contradicts Länder demands for a greater degree of institutional autonomy.

A second problem has to do with the expectations of the German population. A federalism with a much higher degree of autonomy of the Länder would, it is hoped, create competition for the best policy solutions. But the precondition for such competition is diversity. Bavaria has suggested, for example, a regional variation of individual contributions to the social security systems (unemployment and health insurance) and a reorganisation of the administration of the pension system.[23] German federalism would in this way become even more asymmetrical than it became after unification.[24] It is doubtful whether the population of the Länder who are used to uniformity would want to go through a learning process and accept greater diversity, especially if a Land is not only positively affected by a greater diversity of living conditions. Citizens today already complain about differences in the educational systems of the Länder; for example, when they have to move from one Land to another. In a way a new federalism would urgently need a new federal political culture as its precondition which not only measures the success of policy-making by its outputs (they should be positive and uniform), but also sees an advantage in a greater control of a Land over her own affairs in good times as well as in bad times.[25]

## Conclusion

German federalism started as a democratic safety valve against centralised dictatorship. It soon developed into a system of negotiated policy-making which was refined in the late 1960s into a system of interlocking federalism. The kind of executive federalism which transferred political power from the parliaments of the national and Land level to the respective governments could be successful only as long as Germany was rich and homogeneous enough to offer benefits to all partners in the federal bargaining process and as long as the traditional nation-state, above all in economic terms, remained more or less intact. Economic misfortunes, German unification and European integration have, however, changed the picture. Now the same rational choice logic which had determined the preferences of decision-makers for negotiated federalism makes at least some of them rethink their position. Competition-based federalism has for various reasons become the accepted alternative to the federal *status quo*.

There is no doubt that a reform of federalism is on the political agenda. The need for reform is seen with much greater urgency by the richer (all of them West German) Länder than by the poorer Länder. When it comes to details of reform, such as the redrawing of Länder boundaries, the reform of the financial equalisation systems or the redivision of responsibilities between the federal and the Land level, the majority for the *status quo* seems to be stable, however, and it is unlikely that the Constitutional Court will accept the role of problem-solver. Too many interests are affected by reform and the reformers are in the difficult position to argue that for them more autonomy does not mean the end of federal solidarity, though the richer Länder want to pay less for the poorer states and they want to use their resources to their advantage in the future competition between the Länder. Multi-level government of almost all policy fields, which now extends to the European level,[26] is firmly established, and provides strong institutionalised resistance against reform.

The negative coalition of anti-reformers will, however, have difficulties in surviving a double challenge: one are the upcoming new negotiations on the financing of German unification and the other is the economic challenge of non-German regional competitors in the Single European Market.[27] It is doubtful whether constant political bargaining and the permanent search for the smallest political denominator will benefit the poorer Länder more than greater flexibility and autonomy. This has even been admitted by Kurt Biedenkopf, for example, who is Prime Minister of Saxony.[28] Still, as long as some Länder take the short-term view, the tendency is strong to rely on even a greater dose of executive federalism to secure at least the *status quo* of a Land's resources also on the European level, even if this means that an ever-greater part of its population sees this as a kind of conspiracy of the *'politische Klasse'* (political class), as it has become fashionable to be called, and wonders what Länder parliaments and Land politicians who are not members of Land governments are still good for.

## Notes

1  See *OECD 1998 Wirtschaftsberichte: Deutschland* (Paris: OECD, 1998), p. 110.

2  *The Economist*, 29 August 1998, p. 23.

3  See Konrad Hesse, *Der unitarische Bundesstaat* (Karlsruhe: C. F. Müller, 1962).

4  See Heidrun Abromeit, *Der verkappte Einheitsstaat* (Opladen: Leske & Budrich, 1992).

5  Fritz Scharpf, Bernd Reissert and Fritz Schnabel, *Politikverflechtung* (Kronberg/Ts.: Athenäum, 1976).

6  See Wilhelm Hennis, 'Die Chance einer ganz anderen Republik', in Wilhelm Hennis, *Auf dem Weg in den Parteienstaat* (Stuttgart: Reclam, 1998), p. 105.

7  See Walter Döring, *Wie die Krise des Föderalismus überwunden werden kann* (Stuttgart: FDP, Landesverband Baden-Württemberg, 1998), p. 3.

8  See Wolfgang Luthardt, 'Europäischer Integrationsprozeß, deutscher Föderalismus und Verhandlungsprozesse in einem Mehrebenensystem: Beteiligungsföderalismus als Zukunftsmodell', *Staatswissenschaften und Staatspraxis*, 7 (1996), p. 309.

9  See Roland Sturm, 'The Changing Territorial Balance', in Gordon Smith, Peter H. Merkl and William E. Paterson (eds), *Developments in German Politics* (London: Macmillan, 1992), p. 121.

10  Roland Sturm, 'The States as Laboratories', in Franz Gress, Detlef Fechtner and Mathias Hannes (eds), *The American Federal System: Federal Balance in Comparative Perspective* (Frankfurt a.M.: Lang, 1994), pp. 141–5.

11  Fritz W. Scharpf, 'Die Politikverflechtungsfalle', *Politische Vierteljahresschrift*, 26 (1985), pp. 323–56.

12  Mancur Olson, 'The Principle of "Fiscal Equivalence": the Division of Responsibilities between Different Levels of Government', *American Economic Review*, 59 (1969), pp. 479–87.

13  Of the many speeches and papers by politicians on this topic the following are of special interest: Erwin Teufel, *Rede des Vorsitzenden der*

*Ministerpräsidentenkonferenz der Länder beim Festakt '50 Jahre Rittersturz-Konferenz' am 9. Juli in Koblenz* (Staatsministerium Baden-Württemberg: Press release, 1998); W. Döring (note 7); Edmund Stoiber, *Föderaler Wettbewerb. Deutschlands Stärke – Bayerns Chance, Regierungserklärung des Bayerischen Ministerpräsidenten vom 4.2.1998 im Bayerischen Landtag* (Munich: Press release, 1998), and Friedrich-Naumann-Stiftung, *Wider die Erstarrung in unserem Staat – für eine Erneuerung des Föderalismus* (Königswinter: Friedrich-Naumann-Stiftung, 1998).

14 See Fritz W. Scharpf and Arthur Benz, *Kooperation als Alternative zur Neugliederung? Zusammenarbeit zwischen den norddeutschen Ländern* (Baden-Baden: Nomos, 1991).

15 See W. Döring (note 7), p. 8.

16 See *Positionspapier des Landes Baden-Württemberg und des Freistaates Bayern 1998: Stärkung der Eigenverantwortung der Länder – Reform der Finanzverfassung* (Neu-Ulm: Press release).

17 See Hartmut Klatt, 'Reform und Perspektiven des Föderalismus in der Bundesrepublik Deutschland: Stärkung der Länder als Modernisierungskonzept', *Aus Politik und Zeitgeschichte*, B 28/1986, pp. 3–21.

18 See, e.g., Wolfgang Fischer, 'Forderungen der Länder zur Regierungskonferenz 1996/97', in F. H. U. Borkenhagen (ed.), *Europapolitik der deutschen Länder* (Opladen: Leske & Budrich, 1998), pp. 9–27.

19 See Dieter Grimm, 'Blockade kann nötig sein', *Die Zeit*, 10 October 1997, pp. 14–5.

20 See Gerhard Lehmbruch, *Parteienwettbewerb im Bundesstaat*, 2nd edn (Opladen: Westdeutscher Verlag, 1998); Roland Sturm, 'Party Competition and the Federal System: the Lehmbruch Hypothesis Revisited', in Charlie Jeffery (ed.), *Recasting German Federalism: The Legacies of Unification* (London/New York: Pinter, 1999), pp. 197–216.

21 See Sabine Kropp and Roland Sturm, *Koalitionen und Koalitionsvereinbarungen* (Opladen: Leske & Budrich, 1998).

22 See Hendrik Escher, 'Ländermitwirkung und der Ausschuß der Ständigen Vertreter (AStV)', in F. H. U. Borkenhagen (note 18), pp. 51–68.

23 See E. Stoiber (note 13), pp. 30ff.

24 See Roland Sturm, 'The Constitution under Pressure: Emerging Asymmetrical Federalism in Germany?', Paper, IPSA Congress, Berlin, 1994, to be published in Bob Agranoff (ed.), *Asymmetrical Federalism* (Baden-Baden: Nomos, 1998) (forthcoming).

25 See Rainer-Olaf Schultze, 'Wieviel Asymmetrie verträgt der Föderalismus?', in Dirk Berg-Schlosser Gisela Riescher and Arno Waschkuhn (eds), *Politikwissenschaftliche Spiegelungen: Festschrift für Theo Stammen* (Opladen: Westdeutscher Verlag, 1998), pp. 213–15.

26 See Roland Sturm, 'Multi-level Politics of Regional Development in Germany', *European Planning Studies*, 6 (1998), pp. 525–36.

27 See Richard Deeg, 'Economic Globalization and the Shifting Boundaries of German Federalism', *Publius: The Journal of Federalism*, 26 (1996), pp. 27–52.

28 Interview in *Der Spiegel*, 31 August 1998, p. 44.

# 7
# The Electoral System: More Continuity than Change

*Eckhard Jesse*

## Introduction

Elections, in the sense of having a choice, are what characterise democratic constitutional states. That differentiates them from dictatorships of various types. However, in democracies the electoral systems – which translate votes into seats – vary considerably one from another.[1] One basic type of electoral system (the majoritarian system) is intended to promote the formation of stable governments by disproportionality between the share of the vote and the share of seats. Another type (proportional representation) tries to reflect accurately the electoral strengths of various political groups. Apart from these two basic types there is a multiplicity of complex mixed systems, for instance using an electoral 'hurdle' to promote majority creation, or multi-member constituencies which restrict the proportional relationship between vote-share and allocation of seats.

This chapter does not merely deal with how the Federal Republic's electoral system has developed over the course of 50 years; it also considers the reasons for continuity and change. Above all, it is concerned with evaluating the detailed reasons for the very small amount of 'institutional change' in the electoral system. As a brief historical review will show, in its history Germany has possessed a series of very different electoral systems, which differ fundamentally from each other (second section). The electoral system of the Federal Republic tried to draw lessons from the past (third section). That is much more complicated than many people assume. Especially in the first two decades of the Federal Republic efforts were repeatedly made to reform the system in a more majoritarian direction (fourth section). However, all such attempts failed. On the other hand, a series of changes to the electoral law were introduced in the 1950s (fifth section). These, though, did not change fundamentally the basic principles of the electoral system. In the 1990s discussion of electoral reform has been concerned especially with the justification of the *Grundmandatsklausel* (three-seat alternative to the 5 per cent clause) and the *Überhangmandate* (surplus seats). This discussion was originated by the situation in the 1994 Bundestag election, in which both these factors played a significant role. The Federal Constitutional Court confirmed the constitutionality of these two special features of the electoral system, though the counter-arguments are difficult to circumvent (sixth section). The concluding section summarises these considerations.

## Historical review

A brief survey of German history reveals the wide range of variation of the electoral systems that have been utilised. The German Empire (1871–1918) belonged to those few countries in which universal male suffrage existed. However, it was not a parliamentary system, as the chancellor was appointed by the Emperor and parliament could not dismiss him, even though it was becoming ever more influential. The absolute-majority-based electoral system was presented to the end of the Empire. Whoever obtained an absolute majority in a constituency was elected (at first for 3, then from 1888 onwards for 5 years). If nobody obtained an absolute majority in the first round of voting, a second round involving the two leading candidates took place.[2] The situation in the Empire gave many grounds for criticism, because the sizes of the constituencies were never adjusted to take account of the movement of population from rural to urban areas. This 'passive constituency geometry' was disadvantageous especially to the Social Democrats, who needed many more votes than their rivals in order to win a seat. In addition, it was frequently the case that in the second round of voting alliances were formed against the Social Democrats. By 1890 the SPD was the largest party in terms of votes, but not until 1912 was it the largest in terms of seats.[3]

The Council of People's Delegates (*Rat der Volksbeauftragten*) – formed by representatives of the SPD and USPD – proclaimed on 12 November 1918 in its manifesto that in future the parliament would be elected according to proportional representation by both men and women voters over the age of 20. Germany's first democracy, the Weimar Republic (1919–33) brought to perfection the list-based PR system,[4] even though the general view, that 60,000 votes were sufficient to obtain a parliamentary seat, was not really accurate, because of a complicated distribution procedure.[5] The number of members of the *Reichstag* depended on the level of turnout and the size of the electorate. The thesis has persisted that the Weimar electoral system caused the multiplicity of parties. However, what was critical was not so much the large number of parties, but rather the lack of co-operation among the main party groups. The assertion that a major-itarian electoral system could have protected the Weimar Republic from the attacks on it by its enemies on the right and on the left is extremely speculative. Additionally, at the time the demand was less for a majoritarian electoral system, much more for a stronger personal element to be introduced to the electoral system. Criticism of the list system was much greater than criticism of the PR principle.[6]

There is no need to give much attention to the electoral systems of the Third Reich (the *Reichstag* was popularly regarded as the 'most expensive choir in the world' or the GDR (only on the vote concerning abortion time-limits in 1972 was there any case of abstention or dis-senting votes by members of the *Volkskammer* until 1989), since elec-tions, though they continued to be held, were almost a farce. They had only an acclamation function, not a legitimising role. In the Third Reich no election took place after 1938.[7]

The first and last freely-elected *Volkskammer* was produced by an unfiltered PR system in March 1990. A party obtaining at least 0.25 per cent of votes could be certain of winning at least one of the 400 seats. It was an unrestricted PR system. Nevertheless, the CDU-dominated 'Alliance for Germany' won almost 50 per cent of the vote.

The differences in the various political systems depended only in part on the differences in the particular electoral system.[8] Other factors were responsible for the specific deficits of the systems of government. In the Empire democratisation closely connected with parliamentarism did not occur; in the Weimar Republic there was a lack of a sufficiently high democratic consensus among important social groups.[9] A differ-ent electoral system of itself would have produced fundamental change neither in the Empire nor in the Weimar Republic.

## The mode of operation of the German electoral law

The electoral system of the Federal Republic is clearly different from that of the Empire (because of the abolition of the majoritarian princi-ple) as well as from that of the Weimar Republic (because of restric-tions applied to the list system and proportional representation). Put simply, it is a system of proportional representation, restricted by a 5 per cent clause, with a personalised element.

In a Bundestag election, to be held at least every 4 years, each voter has two votes. The first vote is given to a constituency candidate, the second vote for a party list. A differentiated use of the first and the second vote ('splitting') is permitted. In this way a candidate of one party receives the first vote but a different party receives the second-party-list-vote. How the 656 Bundestag seats from 1990 to 1998 (from then on, 598 seats) are allocated among the parties depends on their share of second votes. Once this share for each party is known, it is then calculated for each party how they are shared out among the party's Land lists. The voter has no influence on the ordering of individual candidates on these lists ('fixed lists'). The seats in the 328 (in future 299) constituencies are deducted from the list seats of the parties.

Should it happen that a party in one Land – on account of its first votes – wins more constituency seats than its share of second votes in that Land allows, it retains these surplus seats (*Überhangmandate*). A party participates in the proportional distribution of seats only if it obtains more than 5 per cent of second votes, unless it wins at least three constituency seats (*Grundmandatsklausel*). This clause is an exception to the 5 per cent clause, which itself is an exception to the principle of proportionality. Paradoxically, in such a case the first vote has the function of restoring proportionality.

Is the German electoral system a 'mixed system'? The answer must be – according to one's perspective – 'yes' and 'no'. Whoever assumes that the current electoral system is a mixed system because of the constituency and list seats is mistaken, because the allocation of seats depends almost exclusively on the second vote. The second vote takes priority; the first vote is only secondary. The introduction of the 5 per cent clause means, however, that the German electoral system deviates from pure proportional representation. The argument is valid, though, that the electoral system is a mixed system in relation to direct seats and list seats. One half of the representatives is directly elected in constituencies; the other half indirectly from party lists. In fact, both of the big parties secure a seat for their candidate in a constituency with the help of a list. Thus the significance, that the candidate of party A or party B is successful in a constituency, is often exaggerated. If the candidate of party A is successful, he enters the Bundestag as a constituency representative, whereas the candidate of party B secures a seat by means of the Land list, or vice-versa. In practice the choice made by the voter is not as relevant as many believe, because of the existence of the Land lists.

The electoral laws in the individual Länder do not differ fundamentally from the federal electoral law. In some Länder the electoral period is 5 years, and some Länder employ a one-vote system. Most Länder offset surplus seats by means of compensatory seats (*Ausgleichsmandate*). The Bavarian electoral law provides the voter with the opportunity of varying the order of candidates on the list. The Baden-Württemberg electoral system operates without a Land list. In all the Länder there is a 5 per cent clause.[10]

## Proposals for reform of the electoral system

In order not to make a change of the electoral system difficult, the Parliamentary Council decided not to anchor it in the constitution itself.[11] Nevertheless there is a notable contrast between the stability of the electoral system and the multiplicity of attempts to reform it. In the Parliamentary Council, whose composition reflected party proportionality, the CDU/CSU was unsuccessful with its proposal to introduce a majoritarian electoral system, because of the opposition of the SPD and other small parties (with the exception of the German Party, DP). The electoral system was intended to apply only to the first Bundestag election. In addition the Allies laid down guidelines for a multi-party system. Because of this one can hardly speak of a 'new beginning' (*Stunde Null*). What is remarkable about the years that follow is that an electoral system design, once adopted, has scarcely been changed even though demands for reform were never absent in the first 20 years of the Federal Republic.

In 1953 the CDU/CSU once more pressed for a majoritarian electoral system. The cabinet introduced a proposal (named after Interior Minister Lehr) which would give each voter two votes: a main vote and a supplementary vote. The purpose of this supplementary-vote system was to strengthen the position of the CDU/CSU at the cost of the SPD, because voters for small parties generally were closer to the CDU/CSU than to the SPD. The public regarded this reform proposal as a 'law' to preserve the coalition. The new electoral law, passed after the CDU/CSU had backed down, was also to apply for only one election.

The next controversy was not long in appearing. In 1955/56 the CDU/CSU and the DP wanted to introduce a so-called '*Grabenwahlsystem*': this proposal was based on the idea that direct seats would no longer be included in the proportional distribution of seats from the list. In this case there would be equal quantities of proportionally allocated and directly elected majoritarian seats. A party with a vote-share of 8 per cent but without any constituency seats would accordingly be represented in parliament with only 4 per cent of the seats. The FDP, from which a minority had broken away (the so-called 'ministerial wing'), partly due to this reform proposal, withdrew from the coalition, and shortly beforehand had helped to replace the CDU-Minister President Karl Arnold in North Rhine-Westphalia by means of a constructive vote of no-confidence. In the discussions which followed, the CDU/CSU once more had to concede defeat. The electoral law of 1956, which differentiated itself from its predecessor only in matters of detail, has become definitive and remains valid until today, apart from minor amendments.

Following the 'Spiegel-affair' in 1962, informal exploratory talks between the CDU/CSU and the SPD took place concerning a Grand Coalition and the introduction of a majoritarian electoral system. These talks were at the time unproductive (although they further worsened the relationship between the CDU/CSU and the FDP). However, by the end of 1966 the chances for a reform of the electoral system were good. The Grand Coalition led by Chancellor Kurt Georg Kiesinger (CDU) wanted to install a majoritarian electoral system and made this commitment part of the government policy statement (*Regierungserklärung*). Had this reform occurred a two-party system would have resulted, probably with a strong government and a strong opposition. However, the reform failed due to resistance from a section of public opinion, the FDP, and above all the SPD which on the one hand feared that it would be the permanent loser under such a system and on the other hand was concerned not to repel its future coalition partner, the FDP. Even within the CDU/CSU there were those who were concerned about the unforeseeable consequences of such a reform. In 1967/68 discussion about the 'best electoral system' – at the time perhaps *the* domestic political theme – was intense and at times even emotional.[12] Dogmatism concerning electoral law among social scientists was as prevalent as petty calculation of self-interest on the part of politicians.

Such political – and also academic – discussion in the Federal Republic concerning the 'best' electoral system belongs since the end of the 1960s more or less to the past. Even when the Party of Democratic Socialism (PDS) entered the Bundestag (in 1990, 1994, and 1998), and could have prevented the formation of either a CDU/CSU–FDP coalition or a 'red–green' (SPD–Greens) coalition, there were only insignificant demands for reform. No party of any political importance since the start of the 1970s has called for the introduction of a majoritarian electoral system, and even in academic circles this theme receives no attention – with a few exceptions.[13]

What conclusions should be drawn from the fact that the electoral system has remained unaltered until now? This is almost paradoxical. The main arguments which supporters of a majoritarian electoral system have put forward – the creation of effective governing majorities, in practice the choice of government by the electorate, the ease with which governments can be changed, the requirement of moderation, and the transparency of competition – have all up to now been realised under the conditions of proportional representation. At present there is no fundamental need for reform, the more so because a symmetrical party system has gradually developed. In the 1950s, 1960s, 1970s and even in the 1980s this claim could not be made.

At first an asymmetry existed favouring the CDU/CSU. The SPD was more or less alone, whereas the CDU/CSU received the support of a number of smaller parties. Despite continually improving electoral results for the SPD (*'Genosse Trend'*) the Social Democrats remained without allies. Not until a change of orientation by the FDP in 1969 was the SPD able to elect a federal chancellor. From then on a party-asymmetry existed to the disadvantage of the CDU/CSU. The CDU/CSU managed to obtain 48.6 per cent in the Bundestag election 1976 under Helmut Kohl's leadership. Never again did he obtain such a good result, but nevertheless his party had then to remain in opposition. The SPD and the Liberals had agreed prior to the 1976 election to continue the Social–Liberal coalition. Because of this, from time to time within the CDU/CSU there were ideas regarding the creation of a 'fourth party'. The decision of CSU members of the Bundestag at Wildbad Kreuth in 1976 not to continue the parliamentary alliance with the CDU (although this was soon reversed) was responsible for such schemes.

When the FDP decided in 1982 to form a coalition with the CDU/CSU and Helmut Schmidt was dismissed as chancellor by a constructive vote of no-confidence the SPD was once again put at a disadvantage. However, in the 1980s a 'fourth force' emerged: the Greens, who managed in 1983 to enter the Bundestag. Nevertheless quite some time was to pass before that party proved itself to be willing and able to be regarded as a coalition partner. Through its fusion with Alliance '90 (*Bündnis '90*) in 1993 the Greens have developed further in the direction of pragmatism. So the following paradox has appeared: precisely at the time when a symmetrical party system had begun to take shape the PDS has come on the scene as a 'fifth party' which endangers that system.

Until 1998, on account of this long-lasting party asymmetry, there had been no orthodox change of government (*'Machtwechsel'*), not in 1966, not in 1969, and not in 1982.[14] In 1966, when the FDP left the coalition, the CDU/CSU remained and formed a Grand Coalition with the SPD. In 1969 the SPD remained in government, but this time formed a coalition with the FDP – a coalition occasionally being classified as a 'historical alliance'. In 1982 the FDP who cushioned the change of government remained in government, but as partner with the Christian Democrats. In 1998, with the formation of the 'red–green' coalition, an 'unfiltered' change of government occurred. The previous government went into opposition (where the PDS remained). The voter has up to now under conditions of proportional representation in practice decided which government should be formed.

A reform of the electoral system could be attempted only under the following scenario. A party from the far-right or the far-left, which was regarded as unsuitable as a coalition partner, had seats in the Bundestag sufficient to prevent a 'red–green' coalition or a CDU/CSU–FDP government. In such a case a Grand Coalition would have to face the consequences – if only in order to make itself superfluous and bring in a majoritarian electoral system. Even so, such a scenario is unrealistic. Should for example the PDS continue to be represented in the Bundestag, the indications are that it would be integrated within the left-wing bloc. The first Land-level coalition for the PDS – with the SPD in Mecklenburg-West Pomerania – already points in this direction. What is probable for the left does not apply to the right. Should a party located to the right of the CDU/CSU enter the Bundestag, co-operation of such a party with the Christian Democrats would be improbable. What applies to the right does not apply – any longer – to the left.

## Changes of the electoral law

Even though the fundamental principle of proportional representation established in 1949 – despite much discussion in the first two decades following – has not been undermined, there have in fact been several changes to the electoral system.[15] These have affected the electoral outcome. The following have been the most significant changes.

- The 5 per cent clause (originally introduced after the Parliamentary Council had produced its draft law) was extended to apply to the Federal Republic as a whole in 1953 (for the first Bundestag election in 1949 a party could enter the Bundestag if it obtained 5 per cent in a single Land).[16] Excluded from the application of the 5 per cent clause were parties which obtained at least one constituency seat in 1953. Since 1956 this alternative has been three seats.

- In 1953 the two-vote system was introduced. The voter was given the chance of separating the first and second vote ('vote-splitting'). The first vote anyway has never fulfilled its intended function of being a personalised vote, even though increasing numbers of electors make use of vote-splitting. An important criticism of the two-vote system is that research shows that many voters do not realise that the second vote is the decisive vote.

- The postal vote, introduced in 1956, was the result of the fact that the right to vote is the decisive participatory right of the citizen. It should also be provided for those who cannot attend at the polling station (e.g. through illness or being away from home at the time of the election). Since 1976 about 10 per cent of all voters make use of postal voting.

- In 1970 the voting age was reduced from 21 to 18, and in 1975 the age when one could be elected to the Bundestag was also reduced from 21 to 18. These reforms were intended to bind young people more quickly to the political system. It was a politically wise, but in no sense a necessary, change.

- The introduction in 1987 of voting rights for Germans resident abroad was intended to remove electoral disadvantage for Germans who, perhaps of necessity, had to live outside Germany. A condition was that they must have resided in Germany for at least 3 months prior to moving abroad. Only some 5 per cent or so of such Germans make use of this right to vote.

- In the same year the method of calculating the number of seats for each party was changed from the d'Hondt 'highest number' system to the mathematical-proportion system of the Hare-Niemeyer. The significance of this change is generally overestimated. It removes a very slight disadvantage for small parties: Alliance '90/the Greens or the FDP may, by this new system, receive one additional seat.

- Finally there is a series of proposed alterations that so far have not been introduced. The background of the recent reform debate has been marked by a widespread inclination among both scholars and politicians to interpret more broadly the constitutional requirement that elections should be 'general' (*allgemeine Wahl*). Some thus desire to reduce the voting age to 16, as some Länder (e.g. Hesse, Lower Saxony, Schleswig-Holstein) have already done for Land elections. Others propose a 'family vote', by which parents would vote on behalf of their children, until such time as these children reached voting age. The legislators have been well advised to link voting age to the age of maturity and full legal responsibility. Others suggest that the legislative period should be extended to 5 years, as meanwhile has become the case in most of the Länder. Bundestag President Wolfgang Thierse and (former) SPD chairman Lafontaine have recently indicated that the new government should introduce this change. Another proposal, based on the practice for Bavarian Land elections, is to replace fixed-order party lists with lists in which the voter can influence the final ordering of the candidates. However, this would not mean that the voter could introduce new names onto the list ('free list system').

Though in principle it is legitimate for parties to take account of party advantage in shaping or amending the electoral system (the electoral law), a too-selfish approach to such matters can damage a party rather than benefit it. 'Tailor-made' systems can rarely be realised, if one thinks of the objections from the parliamentary opposition, public opinion and the Federal Constitutional Court. There is another point: the incalculable factors are legion. Even ingeniously designed electoral systems and finely-calculated adjustments to the electoral law cannot take into account the unanticipated decisions of the voter.

## The three-seat alternative and surplus seats as examples of difficulties of introducing reforms

As already described, the three-seat alternative to the 5 per cent clause and the surplus seat provision are two – special and unusual – features of the electoral system which can change the number of seats which parties would otherwise obtain in an election. The first feature benefits small parties; the second (as a rule) the larger parties. Both features concern the 'first votes'. Until the end of the 1980s they had only very incidental effects: the direct-seat alternative in the 1950s, the surplus seats at the beginning of the following decade, and therefore played almost no role in academic or political discussion about the electoral system. This all changed in the 1990s.

In the Bundestag election of 1990 the CDU received six surplus seats. In no previous election had there been so many. All of them came from the new Länder (three in Saxony-Anhalt; two in Mecklenburg-West Pomerania; one in Thuringia). Because there was anyway a substantial majority for the Christian–Liberal coalition neither this large number of surplus seats (in 1961 there had been four, in 1953 and 1957 three each time, in 1949 and 1953 two on each occasion, in 1980 and 1987 only one each time) nor the 'divided' 5 per cent clause caused particular concern. The Federal Constitutional Court, in view of the special circumstances of the first all-German Bundestag election, had required that the 5 per cent clause be applied separately to the old Federal Republic and West Berlin on the one hand, and to the former GDR on the other.[17] Thus the PDS, because of its 11.0 per cent share of second votes in the East German electoral area, entered the Bundestag even though its national vote-share was only 2.4 per cent). Had the version of the 1949 electoral law been applied in 1990, the PDS would have had seats only from those Länder where it won over 5 per cent. Under the 1953 electoral law, because it won one constituency seat, it would have obtained its full proportional share of seats. The law as it was applied from the 1957 federal election onwards would have given the PDS only Gysi's constituency seat – no additional list seats. As this example shows, the share of seats would be substantially changed, according to which electoral law was applied.

Both the three-seat alternative rule and the surplus-seats provision played a significant role in the Bundestag election of October 1994. On the one hand the PDS won four East Berlin constituencies (though, oddly, two of the successful candidates, Stefan Heym and Manfred Müller, were not actually members of the PDS), and thus entered the Bundestag, even though the party obtained only 4.4 per cent of second votes. On the other hand there were 16 surplus seats: more than ever before. The CDU obtained 12 of these (three each in Saxony and Thuringia; two each in Baden-Württemberg, Mecklenburg-West Pomerania and Saxony-Anhalt), the SPD four (three in Brandenburg, one in Bremen). Thus 13 of these 16 seats came from the new Länder. This result had nothing to do with differential allocations of first and second votes. It was much more the consequence of low rates of electoral participation and the small size of constituencies in the new Länder. Also, the relatively good showing of the PDS meant that in East Germany many constituencies were won with less than 40 per cent of the vote. In Brandenburg, Saxony and Thuringia one party won all the constituencies in each case. Because of the surplus seats, the CDU-CSU and FDP coalition secured an overall majority of 10 seats. Because of the entry of the PDS into the Bundestag, the majority for the coalition without these surplus seats would have been only two seats.

There followed a wave of criticism of these special rules. In line with party interests the Christian Democrats attacked the three-seat rule, the SPD the surplus seats provision. This was ironic, since in the past the Christian Democrats had made successful use of the direct-seat alternative to the 5 per cent clause, whereas the SPD had – unsuccessfully, though – attempted in the past to benefit from 'voter initiatives' designed to promote vote-splitting. The connection between the two special provisions was not mentioned by either side. Several experts in public law brought a case against the direct seat alternative rule, the Land of Lower Saxony a case against surplus seats. The Federal Constitutional Court gave a unanimous decision in support of the constitutionality of the direct-seat alternative, and confirmed the constitutionality of the surplus seats rule, although only with a tied decision of 4–4 among the judges.[18]

Victory in constituency elections indicates a special political strength of a party. The direct-seat alternative as a way of by-passing the 5 per cent clause also finds justification in the tradition of German electoral systems. It does not call into question the functionality of the Bundestag, but rather remains a rare exception, as experience shows. Formerly, the Constitutional Court had emphasised very strongly the 'personalisation effect' of this alternative. The justification of the surplus seats provision resides in the special properties of the personalised proportional representation system which by means of the election of constituency candidates guarantees for at least half of the members of the Bundestag a close personal relationship with their constituency. Nevertheless the essence of the proportional representative electoral system must be preserved. Because of this, in conformity with the constitutionally validated 5 per cent clause, the proportion of surplus seats should not exceed 5 per cent of the normal number of seats.

In 1998, in a further decision that was generally not noticed by the public, the Constitutional Court decided that the succession for a vacancy in a *constituency* seat, in a Land which had produced surplus seats at the previous Bundestag election, would be regulated in a different manner than had previously been the case. In future a party which had won surplus seats would lose that constituency seat when a vacancy (e.g. through death or resignation) occurred, thus reducing that party's contingent in the Bundestag.[19]

In the Bundestag election of 1998 the three-seat alternative clause played no role, because the PDS obtained 5.1 per cent of list votes.[20] On the other hand, once more there were numerous surplus seats – all for the SPD, of which 12 arose in the new Länder (four in Saxony-Anhalt; three each in Brandenburg and Thuringia; two in Mecklenburg-West Pomerania) and one in Hamburg. In Brandenburg and Saxony-Anhalt the SPD in fact won all the constituency seats in each Land. Without those 13 surplus seats the SPD–Green coalition would have had a majority of only eight seats. Schröder had declared before the election that a majority of at least 10 seats would be necessary for the formation of a coalition with the Greens. Paradoxically, he obtained this sufficient majority for his government (in his own terms) only by means of a provision in the electoral law which his Land of Lower Saxony had challenged before the Constitutional Court. After the election no-one felt inclined to remind the new chancellor of this fact! The SPD had no interest in doing so, since it did not want the size of its majority to appear to have been obtained 'illegitimately'; the CDU-CSU had no reason for doing so, because, in its opposition role, it wanted at all costs to avoid diminishing the image of the opposing majority.

As a brief review of the history of the electoral system reveals, the introduction of such special provisions was strongly determined by chance. In no way did they originate from the requirements of a systematic design. The rules relating to a direct-seat alternative to the 5 per cent clause[21] and to surplus seats date back to 1949.

Gebhard Müller, the Minister-President of the Land of Württemberg-Hohenzollern, wanted to make entry to parliament dependent upon a victory in at least one constituency, in order to weaken electorally the party of Reinhold Maier, the Liberal Minister-President of the Land of Baden-Württemberg, because of the forthcoming decision about the fusion of the three South-Western Länder. He was not successful in this aim, but the modified version of the electoral system took up his suggestion. Instead of '*at least*' one direct seat, the rule became '*or*' one direct seat, as an alternative to the 5 per cent requirement for an allocation of seats. In 1953 the direct-seat alternative became applicable at the federal (and not just the Land) level. In 1956 it was increased to *three* seats.

In 1953 the DP, which was closely associated with the CDU, entered the Bundestag with 3.3 per cent of the vote; in 1957 it did so with 3.4 per cent, but on this occasion only thanks to an electoral pact with the CDU, by which each party benefited by withdrawal of the other party's candidates in specific constituencies. In 1953 the Centre Party (*Zentrum*), though receiving only 0.8 per cent of the vote, obtained Bundestag seats: but only because the CDU agreed not to nominate its own candidate in one constituency, which the Centre Party candidate won. In return for this, the Centre Party gave a CDU candidate a place on its list, and that candidate was elected.[22] In this manner the Christian Democrats in the past have profited more than a little from the direct-seat alternative clause, which today they so vehemently reject.

The rule imposed by the minister-presidents of the Länder that 60 per cent of seats should come from constituencies, and 40 per cent from party lists made the chances of surplus seats in 1949 greater than would have been the case had the original proposal of the Parliamentary Council (50 per cent from constituencies, 50 per cent from party lists) been adopted. The introduction of a two-vote system in 1953 increased the possibility of surplus seats, though the change to a 50:50 division of constituency and list seats reduced that likelihood. Sometimes, as in 1972, 'voter initiatives' campaigned for 'split votes', in order to 'double' the value of certain votes, though this effect was not in fact produced. Because of so many incalculable factors it is in fact much more difficult to deliberately produce such an effect than many people think. In the whole history of the Federal Republic up until and including the Bundestag election of 1987 there were only 17 surplus seats. Between 1965 and 1976 there were none at all.

Anyone attempting to justify the direct-seat alternative or surplus seats is immediately put on the defensive. The relevant jurisdiction of the Federal Constitutional Court is not convincing.[23] How can the 'direct-seat alternative' in particular be legitimated by the effective integration of the population, as the Federal Constitutional Court points out? This can be held to be true for the 5 per cent hurdle, but not for a provision which in fact by-passes that hurdle. Whoever believes it is sensible to promote stable governing majorities by means of the 5 per cent clause cannot at the same time justify provisions designed to get round that hurdle. It is not logical that a party with 4.9 per cent of the vote should remain without parliamentary representation, but that a party with a lower vote-share should enter the parliament as long as it wins three constituency seats. How can it be held that a stable governing majority – the primary justification for the 5 per cent clause – is not in this way endangered? And how can it be suggested that locally concentrated parties are especially worthy of representation? Apart from that, there is in any case no requirement that the three direct seats must be won within a narrowly defined geographical area.

Clearly, surplus seats are not an inevitable consequence of a personalised electoral system – only in exceptional cases does split-voting lead to surplus seats[24] – but rather derive from other factors (e.g. disproportionately large numbers of constituencies in a Land; a low rate of turnout; a large number of invalid votes; a strong third party). Because these can mutually influence each other, a prediction as to whether there will be surplus seats is just as difficult to make as is an attempt deliberately to create such seats by campaign tactics. The example of the Bundestag election of 1994 reveals the absurdity and accidental nature of surplus seats. Had the CDU in Thuringia had about 400 list votes *fewer*, it would have obtained an additional surplus seat in that Land![25] A more startling paradox is difficult to imagine: if there are fewer votes there will be more seats. *Difficile est satiram non scribere...* . The reason for this: the CDU would have retained all its 232 seats, but its last seat would not have come from the Thuringia Land list, but from the Land list in Hesse.[26]

These two provisions, which tend to confuse and which certainly produce no additional legitimacy for the electoral system, should be abandoned as soon as possible. The case for eliminating them is not urgent because they distort the proportional relationship between votes and seats (the 5 per cent clause also does this), but rather because no sufficient reason for their preservation has been offered. The 5 per cent clause can be justified, because it contributes to the formation of stable government majorities. For the three-seat alternative and surplus seats no such logical justification exists. The claim that they contribute to the personalisation of the act of voting cannot be upheld. Only a small minority of voters know the name of 'their' constituency candidate. Hardly anyone makes his/her vote dependent on the personal qualities of the constituency candidate, though many make it dependent on the qualities of the rival chancellor-candidates. The FDP last won constituency seats in 1957 and 1990; the Greens have never done so.

The three-seat alternative could be simply eliminated, without affecting the 5 per cent clause. Surplus seats would no longer exist if constituency seats were immediately deducted from the total seats allotted to a party – that is, before the allocation of seats for a party to the various Länder. The potential argument that surplus seats will be less likely to arise once the size of the Bundestag is reduced (to 598) as from the next federal election and the constituencies are accordingly redesigned, is simply a pragmatic point. It does not deal with the principle of surplus seats. The problem would not be removed, but simply reduced. The introduction of compensatory seats (*Ausgleichsmandate*), as occurs in several of the Länder for Landtag elections, would be a second-best solution. That would still involve an unpredictable increase in the size of the Bundestag from time to time.

The situation today is favourable to reform. No party benefited in the Bundestag election 1998 from the three-seat alternative. The SPD is still vehemently opposed to surplus seats, even though at the 1998 election it profited from them itself. Thus no accusation of manipulation can be levelled at any party proposing abolition of these special provisions.

The political system of the Federal Republic should in future be spared from the risk that illegitimate provisions of the electoral system, such as the three-seat alternative and surplus seats, could, in a very close election, take on decisive importance. In this respect there is an urgent need for reform.

## Conclusion

Legislation concerning the electoral system in the Federal Republic has been marked by a high level of continuity. In its basic characteristics the electoral system has remained unchanged until today. This assertion is indisputable. The assessment of the system, however, is a matter for controversy. Has the Bundestag not changed because the electoral system has proved itself to be especially effective? Or is there a pressing need for its reform because of grave shortcomings? A clear-cut answer is not easy to give.

The proportional representation system has, on the whole, proved itself.[27] The very length of its existence as a system conveys legitimacy. There is no question now of changing this. The parties quite rightly do not press for its reform. In the Federal Republic voters know *before* an election which parties wish to form coalitions with each other, if that proves possible. To that extent the voter also decides indirectly which government should form, and which parties should go into opposition. Under these conditions of proportional representation, many outcomes have in fact occurred which *opponents* of proportional representation claim would be produced by a majoritarian electoral system.

The list of various changes to the electoral system must be assessed in different ways. Judgements range from 'necessary' (introduction of postal voting), or 'sensible' (reduction of the voting age), to 'questionable' (two-vote system). There are also missed opportunities to regret.

As the cases of the surplus seats and the direct-seat alternative clearly illustrate, the passivity of the legislators is sometimes difficult to justify.

In passing laws which affect the electoral system the legislator has considerable latitude with regard to reform of the system. It is thus perfectly possible to reduce the 5 per cent clause or even to eliminate it altogether. One could also introduce a majoritarian system on British lines, for example to avoid the need for a Grand Coalition always assuming the political will is there. On the other hand, this does not mean that any combination whatsoever of pure proportional representation and the majoritarian system would be acceptable, as the example of the direct-seat alternative and the surplus seats clearly demonstrates. They deserve to be abolished as swiftly as possible.

## Notes

1  See Dieter Nohlen, *Wahlrecht und Parteiensystem* (Opladen: Leske & Budrich, 1986); David M. Farrell, *Comparing Electoral Systems* (London: Prentice Hall/Harvester Wheatsheaf, 1997).

2  See Alfred Milatz, 'Reichstagswahlen und Mandatsverteilung 1871 bis 1918. Ein Beitrag zu Problemen des absoluten Mehrheitswahlrechts', in Gerhard A. Ritter (ed.), *Gesellschaft, Parlament und Regierung: Zur Geschichte des Parlamentarismus in Deutschland* (Düsseldorf: Droste, 1974), pp. 207–33.

3  At any rate, these facts have to be modified in so far as, from the beginning, the SPD has nominated candidates everywhere due to its idea of equality, whereas other parties have not done so to the same degree but first of all concentrated on promising constituencies.

4  See Eberhard Schanbacher, *Parlamentarische Wahlen und Wahlsystem in der Weimarer Republik: Wahlgesetzgebung und Wahlreform im Reich und in den Ländern* (Düsseldorf: Droste, 1982).

5  A party which obtained less than 60,000 votes in any of the 35 constituencies was excluded from the distribution of *Reichstag* seats. In the *Reichstag* election of 1928 a total of 1,546,762 votes were in this way without effect.

6  See Eckhard Jesse, *Wahlrecht zwischen Kontinuität und Reform: Eine Analyse der Wahlsystemdiskussion und der Wahlrechtsänderungen in der Bundesrepublik Deutschland 1949–1983* (Düsseldorf: Droste, 1985), pp. 51–90.

7  See Otmar Jung, 'Wahlen und Abstimmungen im Dritten Reich 1933–1938', in Eckhard Jesse and Konrad Löw (eds), *Wahlen in Deutschland* (Berlin: Duncker & Humblot, 1998), pp. 69–97.

8  See Hans Fenske, *Wahlrecht und Parteiensystem: Ein Beitrag zur deutschen Parteiengeschichte* (Frankfurt a.M: Athenäum, 1972).

9  See Eckhard Jesse, 'The West German Electoral System: the Case for Reform 1949–1987', *West European Politics*, 10 (1987), pp. 434–48; Max Kaase, 'Personalized Proportional Representation: The "Model" of the West German Electoral System', in Arend Lijphart and Bernhard Grofman (eds),

*Choosing an Electoral System: Issues and Alternatives* (New York: Praeger, 1984), pp. 155–64; Peter Pulzer, 'Germany', in Vernon Bogdanor and David Butler (eds), *Democracy and Election: Electoral Systems and their Political Consequences* (Cambridge: Cambridge University Press, 1983), pp. 84–109; Geoffrey K. Roberts, 'The Federal Republic of Germany', in Samuel E. Finer (ed.), *Adversary Politics and Electoral Reform* (London: Anthony Wigram, 1975), pp. 203–22; Hans Meyer, 'Wahlgrundsätze und Wahlverfahren', in Josef Isensee and Paul Kirchhof (eds), *Handbuch des Staatsrecht der Bundesrepublik Deutschland*, vol. 2 (Heidelberg: C. F. Müller, 1987), pp. 269–311.

10  With the minor exception which exists in the Land of Bremen. Here it is sufficient to obtain 5 per cent either in the Bremen electoral area or in the Bremerhaven electoral area in order to win seats. In this way the extreme right wing DVU (German People's Party) managed to win one seat in 1987, even though it only secured 3.4 per cent of the vote, because it obtained 5.4 per cent in Bremerhaven.

11  See Erhard H. M. Lange, *Wahlrecht und Innenpolitik: Entstehungsgeschichte und Analyse der Wahlgesetzgebung und Wahlrechtsdiskussion im westlichen Nachkriegsdeutschland 1945–1956* (Meisenheim am Glan: Hain, 1975).

12  Rüdiger Bredthauer, *Das Wahlsystem als Objekt von Politik und Wissenschaft: Die Wahlsystemdiskussion in der BRD 1967/68 als politische und wissenschaftliche Auseinandersetzung* (Meisenheim am Glan: Hain, 1973); David P. Conradt, 'Electoral Law Politics in West Germany', *Political Studies*, 18 (1970), pp. 341–56.

13  See Ferdinand A. Hermens, 'Evaluating Electoral Systems', in Max Kaase (ed.), *Politische Wissenschaft und politische Ordnung: Analysen zu Theorie und Empirie demokratischer Regierungsweise. Festschrift zum 65. Geburtstag von Rudolf Wildenmann* (Opladen: Westdeutscher Verlag, 1986), pp. 233–53.

14  See Ludger Helms, '"Machtwechsel" in der Bundesrepublik Deutschland. Eine vergleichende empirische Analyse der Regierungswechsel von 1966, 1969 und 1982', *Jahrbuch für Politik*, 4 (1994), pp. 225–48.

15  See Eckhard Jesse, *Elections: The Federal Republic of Germany in Comparison* (Oxford/New York: Berg, 1990), pp. 79–85.

16  This change in 1953 is frequently seen as a tightening of the 5 per cent clause. This is on the one hand correct, in as much as only parties with 5 per cent or more of list votes enter the Bundestag. On the other hand it is a relaxation of the clause, since under the previous law a party only received seats in Länder in which they obtained at least 5 per cent.

17  See Eckhard Jesse, 'Die institutionellen Rahmenbedingungen der Bundestagswahl vom 2. Dezember 1990', in Hans-Dieter Klingemann and Max Kaase (eds), *Wahlen und Wähler: Analysen aus Anlaß der Bundestagswahl 1990* (Opladen: Westdeutscher Verlag, 1994), pp. 15–41.

18  See Hans-Jörg Bücking, 'Der Streit um Grundmandatsklausel und Überhang-mandate', in E. Jesse and K. Löw (note 7), pp. 141–215; Eckhard Jesse, 'Grundmandatsklausel und Überhangmandate. Zwei wahlrechtliche Eigentümlichkeiten in der Kritik', in Max Kaase and Hans-Dieter Klingemann (eds), *Wahlen und Wähler: Analysen aus Anlaß der Bundestagswahl 1994* (Opladen: Westdeutscher Verlag, 1998), pp. 15–41; Christofer Lenz, 'Grundmandatsklausel und Überhangmandate vor dem

Bundesverfassungsgericht', *Neue Juristische Wochenschrift*, 50 (1997), pp. 1534–7.

19  Had this rule applied during the 1994–98 legislative period the CDU would have lost two Bundestag seats.

20  Thus the party obtained seats in the Bundestag in three different ways since 1990. In 1990 it benefited from the special role for that election, whereby the 5 per cent clause applied separately to the West German and to the East German electoral areas; in 1994 it qualified by means of the three-seat alternative clause; in 1998 it obtained seats 'normally' by getting over the 5 per cent hurdle.

21  See Ulrich Wenner, *Sperrklauseln im Wahlrecht der Bundesrepublik Deutschland* (Frankfurt a.m.: Peter Lang, 1996).

22  In this way the CDU/CSU obtained an absolute majority of seats (244 out of a total of 487 seats).

23  See Jochen Frowein, 'Die Rechtsprechung des Bundesverfassungsgerichts zum Wahlrecht', *Archiv des öffentlichen Rechts*, 99 (1974), pp. 72–110; Hans Meyer, *Wahlsystem und Verfassungsordnung: Bedeutung und Grenzen wahlsystematischer Gestaltung nach dem Grundgesetz* (Frankfurt a.m.: Metzner, 1973); Christofer Lenz, 'Die Wahlrechtsgleichheit und das Bundesverfassungsgericht', *Archiv des öffentlichen Rechts*, 121 (1996), pp. 337–58.

24  Leaving aside the fact that split-voting is only in very occasional cases caused by 'personalised' voting. In most cases it is due to strategic considerations of the voter, concerned to bring about a particular coalition. See Eckhard Jesse, 'Split-voting in the Federal Republic of Germany: an Analysis of the Federal Elections from 1953 to 1987', *Electoral Studies*, 7 (1988), pp. 109–24; Geoffrey K. Roberts, 'The "Second-Vote" Strategy of the West German Free Democratic Party', *European Journal of Political Research*, 16 (1988), pp. 317–37; Rüdiger Schmitt-Beck, 'Denn sie wissen nicht, was sie tun … Zum Verständnis des Verfahrens der Bundestagswahl bei westdeutschen und ostdeutschen Wählern', *Zeitschrift für Parlamentsfragen*, 24 (1993), pp. 393–415; Harald Schoen, 'Stimmensplitting bei Bundestagswahlen: eine Form taktischer Wahlentscheidung?', *Zeitschrift für Parlamentsfragen*, 29 (1998), pp. 223–43; Heinrich Pehle, 'Ist das Wahlrecht in Bund und Ländern reformbedürftig? Eine Bilanz seiner Mängel und Ungereimtheiten nach 50 Jahren', *Gegenwartskunde*, 48(1999), pp. 233–56.

25  See Hans Meyer, 'Der Überhang und anderes Unterhaltsames aus Anlaß der Bundestagswahl 1994', *Kritische Vierteljahresschrift für Gesetzgebung und Rechtswissenschaft*, 77 (1994), pp. 312–62.

26  The same applied to Saxony. Approximately 41,000 fewer votes in their Land would have gained an additional CDU surplus seat. The Land list seat would have been lost in Saxony, but the Lower Saxony CDU list would have elected one more Member of the Bundestag.

27  See E. Jesse (note 9); D. Nohlen (note 1).

# 8
# Monetary Institutions: Maintaining Independence in Times of Fiscal Stress

*Uwe Wagschal*

## Introduction

The most important task of a central bank is to preserve the value of a nation's currency. However, during this century monetary institutions in Germany failed three times to guarantee price stability. Firstly, in 1923 hyperinflation arose as a consequence of the First World War. Secondly, after the Second World War Germany experienced high inflation, which was ended in 1948 by a successful currency reform in the Western occupation sectors and a fruitless one in the Soviet sector. Thirdly, the breakdown of the German Democratic Republic was accompanied by massive hidden inflation. The experiences of the first two inflation processes have led to an impressive macroeconomic success story: the Federal Republic of Germany went through a period of price stability lasting 50 years. Not only did the Deutschmark remain stable, but also Germany has experienced the lowest inflation rate (2.7 per cent) of all the OECD countries. Two institutions can be held responsible for this: the *Bank Deutscher Länder* (BdL), acting as a central bank between 1948 and 1957, and its immediate successor, the *Deutsche Bundesbank* (DBB). This chapter aims to analyse Germany's monetary institutions and the institutional changes that occurred in their history. As we will see, the judicial rules of central banking have often been altered. The latest reform of the mid-1990s was the most dramatic one: the 'taming' of the German Bundesbank through the establishment of a European Central Bank. Furthermore, the political complexion of the central bank and several historical struggles for independence and price stability between 1948 and 1998 will be analysed, predominantly taking place in times of fiscal stress.

## The development of central banking institutions

The first national central bank in Germany, the *Reichsbank*, established in 1876, came about as a consequence of Germany's nation-building. The new currency, the Mark, was tied to Gold. It was valid for the whole Reich and in the long run replaced all other currencies.[1] However, central banks still existed in the bigger German Länder, such as Bavaria or Saxony, with the right to issue money.[2] Institutional central bank independence was not of great concern. The Board of Directors (*Direktorium*), led by the president of the *Reichsbank*, was fully dependent on a supervisory board headed by the *Reichskanzler*, although the bank was owned privately.[3] Financial independence was not ensured either, because the Empire levied a bank-note tax that yielded an important contribution to the state revenues.

The First World War resulted not only in a disastrous defeat but also in an oversupply of money and massive inflation that started in 1914 and culminated in the hyperinflation of 1923. The *Reichsbank* was fully dependent on the Ministry of Finance. As a consequence of massive inflation the victorious powers exercised their authority on the German government to make the *Reichsbank* independent (this was achieved in May 1922). Still it was neither able nor willing to reduce monetary inflation. In the wake of this crisis two other central banks worked in parallel,[4] and a token currency, the *Rentenmark*, was issued to overcome the monetary crisis. After the stabilisation process a new central bank law became effective in August 1924, in which the central bank was granted more independence from the government. On the other hand the law created a new dependency from foreign supervisors acting together with the same number of Germans in the supervisory board (*Generalrat*). In 1933 the government suspended this board and took over the control of the *Reichsbank*, which took an active part in financing Germany's military expenditures. After a protest of several directors against the inflationary politics in 1939 the central bank became fully dependent upon the *Reichskanzler*.

After the Second World War there was massive hidden inflation. This second period of inflationary politics was ended by the currency reform of 20 June 1948. Although the BDL and most of the Land Central Banks had already been established, the monetary reform was mainly planned and conducted by the Allies, whereas German specialists, the so-called '*Rothwesten conclave*' were only partly involved.[5] In the American and British Zones the BdL had been established on 1 March 1948. The Land Central Banks of the French Zone joined

3 weeks later. Thus, the BdL was the first German public institution that worked in all three Western zones.[6]

Parallel to the institutional formation of the BdL the *Reichsbank* was abolished. This reform was radical in terms of the institutional structure and different criteria of independence. Starting from a highly decentralised bank system in 1876, there were ups and downs between the two modes of centralisation. The BdL was organised in two tiers (whereas the Bundesbank until today has only one tier). One tier comprised the autonomous Land Central banks, that existed in all 11 (since 1952 nine) newly formed Länder. The second tier comprised the Board of Directors (*Direktorium*) which executed the policies of the bank and served as a clearing and co-ordination agency between all other Land Central Banks. The decisive policy-making institution was the Central Bank Council (*Zentralbankrat*, ZBR), consisting of a chairman, the president of the Board of Directors and the presidents of each of the member Land Central Banks. Both chairman and president of the Board of Directors were elected by a simple majority from the presidents of the Land Central Banks. The latter were appointed by the minister-presidents of the Länder.

With regard to political independence the BdL was autonomous from governmental directives. However, the Allied Bank Commission, made up of representatives from the three Western Military Governments, had veto rights and the right to give orders. Despite these reservations the ZBR was able to determine its policies without much interference from the Allies,[7] except some personnel decisions. These influences occurred in connection with the filling of the top positions in 1948.[8] During its first eight sessions the ZBR was busy with the election of the chairman and the president of the Board of Directors, where the Allies rejected the appointment of several candidates (Schniewind, Abs), whilst other candidates (von Wedel, Vocke) refused to be elected. Finally, Bernard and Vocke accepted their election as chairman and president respectively in May 1948, and both kept their positions until the transformation of the BdL into the Bundesbank. Shortly afterwards, in spring 1951, the Allies renounced their veto rights. After that the German government tried to appropriate these powers, resulting in a hot domestic debate over the legal status of the central bank. In March 1951 the Ministry of Finance introduced a bill suggesting that all rights of the Allies should be transferred to the government,[9] but in the end this attack failed. The result was a compromise in the BdL Act (*Übergangsgesetz*, 10 August 1951), which stipulated that the central bank should support the economic policies of the government, within the scope of their tasks. Governmental representatives were given the right to attend and to speak at meetings of the ZBR, but they did not have any voting rights. Their only power was a suspensive veto for 8 days.

Functional independence affects the clear competence for monetary stability and the application of the instruments, the possession of adequate instruments, and unequivocal priorities for low inflation.[10] According to these measurements the BdL as the final legal authority for monetary policy was granted a high degree of functional independence. It possessed a variety of conventional instruments, e.g. it was responsible for fixing the interest and discount rates and for conducting open-market operations with the Land Central Banks. Those again were responsible for the transactions with banks and enterprises. Moreover, the number of instruments had been even further enlarged: the Bank was authorised to fix reserves, which was a new power. On the other hand the right to issue money was restricted to a total amount of up to 10 billion Deutschmarks.

Financial independence was also guaranteed to a relatively great extent. Except for short-term advances no long-term credits for the government had been allowed, so that the government had only very limited access to central bank credit. Each Land Central Bank was entitled to participate in the net profits of the BdL according to their shares. In 1951 this provision was also changed by another law affecting the status of the BdL, whereby the government obtained a claim on the net profits.

Personal independence was higher than it had ever been, though political institutions were strongly involved in the selection of the central bankers. There were no governmental representatives in the Central Bank Council and the government did not have the possibility to recall members of the Council. On the other hand the presidents of the Land Central Banks were appointed by the minister-presidents of the Länder, which offered a potential for political influence. Possible protection against such pressures can be achieved by long terms without the possibility of re-election. However, the chairman's term of office was only 3 years, but with the possibility of re-election. The term of president of the Directorate had not been fixed in the BdL Act, since the contract was drawn up by the Central Bank Council. Re-election of the president of the Directorate was also possible.

Even though the bank was organised in a decentralised way it behaved like a centralised institution.[11] Several reasons led to this unintended result. First of all, the ZBR had the authority to issue directives to the Land Central Banks and these decisions were usually prepared by the Directorate. Secondly, most members of the ZBR had been former members of the *Reichsbank*, which had a long-lasting tradition as a centralised institution, and most did not agree with the measures imposed upon by the Allies. Thirdly, Wilhelm Vocke, the President of the Directorate and the most influential member of the ZBR, was a convinced advocate of centralism.

The BdL was a child of the Allies. The Basic Law (Article 88) called as early as 1949 for a new central bank, the Bundesbank. In 1951 also the Allies urged the government to establish a new central bank. However, it was a lengthy and highly politicised conflict between the government, the Länder, the BdL and parties to create the Bundesbank in 1957.

Though the two banks were similar in structure, several changes were made: the first most visible change was the abolition of the two-tier system, with independent Land Central Banks, and the foundation of a single-stage central bank system with a push towards more centralisation. Land Central Banks were downgraded to head offices with only minor responsibilities. Secondly, the position of the Directorate was upgraded. It now consisted of the president, the vice-president and up to eight additional members, all of whom were given voting rights in the Central Bank Council. Personal independence was relatively great, though the federal government's potential of influence in the appointment process was enlarged. The federal government selected the members of the Directorate who were appointed between a minimum period of 2 years up to a maximum period of 8 years by the federal president. Re-election was possible and usually occurred without major problems. The average term of more than 14 years for members of the ZBR can be seen as an indicator of the high degree of personal independence.[12] The Directorate is the central executive body of the Bundesbank and implements the resolutions taken by the ZBR. Thirdly, as a consequence of this shift the overall number of members in the ZBR increased to a possible maximum of 21. However, the average number of ZBR members between 1957 and the reform of 1992 was around 19 (18.8). The federal component outweighed the central one because the 11 presidents of the Land Central Banks still had the absolute majority. Nevertheless that meant a change in the power structure of this decision-making body. Fourthly, the selection process of the presidents of the Land Central Banks was changed. The federal president appointed them on the basis of a proposal from the Bundesrat. *De jure* this seemed to be a weakening of the Länder influence, due to higher transaction costs. However, it was *de facto* still a decision by the respective Länder governments. Fifthly, the twin executive structure was abolished, since the position of the chairman was cancelled. The Central Bank Council was now headed by the president or, in case of his absence, by the vice-president of the Directorate (§ 6 of the Bundesbank Act). Though the president represents the Bundesbank to the outside, he is just *primus inter pares*, having the same vote as any other ordinary member of the ZBR.

During the lengthy debate over the new Bundesbank Act, political and functional independence of the bank, secured in § 12 of the Bundesbank Act, had been discussed controversially,[13] especially its policy objectives and its role in supporting governmental trade-cycle and fiscal policies. In this conflict the Bundesbank was able to defend its independence, with aid of an important minister (Erhard), the Bundesrat, and the public opinion against Chancellor Adenauer.[14] Price stability remained the prime objective, whereas supporting the governmental economic policy remained a secondary objective for the Bundesbank (§ 12). On the other hand the federal government is now able to make inquiries from the Bundesbank (§ 13(1)) and members of the government are allowed to attend the ZBR without voting rights but with the right to place applications. With its most prominent power, the suspensive veto, the government may postpone decisions up to 2 weeks (§ 13(2)).

During the exchange rate crisis, from the 1950s up to the early 1970s, the instruments appeared to be rather limited. Fixed exchange rates can cause many inflationary troubles, when a currency is expected to be overrated, as was partly the case for the Deutschmark until the breakdown of the Bretton Woods system in 1973. When the full convertibility of the Deutschmark was established by the end of 1958 it was difficult to control the monetary base.[15] Due to these problems the Bundesbank was forced to increase the reserve rate for foreigners several times, raising it up to 100 per cent. This meant all inflowing foreign currency, which was changed into Deutschmarks, had to be transferred to the Bundesbank through the banking system (e.g. December/1968 to November/1969).

Since 1985 central bank money has mainly been provided through a new instrumental innovation, the securities repurchase transactions (*Wertpapierpensionsgeschäfte*), which were first used in 1979.[16] Since 1962 the Bundesbank, together with the Federal Banking Supervisory Office in Berlin, acts as a supervisor for the German banking system. As early as in 1974 it targeted the monetary base as the decisive goal of its policies, some years earlier than other central banks. Since 1975 the Bundesbank has every year announced a monetary target, or a target corridor, but it was not able to reach this goal in nearly half of all the years (11 out of 23).[17] This appears to be a very poor performance. However, the missing of the target was in most cases not severe. Only in a small number of cases, such as those in 1978 and 1992, did a severe target overshooting occur, which could be explained by external (e.g. foreign) factors. Nevertheless, the annual announcement of a monetary target corridor remains a symbol for Germany's 'stability culture'.

Personal independence is visible not only in the regulations concerning the terms, but also in the appointment or recall of the executive board. It is moreover manifested in the reputation and ethos of the members of the Central Bank Council.[18] During its history this board showed some peculiarities. So far it has been dominated by men; only one woman ever served in this institution. Moreover, most members joined the ZBR at an advanced age, 52 years on average.[19] In conjunction with a long tenure this constitutes an incentive to show no considerations for political demands (Thomas Becket effect). Astonishingly, compared to the intentions of the Allies, the share of former members of the NSDAP in the ZBR was very high in the initial decades: e.g. in 1968 it amounted to 40 per cent within the ZBR. Taking all leading members into account it even reached 58 per cent.[20] Some appointments of presidents of the Land Central Banks have been controversial, not only among the political parties but also among the Bundesbank and the government concerned. All members of the ZBR should have special professional qualifications, and this was in some cases proved doubtful. The last incident occurred in 1991 (Koebnick from Saarland). Nevertheless, all proposed candidates were eventually appointed.

Three different kinds of central bankers can be identified. Firstly, technocrats and specialists, mainly produced by the Bank itself and serving usually in the Directorate, which carries out the daily business. Secondly, a group of economists and monetary experts with an university background. Thirdly, there is a large group of politicians, who mainly took up their office through the Bundesrat, though some of them were also appointed to the Directorate. By May 1998 six former Ministers of Finance (from the Länder) were elected to the Central Bank Council (Gaddum, Meister, Kühbacher, Palm, Krupp, Welteke), two former Secretary of States from the Federal Ministry of Finance (Tietmeyer, Zeitler), and one former Commissioner of the European

Union (Schmidhuber). During the past 50 years this group has constituted the largest share of Central Bank Council members. It can be said that personal independence was high, which was also a merit of the presidents of the Bundesbank (Table 8.1), who all had a high reputation.

Although there have been quite a lot of changes to the Bundesbank Act, mostly through other laws, few have been of major relevance. The changes by the Stability Act (*Stabilitätsgesetz*) of 1967 had only been of minor consequence, though some observers argued that this was a severe impeding of its status and a shift towards more planning and Keynesianism.[21] These fears proved to be groundless, as the Bundesbank became the first bank explicitly attached to Monetarism and never played a vital role in the concept of global planning. Between 1957 and German unification in 1990 only minor changes occurred, which affected technical adjustments or the creation of new instruments to fight speculations, such as the possibility to raise reserves up to 100 per cent for foreign money flowing into Germany (June 1969).

The most important changes since 1957 have taken place in connection with German unification and the European Monetary Union (EMU).[22] On 1 July 1990 the reign of the Deutschmark was expanded to the territory of the German Democratic Republic (GDR) – 3 months before unification. This expansion was accompanied by severe tensions between the government and the Bundesbank, mainly over the design of the Monetary Union. The aftermath was dramatic: President Pöhl resigned 1 year later and the Bundesbank tightened its monetary policies due to this lack of co-operation and information. The Unification Treaty called for a reform of the Bundesbank Act within a year, but it took another 2 years until it was passed. This law, promulgated in July 1992, abolished the provisional rules for the transition period, which made some technical adjustments and reorganised the structure of the central bank. One year earlier the Bundestag had adopted another change of the Bundesbank Act, which was uncontroversial but had an important symbolic meaning: Frankfurt was fixed as the seat of the central bank, so far only a provisional rule.

The debate over the restructuring of the Bundesbank was controversial, mainly between centralists and federalists which, in fact, represented the government and the Bundesrat (then dominated by the opposition). A third actor was the President of the Bundesbank Pöhl, backed by the Directorate. All these actors presented proposals for a modification of the Bundesbank Act. Pöhl tried to gain more influence

**Table 8.1  Chairmen and presidents of the Central Bank Council and the Directorate**

| Name | Party affiliation | Begin term | End term | Tenure (years /months) | Other positions held earlier in the Central Bank system |
|---|---|---|---|---|---|
| *Chairman Central Bank Council of BdL* | | | | | |
| Bernard, Karl | CDU | 20.05.48 | 31.12.57 | 9 / 7 | |
| *President Directorate of BdL* | | | | | |
| Vocke, Wilhelm | CDU | 20.05.48 | 31.12.57 | 9 / 7 | Director of the Reichsbank (20 years) |
| *Presidents of the Directorate/Bundesbank* | | | | | |
| Blessing, Karl | CDU | 01.01.58 | 31.12.69 | 12 / 0 | Director of the Reichsbank (3 years) |
| Klasen, Karl | SPD | 01.01.70 | 31.05.77 | 7 / 5 | President LZB Hamburg (01.04.48–31.05.52) |
| Emminger, Otmar | CDU | 01.06.77 | 31.12.79 | 2 / 7 | Director DBB (01.04.53–31.12.69) Vice-President (01.01.70–31.05.77) |
| Pöhl, Karl Otto | SPD | 01.01.80 | 31.07.91 | 10 / 7 | Vice-President (01.06.77–31.12.79) |
| Schlesinger, Helmut | CDU | 01.08.91 | 30.09.93 | 2 / 2 | Director DBB (01.07.72–31.12.79) Vice-President (01.01.80–31.07.91) |
| Tietmeyer, Hans | CDU | Since 01.10.93 | | | Director DBB (01.01.90–31.07.91) Vice-President (01.08.91–31.09.93) |

*Source:* Deutsche Bundesbank, Historisches Archiv; R. Vaubel (note 28); DBB = Deutsche Bundesbank.

and proposed to reduce both the number of Land Central Banks and the members of the Directorate to eight (first he proposed seven, which was voted down). In this plan the President should have a tie-breaking vote.[23] This proposal found a majority in the Central Bank Council (September 1990), though a minority of seven LZB-Presidents expressed their severe discontent, resulting in a letter by Jochimsen (LZB-President of North Rhine-Westphalia) to Chancellor Kohl,[24] an event unparalleled in the Bundesbank's history. Their proposal, which was similar to the one from the Bundesrat, aimed at establishing 16 Land Central Banks, one each for every Land.[25] This would have led to a Council with about 25 members, presumably too large a body to perform its duties efficiently. Meanwhile, the Bundesrat introduced a very similar bill which, after 1 year of discussion, was rejected by the Bundestag.

At last a compromise proposal put forward by the Minister of Finance Waigel in June 1991 cut the Gordian knot. The 'Waigel-plan' suggested reducing the number of Land Central Banks to nine and the maximum of members in the Directorate to eight. It was first rejected by a two-thirds majority of the Bundesrat and went to the committee of mediation (*Vermittlungsausschuß*) for further negotiation.

The outcome of the committee of mediation was as follows: the Central Bank Council should consist of eight directors and nine Land Central Banks presidents. However, the composition of the merged banks was different from the suggestions in the 'Waigel-plan'. Again, the Bundesrat rejected this compromise by an absolute majority because the smaller Länder governed by the CDU (Thuringia, Saxony), now voted in favour of it. This objection was finally rejected by a large majority of the Bundestag, where many members of the opposition also voted together with the government. The modification created five merged central banks: (1) Berlin and Brandenburg; (2) Saxony and Thuringia; (3) Rhineland-Palatinate and Saarland; (4) Bremen, Lower Saxony and Saxony-Anhalt; and (5) Hamburg, Mecklenburg-West Pomerania and Schleswig-Holstein, while Bavaria, Baden-Württemberg, Hesse and North Rhine-Westphalia remained unchanged.

Since 1 January 1999 the Bundesbank is no longer the sovereign of price stability in Germany. Now the European System of Central Banks (ESCB) is responsible for monetary policy in Euroland. This consists of the European Central Bank (ECB), seated in Frankfurt, and the central banks of the countries participating in the EMU. Although the Bundesbank has not ceased to exist, the creation of a common currency must be seen as a serious defeat of the Bundesbank. Within only 3 years the Bank lost its two most important battles: German unification and European Monetary Union. The 'enemies' in the last fight came mainly from abroad: French and Italian politicians had been striving for reining in the Bundesbank because of its tight policies. In the end they succeeded, as Germany's politicians sacrificed the Deutschmark in exchange for the unity of the EU. However, the defeat of the Bundesbank was not total and perhaps the victory of the advocates of a loose monetary policy was a kind of Pyrrhic victory, as the Bundesbank Act served as a blueprint for the new ESCB.

In order to build the ESCB, several changes in the Basic Law and the Bundesbank Act were necessary. These affected the structure and the policy instruments of the Bundesbank and in connection with the Maastricht Treaty also Article 88 of the Basic Law. According to this revised Article the ECB has to be independent with its priority goal on price stability. The new Article 88 moreover allowed the delegation of monetary powers to the ESCB and the foundation of the EMU which passed the Bundstag against only one dissenting vote. In stark contrast, opinion polls showed – and still do – severe discontent with the abolition of the Deutschmark.

A three-stage approach outlined the creation of the EMU (Delors-Plan). During the first stage (1990–93), no institutional changes of the Bundesbank were necessary. Within the second stage (1994–98) some minor modifications took place, most of them affecting technical provisions. The most important one affected financial independence, since short-term credits for public authorities were no longer allowed. Furthermore, administrations were no longer forced to hold their savings on Bundesbank accounts, diminishing its role as state bank. This law passed all three readings without any problems (5. *BBankGÄndG* from 8 July 1994).

The final thrust hit the Bundesbank when being prepared for the third stage of the EMU. The 'sixth law for changing the Bundesbank Act (6. *BBankGÄndG*)', adopted on 12 December 1997 had severe consequences for the status of the Bank:

- The Bundesbank has been fully integrated into the final stage of the EMU since 1 January 1999. The Bundesbank is obliged to execute directives from the Council of the ESCB, which means no less than the end of its independence (§ 3 Bundesbank Act).
- Any national monetary policy has ceased to exist (§ 15 and § 16 abrogated).

- The suspensive veto (§ 13), which gives the government the right to postpone decisions of the Central Bank Council, has been abolished. Under 'normal' circumstances this would imply a higher degree of functional and political independence.
- Personal independence has been enlarged by alteration of the term-of-office of the executive members. According to the old wording (§ 7 and § 8) the minimum term for the president and the directors was at least 2 years. That has now been changed to 5 years in accordance with the provisions for executive members of the ESCB.
- The president of the Bundesbank, who is a member of the Council of the European Central Bank, is not subject to any directives from inside or outside the Bundesbank (§ 6).
- The Bundesbank has lost its right to issue money. During a transition period, until the Euro is the only currency, the Bundesbank is allowed to issue money (§ 14), but only with the explicit approval the Council of the European Central Bank.
- Compared to other political conflicts between government and opposition this most recent reform was not a serious matter of conflict in the parliamentary arena, in contrast to the situation among the public and among scholars. Undoubtedly this transformation of power marked the greatest modification in its history, though the Bundesbank's internal structure, as well as the number of Land Central Banks and directors, remained untouched.

## Maintaining independence in conflicts

In international comparative studies on central banks the Bundesbank is usually considered to be the most independent one. Yet to be a member of the Central Bank Council is a matter not only of competence, but also of political partisanship. Most of the time the BdL and the Bundesbank have been led by presidents attached to the CDU/CSU. Two presidents, ruling the bank for 18 years, were members of the SPD (see Table 8.1, above). The composition of the ZBR and the voting behaviour of its members seems to be dominated by a Grand Coalition. Usually the CDU and the SPD shared the two top positions (president and vice-president). Only during the period of the BdL, and since 1991, have members of the CDU controlled both positions.

Although the parties try to achieve a majority in the ZBR, the filling of the posts is not exclusively dominated by partisanship aspects. The SPD government appointed Emminger (CDU) as President and a number of other directors without a Social Democratic background (e.g. Schlesinger and Werthmöller), and even re-appointed some (e.g. Irmler and Lucht). Therefore, it took until 1980 for the SPD to achieve a majority in the Directorate, though it already had the majority in the ZBR in 1975 and 1976. Since 1973 one member of the Directorate can be ascribed to the FDP. Due to the long tenures it was difficult for all governments to change the party complexion in the Directorate after major changes of government at the federal level (1969 and 1982). Even the Christian Democrats had to wait until 1990 for a majority in the ZBR. Only in 26 years (out of 51) has there been a clear majority for one party: almost 7 years for the SPD and 19 years for the CDU/CSU.

To stress the cleavage between the parties implies different objectives of parties towards inflation, and suggests that the central bankers are acting as mere agents of the parties. Both can be doubted for Germany. Price stability is a public good. It is non-exclusive, because everybody benefits from low inflation and there is no rivalry whilst consuming this good. Besides, the historical experiences push all major parties to similar positions on this issue. Empirical evidence is rather weak for this partisan hypothesis, since there is a zero correlation for the OECD countries.[26] Concerning the agent hypothesis several arguments can be raised against it. Again, the historical experience works as a cramp for all central bankers to establish price stability. Furthermore the institutional framework of the Bundesbank ensures a high degree of personal independence. Also the tradition and ethos of the Bundesbank are not a *quantité négligeable*.[27]

In contrast to this line of reasoning there is a vast body of empirical literature produced in an altempt to identify a political business cycle, or at least specific patterns, in the behaviour of the Bundesbank.[28] The policies of the Bundesbank are not determined by a single factor, as it has to face other constraints.[29] Therefore it might be a critical statement to identify partisanship as the decisive factor concerning the monetary policy of the Bank. Nevertheless, some hypotheses seem worth discussing:

- The Bundesbank supports the incumbent government during the run-up to elections irrespective of the political composition of both institutions (simple political business cycle hypothesis $H_1$).
- A Central Bank Council dominated by a party supports, during the pre-election period, a government with the same political complexion, while it obstructs a government with a different one (simple partisan political business cycles hypothesis PPBC $H_2$).

- A Central Bank Council dominated by the CDU produces a tighter monetary policy than a Central Bank Council led by a SPD majority (partisan hypothesis $H_3$).
- The use of monetary instruments is not influenced by electoral or partisan effects (null hypothesis $H_0$).

Since 1949 14 national elections have been held. If the first hypothesis is significant the interest rates should behave in the postulated way, i.e. they should go down pre-election. As Figure 8.1 and Table 8.2 reveal, this happened only in seven out of 14 cases, when considering a 1-year period preceding the election. In three cases interest rates remained unchanged in the last 12 pre-election months and in four they increased.

There is also no clear evidence for the second hypothesis $H_2$. The majority within the ZBR can be portrayed with a five-point indicator: clear CDU (SPD) majority (i.e. more than 50 per cent of ZBR members can be ascribed to the CDU (SPD)); weak CDU (SPD) majority (i.e. independent members – not exceeding 50 per cent of their share – are required to manufacture a majority) and a draw. Table 8.2 displays the relevant information for all elections between 1948 and 1998. Testing $H_2$ should reveal that a Central Bank Council dominated by SPD members supports a SPD-led government before elections and obstructs a CDU-led government. For a ZBR dominated by the CDU this should be the other way around. However, the PBC theory can imply several alternatives of central bank behaviour after the election, which are not considered here. There is no significant relation: four cases fit and four contradict the hypothesis, three cases are neutral, because the Bundesbank took no pre-election action and three cases are only partly in favour of the PPBC. However, in two cases (1949 and 1972) the Bank had to anticipate the electoral outcome.

In case the simple partisan hypothesis ($H_3$) is valid, one should expect that the average discount rate produced by a Central Bank Council with a majority of CDU members is significantly lower than the average discount rate manufactured by SPD members, assuming all other factors to be equal. Table 8.3 displays the average discount rates (based on monthly data) under different political conditions. It is obvious that our postulated hypothesis does not hold. Additional breakdown of the data along the political complexion of the governments likewise reveals no systematic relations.

All in all one might conclude that there are no political factors such as partisanship and elections at work, because all three hypotheses

157

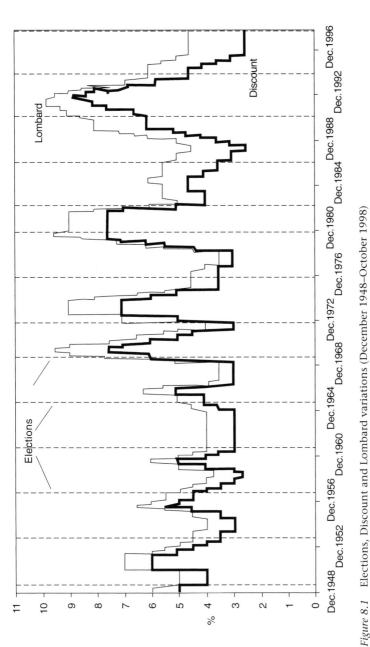

*Figure 8.1* Elections, Discount and Lombard variations (December 1948–October 1998)

*Note*: Monthly data; the broken lines indicate the month of the election; the bold line represents the discount rate and the thin line the rate for loans on securities (Lombard).

Table 8.2 Elections, variations of interest rates and political business cycle (1949–98)

| Election | Variation of interest rates before election[a] | Majority within Central Bank Council | Government complexion before election | Government complexion after election | Variation of interest rates after election[b] | Does pre-election fit the PPBC Hypothesis? |
|---|---|---|---|---|---|---|
| (1) 14.08.49 | Reduced | Weak CDU | | CDU/CSU; FDP; DP | Reduced | Partly pro-PPBC (if anticipated) |
| (2) 06.09.53 | Reduced | Draw | CDU/CSU; FDP; DP | CDU/CSU; FDP; DP; BHE | Reduced | Partly pro-PPBC |
| (3) 15.09.57 | Reduced | Clear SPD | CDU/CSU; FDP; DP; BHE | CDU/CSU; DP | Reduced | Against PPBC |
| (4) 17.09.61 | Reduced | Weak CDU | CDU/CSU | CDU/CSU; FDP | Reduced | Pro-PPBC |
| (5) 19.09.65 | Increased | Weak CDU | CDU/CSU; FDP | CDU/CSU; FDP | Increased | Against PPBC |
| (6) 28.09.69 | Increased | Clear CDU | CDU/CSU; SPD | SPD; FDP | Increased | Partly pro-PPBC (if anticipated) |
| (7) 19.11.72 | Increased | Clear CDU | SPD; FDP | SPD; FDP | Increased | Pro-PPBC |
| (8) 03.10.76 | Unchanged | Clear SPD | SPD; FDP | SPD; FDP | Reduced | Neutral |
| (9) 05.10.80 | Increased | Clear SPD | SPD; FDP | SPD; FDP | Increased | Against PPBC |
| (10) 06.03.83 | Reduced | Clear SPD | CDU/CSU; FDP | CDU/CSU; FDP | Reduced | Against PPBC |

**Table 8.2** Continued

| Election | | Variation of interest rates before election [a] | Majority within Central Bank Council | Government complexion before election | Government complexion after election | Variation of interest rates after election [b] | Does pre-election fit the PPBC Hypothesis? |
|---|---|---|---|---|---|---|---|
| (11) | 23.01.87 | Reduced | Weak CDU | CDU/CSU; FDP | CDU/CSU; FDP | Reduced | Pro-PPBC |
| (12) | 02.12.90 | Unchanged | Clear CDU | CDU/CSU; FDP | CDU/CSU; FDP | Unchanged | Neutral |
| (13) | 16.10.94 | Reduced | Clear CDU | CDU/CSU; FDP | CDU/CSU; FDP | Reduced | Pro-PPBC |
| (14) | 27.09.98 | Unchanged | Clear CDU | CDU/CSU; FDP | SPD; Green | Unchanged [c] | Neutral [c] |

*Note:* PPBC = Partisan Political Business Cycle; [a] = variation within the pre-election year (12 month); [b] = first variation within 12 months after the general election; [c] = situation by the end of October 1998.

Table 8.3  Average discount rates under different political conditions (September 1949–October 1998)

| Majority in Central Bank Council | CDU/CSU-led government | | SPD-led government | | Grand coalition | | Overall | |
|---|---|---|---|---|---|---|---|---|
| Clear CDU | 4.96 | (117) | 5.27 | (72) | 3.53 | (35) | 4.84 | (224) |
| Weak CDU | 3.64 | (111) | – | – | – | | 3.64 | (111) |
| Draw | 4.04 | (116) | 4.08 | (25) | – | | 4.05 | (141) |
| Weak SPD | 3.49 | (32) | 5.67 | (3) | – | | 3.68 | (35) |
| Clear SPD | 4.61 | (23) | 5.91 | (55) | – | | 5.53 | (78) |
| Overall average | 4.19 | (399) | 5.32 | (155) | 3.53 | (35) | 4.45 | (589) |

*Note:* The averages are based on monthly data. Numbers of months in parentheses.

have to be rejected. Therefore it would be easy to accept the null hypothesis ($H_0$) deducing that the Bundesbank is independent and in fact ruled by technocrats. However, this would neglect the fact that there have been several serious dealings with the government. Two failures of government (Erhard 1966 and Schmidt 1982) and one resignation of an important minister (Schiller 1972) are connected with the politics of the Bundesbank.

In 1951 the Adenauer administration tried to destroy central bank independence by taking over the veto rights of the military powers, which marked the first attempt to weaken the BdL. A few years later in 1955, and especially in 1956, the first severe quarrels concerning rising interest and reserve rates occurred. During that time the economy boomed and wage settlements were also above the previous years, so that the Bundesbank reacted by increasing the discount rate in three steps from 3 per cent (August 1955) to 5.5 per cent (May 1956). Having his re-election in mind Adenauer was not pleased with these policies. He therefore forced the Bundesbank to postpone a decision with a suspensive veto. Two months later the Bundesbank again increased interest rates – this time two important ministers (Erhard and Schäffer) attended the conference and supported the decision. This caused a dramatic response by Adenauer, who blamed the Bundesbank and the ministers as being the guillotine of the ordinary man in the street.[30] His so-called 'Gürzenich speech' provoked reactions from all major newspapers and interest groups which declared their solidarity with those he attacked,[31] although Adenauer knuckled under to soaring public opposition he did not refrain from attacking the Bank. In September 1956 he proposed transferring the Bundesbank from Frankfurt to Cologne so as to increase the influence of the government, but failed in this attempt.

Also in 1965 and 1966 the Bundesbank proved to be stronger than the government. Erhard, who replaced Adenauer in 1963, went on a spending spree prior to the pending federal election. The Bundesbank took countermeasures and increased interest rates in two steps before the election and raised reserves, to prevent an overheating of the economy and to 'punish' the government for its procyclical behaviour.[32] In May 1966 the Bank – unanimously – raised interest rates again. When the first major economic crisis in the Federal Republic's history emerged in 1966, conflicts over the financial recovery began and Erhard finally resigned. It is widely acknowledged that the policies of the Bundesbank played a significant role in his resignation.

Other attacks on central bank independence appeared in connection with the monetary crisis during the Bretton Woods system. As massive flights of capital from the Dollar, the Franc and Sterling occurred, the Deutschmark was twice up-valued (in 1961 and in 1969). Up to the early 1970s the Bundesbank, and its President Blessing in particular, opposed any exchange rate adjustments, while Erhard and Schiller (the Ministers of Economics during the crisis) favoured them. The underrating of the Deutschmark led to huge surpluses in the current account over many years and caused inflationary troubles. Although the final decision on a realignment of exchange rates is up to the government, the Bundesbank was able to postpone the decision several years until 1961. In 1969 a second realignment occurred shortly after the federal election, though the turbulences at the financial markets were present for more than a year. Also in the early 1970s conflicts between Schiller and the Bank happened and finally Schiller, who lost backing in the cabinet, resigned.

The change of government in 1982 was also influenced by the Bundesbank. Though the Central Bank Council displayed a clear majority of members with a SPD party affiliation, it raised interest rates to a unpopularly high level, due to the excessive spending of the SPD–FDP government. When the new government assumed office it lowered its interest rates in three consecutive steps. The previous government had blamed the Bundesbank for its tight monetary policy, resulting in a recession. When the new government promised a reliable policy change the Bundesbank gave it a reward in advance. The CDU/CSU-FDP government repaid this mark of confidence and performed an austerity policy reducing the deficit.

However, the relationship between the Kohl government and the Bundesbank was not free of irritation, especially during the establishment of the German–French Finance and Economic Council in 1987/88 and the process of German unification. Several affronts could be observed, such as the government's deficient information policy concerning crucial properties over the Monetary Union. In 1991 Pöhl resigned mainly because of these conflicts.[33] This shift from austerity towards a large debt financing and the disregarding by the federal government forced the Bank to react. Since inflation rose to nearly 9 per cent in 1992, the Bundesbank increased interest rates to an all-time high, which was remarkable as during the 1970s inflation had at some stage been three percentage points higher.

## Conclusions

In Germany the importance of central bank independence has been recognised early. Some observers labelled the Bank as 'contre-gouvernement'.[34] Although the Bundesbank never agreed in public to this position, it was always well aware of its power. All in all it was one of the most successful public institutions in Germany's history. However, to ensure that inflation is kept on a very low level, several more factors are needed for such an outstanding performance, including low public expenditures, reasonable wage settlements and few macroeconomic problems.

The Bundesbank won most of its conflicts with the government. That is why the Bundesbank is one of the most pivotal institutions in Germany, exercising a kind of veto power against governmental policies. On the other hand it lost some fights, such as the struggles for the revaluation in the 1960s and 1970s and the conflicts over the German and European Monetary Union.

What are the prospects for the Bundesbank in the future? With the establishment of the EMU the old institutional structure has become obsolete. The Central Bank Council has no means to influence the president of the Bundesbank in any way, as he is an autonomous member of the ESCB. For that reason also the Central Bank Council seems to be superfluous, as it no longer has any power or authority to issue directives. Therefore the Bundesbank has to find a new role.

## Notes

1 See Knut Borchardt, 'Währung und Wirtschaft', in Deutsche Bundesbank (ed.), *Deutsches Geld- und Bankwesen in Zahlen, 1876–1975* (Frankfurt a.M.: Fritz Knapp, 1976), p. 9.

2 See Joachim von Spindler, Willy Becker and Ernst Starke, *Die Deutsche Bundesbank: Grundzüge des Notenbankwesens und Kommentar zum Gesetz über die Deutsche Bundesbank* (Stuttgart: Kohlhammer, 1973), p. 7

3 Harold James, 'Die Reichsbank 1876 bis 1945', in Deutsche Bundesbank (ed.), *Fünfzig Jahre Deutsche Mark: Notenbank und Währung in Deutschland seit 1948* (Munich: Beck, 1998), p. 36.

4 *Ibid.*, pp. 53–4.

5 See Hans Roeper and Wolfram Weimer, *Die D-Mark: eine deutsche Wirtschaftsgeschichte* (Frankfurt a.M.: Societäts-Verlag, 1996), p. 23; Hans Möller, 'Die Westdeutsche Währungsreform von 1948', in Deutsche Bundesbank (ed.), *Währung und Wirtschaft in Deutschland, 1876–1975* (Frankfurt a.M.: Fritz Knapp Verlag, 1976), pp. 433–83.

6. See Eckhard Wandel, *Die Entstehung der Bank deutscher Länder und die deutsche Währungsreform 1948. Die Rekonstruktion des westdeutschen Geld- und Währungssystems 1945–1948 unter Berücksichtigung der amerikanischen Besatzungspolitik* (Frankfurt a.M.: Fritz Knapp Verlag, 1980), p. 73; Christoph Buchheim, 'Die Errichtung der Bank deutscher Länder und die Währungsreform in Westdeutschland', in Deutsche Bundesbank (note 3), p. 112.

7   Deutsche Bundesbank 'Der Zentralbankrat vor fünfzig Jahren', *Deutsche Bank Monatsbericht März 1998*, pp. 29–31.

8   See H. Möller (note 5), p. 455.

9   See Volker Hentschel, 'Die Entstehung des Bundesbankgesetzes 1949–1957: Politische Kontroversen und Konflikte' (Teil I und Teil II), *Bankhistorisches Archiv: Zeitschrift zur Bankengeschichte*, 14 (1988), pp. 3–31 and 79–115.

10  See Rolf H. Hasse, *Die Europäische Zentralbank: Perspektiven für eine Weiterentwicklung des Europäischen Währungssystems* (Gütersloh: Bertelsmann Stiftung, 1989), pp. 116–7.

11  See Monika Dickhaus, *Die Bundesbank im westeuropäischen Wiederaufbau: die internationale Währungspolitik der Bundesrepublik Deutschland 1948 bis 1958* (Munich: Oldenbourg, 1996), pp. 60–4.

12  See Manfred J. M. Neumann, 'Geldwertstabilität: Bedrohung und Bewährung', *Fünfzig Jahre Deutsche Mark: Notenbank und Währung in Deutschland seit 1948* (Munich: Beck, 1998), p. 319.

13  See V. Hentschel (note 9).

14  See Ludwig Gramlich, *Bundesbankgesetz, Währungsgesetz, Münzgesetz: Kommentar* (Köln/Berlin: Carl Heymanns, 1988), p. 86; V. Hentschel (note 9).

15  See Carl-Ludwig Holtfrerich, 'Geldpolitik bei festen Wechselkursen (1948–1970)', in Deutsche Bundesbank (note 3), p. 407.

16  See Deutsche Bundesbank (ed.), *Die Geldpolitik der Bundesbank* (Frankfurt a.M.: Deutsche Bundesbank, 1995), pp. 113–7.

17  See Peter Schmid, 'Monetary Policy: Targets and Instruments', in Stephen Frowen and Robert Pringle (eds), *Inside the Bundesbank* (London: Macmillan, 1998), p. 36.

18  See Ellen Kennedy, *The Bundesbank: Germany's Central Bank in the International Monetary System* (New York: Council on Foreign Relations Press, 1991); Jeremy Leaman, 'The Bundesbank. Unelected Government of Germany and Europe?', *Debatte*, 1 (1993), pp. 8–32.

19  See M. Neumann (note 12), p. 319.

20  See David Marsh, *Die Bundesbank: Geschäfte mit der Macht* (Munich: Bertelsmann, 1992), p. 207.

21  See Heiko Faber, *Wirtschaftsplanung und Bundesbankautonomie* (Baden-Baden: Nomos, 1969).

22  See Klaus Stern, 'Die Notenbank im Staatsgefüge', in Deutsche Bundesbank (note 3), pp. 141–98.

23  See Susanne Lohmann, 'Designing a Central Bank in a Federal System: the Deutsche Bundesbank, 1957–1992', in Pierre Syklos (ed.), *Varieties of Monetary Reforms: Lessons and Experiences on the Road to Monetary Union* (Boston: Kluwer Academic Publishers, 1994), p. 267.

24  See D. Marsh (note 20), p. 292

25  See Karl Kaltenthaler, 'The Restructuring of the German Bundesbank: the Politics of Institutional Change', *German Politics and Society*, 14 (1996), pp. 36–7.

26  See Andreas Busch, *Preisstabilitätspolitik: Politik und Inflationsraten im internationalen Vergleich* (Opladen: Leske & Budrich, 1995).

27  E. Kennedy (note 18); Hans Tietmeyer, 'The Bundesbank: Committed to Stability', in S. Frowen and R. Pringle (note 17), pp. 1–10.

28  See Bruno S. Frey and Friedrich Schneider, 'Central Bank Behaviour: a Positive Empirical Analysis', *Journal of Monetary Economics*, 7 (1981), pp. 291–315; Günter Lang and Peter Welzel, 'Budgetdefizite, Wahlzyklen und Geldpolitik: Empirische Ergebnisse für die Bundesrepublik Deutschland 1962–1989', *Institut für Volkswirtschaftslehre der Universität Augsburg*, Beitrag no. 63 (1991); Roland Vaubel, 'Eine Public-Choice-Analyse der Deutschen Bundesbank und ihre Implikationen für die Europäische Währungsunion', in Dieter Duwendag and Jürgen Siebke (eds), *Europa vor dem Eintritt in die Wirtschafts- und Währungsunion* (Berlin: Duncker & Humblot, 1993), pp. 23–79; Helge Berger, *Konjunkturpolitik im Wirtschaftswunder, Handlungsspielräume und Verhaltensmuster von Bundesbank und Regierung in den 1950er Jahren* (Tübingen: Mohr Siebeck, 1997); Helge Berger and Friedrich Schneider, 'Does the Bundesbank Give Way in Conflicts with the West German Government?', *University of Linz Working Paper*, 9716 (1997); S. Lohmann (note 23); M. Neumann (note 12).
29  See B. S. Frey and F. Schneider (note 28), pp. 294–5.
30  See H. Roeper and W. Weimer (note 5), p. 90.
31  See M. Neumann (note 28), pp. 330–2.
32  See Wolfram Bickerich, *Die D-Mark. Eine Biographie* (Berlin: Rowohlt, 1998), pp. 198–200.
33  See D. Marsh (note 20); Dieter Balkhausen, *Gutes Geld & schlechte Politik: Der Report über die Bundesbank* (Düsseldorf: Econ, 1992); H. Roeper and W. Weimer (note 5); W. Bickerich (note 32).
34  Rudolf Wildenmann, 'Die Rolle des Bundesverfassungsgerichts und der Deutschen Bundesbank in der politischen Willensbildung. Ein Beitrag zur Demokratietheorie', *Veröffentlichungen der Universität Mannheim*, vol. 23 (1969), p. 10.

# 9
# Parties and the Party System: Pluralisation and Functional Change within Limits

*Oskar Niedermayer*

When studying institutional change in the party sphere one has to distinguish two levels of analysis, the party and the party system level, as well as two dimensions of analysis, the structural and the functional dimension. This chapter will first concentrate on the party level, discussing the structural development of the German parties and how they perform the functions assigned to them. The second part of the chapter then deals with the core characteristics of the party system and their stability or change.

## The four faces of party

It is widely agreed among party scholars that structural change at the party level cannot be studied taking the party as a whole as the unit of analysis. However, there is a lack of consensus regarding the number and type of sub-units that have to be distinguished: Michels' famous law of oligarchy is based on a simple leaders–followers dichotomy.[1] Sorauf supplements the extra-parliamentary party (in his words: the organisation proper) by the party in office and the party-in-the-electorate.[2] Katz and Mair suggest distinguishing three faces of party: the party in public office, the party central office and the party on the ground.[3] The party in public office is dominated by those occupying public office in parliament and government, the party central office consists of the national executive committee(s) and the central party staff. According to Katz and Mair, 'in the case of parties with formal mass membership, the members are the basis of the party on the ground, but more loosely it can be taken to include the core of regular activists, financial supporters, and even loyal voters, whether or not they are formally enrolled as party "members"'.[4] We think that such a definition mixes up two groups of people which should be separated: those who are entitled to take part in the intra-party decisions concerning the performance of the party's functions and those who do not have this possibility. Therefore, we suggest to dividing this subsystem into two: the party's basis consisting of those who can participate in intra-party decision-making, and the party-in-the-electorate, which is 'composed of those partisans who attach themselves to the party either by regular support at the polls or through self-identification with it'.[5]

The four subsystems are differently located in the wider political system. The party in public office is part of the governmental system, because its members belong to the constitutional political institutions. The party central office and the party's basis belong to the intermediary system which mediates between the government system and the politicised citizens, while the party-in-the-electorate is part of the latter. Since political parties penetrate the whole political system, they participate in all the functions assigned to it, that is the formulation, implementation and control of political decisions, the articulation and aggregation of interests (interest mediation), the communication of political decisions to the citizens (policy mediation) and the recruitment of political personnel.[6]

The performance of these functions is not evenly distributed among the different subsystems, however. It is not even absolutely necessary that all four subsystems exist, because other actors can provide functional equivalent contributions. We will therefore develop a structural-functional typology of parties by using the existence of the party subsystems and their relevance for the performance of the party's functions within the political system as criteria for classification.

If one agrees with the crudely realistic view of Schattschneider, according to which a political party is nothing more than an 'organised attempt to get power'[7] through elections, than only two of the four subsystems of party are really indispensable: the party in public office as the party's 'raison d'être', and the party-in-the-electorate, because it provides the necessary resources to achieve it. The other two subsystems are non-essential, as their activities and contributions can be provided by other actors and sources. When a party is reduced to these absolutely necessary core elements the party in public office is the subsystem performing all party functions except its own recruitment. Here, it selects the candidates who are then elected by the party-in-the-electorate. We will call this type of party 'mandate party' because the central actors are those holding a mandate in parliament or are members of government.

The type of party in which all four subsystems exist will be called a 'membership party', because it is characterised by a more or less pronounced membership organisation outside the party in public office. Membership parties can be subdivided using the dominance structure between the subsystems concerning the performance of the party's system functions except: (1) the policy implementation, which is always the task of the party in public office, and (2) the election of the party in public office as part of the recruitment of political personnel, which is always performed by the party-in-the-electorate.

Firstly, the party can still be dominated by the party in public office, although an extra-parliamentary organisation exists. Secondly, the party can be dominated by the party's central office. In this case the party's central office is the real centre of decision-making and the party in public office only implements the political decisions formulated and controlled by the party's central office. The party's central office also takes control of the communication of political decisions to the party's basis and the party-in-the-electorate including the guidance of the party's basis in electoral campaigns, defines the 'true' interests of the other subsystems and dominates the selection of political personnel. Thirdly, the party can be dominated by the party's basis. Here, the party's central office and the party in public office are only agents of the party's basis bound by imperative mandates to carry out its decisions. The next group of subtypes consists of parties which are not dominated by one but by two subsystems. Here we can distinguish between three types of party: (1) parties dominated by their leadership, where the party in public office and the party's central office – at least partly linked by a personal union – dominate the performance of the party's functions; (2) bipolar parties, where this is the case with the party in public office and the party's basis; and (3) those parties dominated by the extra-parliamentary party organisation, that is the party's central office and the party's basis. Last but not least, there is the possibility that no clear dominance structure exists. This type will be called a 'multicentric' party.

The eight types of party of our typology are 'ideal types', that is theoretical constructs and not real party organisations. However, in German history we find parties which come close to this ideal type and we do have a sequence in the types of party dominating in specific historical periods from the beginning of Imperial Germany to the present day.[8] Which ideal types of party the real party organisations come close to depends on a variety of factors which can be separated into three groups: (1) factors defining the framework to which the party competition is subject; (2) factors affecting the demand side of party competition, that is the party-in-the-electorate; and (3) factors affecting the supply side of party competition, that is the other three subsystems.

## The structural development of the German parties

As in other European countries, the German parties developed along the main conflict lines which emerged during the processes of nation-state building and industrial revolution in the 19th century.[9] The first party organisations emerged during the 1860s. In the formative years four main ideological pillars took shape: the Liberals, the Conservatives, the Catholics and the Socialists. The Liberals and the Conservatives were based on the conflict between the conservative feudal political elite in the monarchy and bureaucracy and the liberal forces of the emerging bourgeoisie. The confessional conflict in Germany, dating back to the Reformation in the first half of the six-teenth century, gained political relevance when the Catholics became a national minority in the course of the foundation of Imperial Germany and organised themselves into the Catholic Centre Party. The emer-gence of the Socialists was due to the replacement of the traditional agrarian by the industrial society and the development of a new social group, the industrial working class. In addition, the centre–periphery conflict lead to a variety of small parties representing ethnical groups and minorities.

In the beginning the Liberals and the Conservatives, which in each case were organised in more than one party, were clearly mandate parties. Beyond the party in public office a party organisation and a broad membership did not exist. Electoral support for the parliamen-tarians was provided by loose local groups. Interest mediation as well as policy mediation functions were performed by personal communica-tion between the relatively few people involved. In the course of time, however, the extension of the suffrage and the growing party competi-tion necessitated the development of rudimentary extra-parliamentary organisations with more stable local electoral associations and a shift from personal to media communication with the party-in-the-electorate via the party press. The parties remained clearly dominated by the party in public office, however. This was also the case for the Catholic Centre Party. The Socialists, however, emerged as a political movement outside parliament dominated by the party's central office and became the organisationally well-structured mass membership party par excellence. The party's central office was weakened in favour of the party in public office since 1878, when the oppression policy of the Bismarck government led up to the ban on the extra-parliamentary organisation. At the time of the so-called *Kulturkampf* the Catholics, too, were oppressed and discriminated. This for a long time hindered a wider social integration of workers and Catholics and promoted the encapsulation of these social groups in socio-cultural milieus. These milieus, in a weaker form also to be found among the Liberals and Conservatives,[10] were common ways of living produced by the coincidence of specific economic, cultural and regional factors. Supported by a variety of organisations they formed a unidimensional political socialisation environment, which produced relatively stable, emotionally and normatively embodied ties with the parties.

In his classic work on the sociology of parties, which concentrated on the Socialists (SPD), Michels insisted on the inability of organisations to realise intra-organisational democracy.[11] Although his 'iron law of oligarchy' is often denied,[12] it is consensus that neither the Socialists nor the other parties of Imperial Germany were internally very democratic. Perfect examples of a membership party dominated by the party's central office did not emerge until the beginning of the Weimar Republic, however. On the left side of the political spectrum the secession of the SPD's radical left wing in 1918 led to the foundation of the Communist Party (KPD) with its top-down model of intra-party decision-making according to the principle of 'democratic centralism'. On the right the National Socialists (NSDAP) realised the leader–followers principle of fascist parties with strict hierarchical structures and a giant power apparatus. Even the liberal and conservative parties became membership parties with generally more formalised extra-parliamentary organisational structures. The intra-party dominance structures varied from party to party, however.

With the take-over by Adolf Hitler the NSDAP became official state party (*Staatspartei*) and the other party organisations dissolved or were smashed. The historical party traditions could not totally be erased during the Third Reich, however. Therefore, the development of the German parties immediately after the war was characterised not only by innovations but also by continuities.[13] The SPD and the KPD more or less leaned on their pre-war organisational traditions. In the Western zones of occupation the KPD became more and more isolated and marginalised because of the East–West conflict, however. The

Liberals for the first time in their history overcame their fragmentation by founding the Free Democratic Party (FDP). The most important new development, however, was the foundation of the Christian Democratic Union (CDU) – in Bavaria the Christian Social Union (CSU)[14] – which did not resume the pre-war tradition of the purely Catholic Center Party but offered a home for a broad range of people with Christian, liberal or conservative value orientations. In addition to these main parties there emerged a series of small right-wing, regional and expellee parties. In the Soviet zone of occupation the SPD and the KPD were united in the SED, a party clearly dominated by its central office which became the state party of the German Democratic Republic since 1949 and pushed through its absolute claim to leadership against the other parties.

In the Federal Republic of Germany the parties' structural development was and still is shaped by a variety of factors influencing the dominance structure between the four subsystems of party in different and even contradictory ways. First of all, a considerable part of the legal framework of party competition promotes the multicentric type of party, because these factors prevent the concentration of formal decision-making power within one of the subsystems. Among these factors are:

- German federalism which necessitates the development of full-fledged party organisations not only at the federal but also at the Land level, thereby diversifying the power structure.
- Article 21 of the Basic Law and the party law which prescribe that the internal organisation of the parties has to be democratic, thereby giving the party's basis the formal right to decide details of the statute and programme, as well as to elect the members of the party's central office and to select the candidates for public office.
- Article 38 of the Basic Law which guarantees the freedom of conscience of the members of parliament, so that the party in public office is formally independent from the party's central office.

A second group of factors promotes the type of party which is dominated by the leadership or even only by the party in public office because these factors reduce the functional relevance of the party's basis or even the party's central office and/or strengthen the party in public office. The relevance of the party's basis concerning the performance of policy mediation is reduced by the mass media, above all television, which has become more and more the main communication instrument in the process of policy mediation. Its relevance concerning the articulation of interests is diminished by the extensive use of public-opinion polls. Also its intra-party function to provide the necessary financial resources for the performance of the party's system functions in the form of membership fees has been reduced by the generous German system of public party finance. Even its relevance concerning the selection of candidates for public office has recently been questioned,[15] as has its general ability to perform any function given the considerable drop in membership figures.[16] Most of these factors also threaten the functional relevance of the party's central office, because the use of the functionally equivalent instruments can in principle be organised by the party in public office alone. In addition, the position of this subsystem is strengthened due to its better equipment with resources.

Concerning their intra-party organisational reality, the present SPD and CDU[17] are characterised as 'loosely coupled anarchies' (Wiesendahl), 'organised anarchies' (Schmid) or 'stratarchies' (Alemann).[18] There is no clearly hierarchical intra-party organisational structure with the party's central office at the top co-ordinating, harmonising, synchronising and combining the activities of the various subsystems or organisational entities. The organisational goals are controversial, the members lack clear behavioural rules, competences are not clearly determined, there is no continuous flow of communication and the various organisational entities have a considerable amount of autonomy. This purely structural characterisation does not mean, however, that they can be seen as multicentric parties according to our structural–functional typology. Both parties have a clear dominance structure concerning the performance of their system functions. The factors mentioned above have led to a general decline of the functional relevance of the parties' bases. With regard to the performance of their functions the parties are dominated by their leaderships, especially their party in public office. Their organisational structure promotes this dominance because the loose coupling, that is the flexible links between the subsystems, give the party leadership the necessary autonomy to dominate the performance of the party's system functions.

The small traditional FDP can even more be characterised in this way because in addition it lacks the mass membership of the two big parties which further reduces the relevance of the party's basis. In the 1980s and 1990s there emerged two new parties, however, which did not fit the predominant party type. In the 1980s the new cleavage between the economy and the ecology found its organisational expression in the establishing of the Greens as a relevant party at the federal level.

Based on its roots in the new social movements the performance of this party's functions in the beginning was clearly dominated by the party's basis.[19] Several organisational principles (mandate rotation, separation of public and party offices, claim for an imperative mandate) expressed this grass-roots orientation. In the course of time, however, the general factors mentioned above and the parliamentary representation of the Greens at the Land level led to an increasing adaptation to the predominant party type[20] and it seems that their new role as government party after the 1998 federal election accelerates this process considerably. The other new party, emerging at the federal level in the 1990s as a result of German unification, was the Party of Democratic Socialism (PDS). Its precursor, the SED, was structured according to the principles of a marxist–leninist party and therefore clearly dominated by its central office. As early as in December 1989 and thereafter twice in 1990 and 1993, however, the PDS changed its statutes considerably, especially accentuating the role of the party's basis,[21] and the organisational reality of the PDS more and more adapted to that of the other parties.

The general trend of a declining functional relevance of the parties' bases has led to a broad discussion concerning party reforms, where the pleading for a renewed membership party[22] stands against the proposal to advance into the direction of a mandate party,[23] thereby closing the historical circle to the party type dominating at the beginning of party development in Germany.

## The debate on the performance of party functions

While the structural analysis of the German parties was based on the question of *where* the parties' functions are performed, the following functional analysis deals with the question of *how* they are performed. The German discussion about this topic is loaded with normative considerations and historically burdened with the traditional German 'anti-party affect',[24] e.g. a fundamental aversion to political parties as part of the traditional political culture with conservative, left-wing and liberal varieties.[25] The scientific debate of the 1960s was dominated by the 'one-party-state' hypothesis.[26] In the 1970s the 'legitimation crisis'[27] of the parties was discussed. An attempt to systematise the empirical facts, however, came to the conclusion that one could not speak of a crisis of the German party democracy.[28] In the 1980s the increasing problems of the big parties concerning their memberships and the mobilisation and integration of their party-in-the-electorate[29] led to a new wave of publications dealing with the party crisis.[30] In the 1990s the scientific debate was superimposed by a broad public debate about 'party weariness'. In 1992 and 1993 not only were the mass media full of critical articles but the parties were also criticised by the then Federal President Richard von Weizsäcker[31] and a series of publications which were broadly noticed.[32] The debate regarding party weariness can be summarised in two contradictory positions:[33] the first position sees the parties as functionally all-embracing octopuses which have subjected the whole political system and the society to them. The second one sees them as helpless giants which have not noticed how functionally needless they have become. In view of the empirical facts, none of these extreme positions seems to be justified, however.

## Analysing party system change

A party system consists of political parties and the relationships between them or their attributes. These relationships can be considered as party system properties. To analyse structural party system change one therefore has to focus on the development of its various properties. However, it is controversial which system properties have to be included in such an analysis. A review of the literature[34] shows that party systems can be characterised by the number of parties involved (format), by the relative size of all parties (fragmentation) or of the two biggest parties (asymmetry) at a specific point in time or by the change of the proportions in two consecutive elections (volatility). In addition, one can look at the ideological distances between the parties or the relevance of anti-system parties (polarisation), the citizens' support for the totality of the parties (legitimacy) and at the inter-party relationships based on their governmental role, thereby distinguishing two system properties: the first dealing with the possibilities and difficulties of the formation of governments (segmentation), the second with their duration (government stability). In the German case the three most important properties are fragmentation, polarisation and segmentation of the party system.

To measure the fragmentation of party systems a number of indicators have been proposed, taking into account the number and relative size of the parties involved, whereby the size of a party is measured by the strength of the party-in-the-electorate. Only two of these indicators, however, have found a wider dissemination: Rae's 'fractionalisation of vote shares'[35] and its linear transformation called the 'effective number of parties',[36] which will be used here.[37] The measurement of the second property important for the German party system, the polarisation, is also controversial. As a quantitative indicator we will use Sartori's first distinctive feature of a polarised pluralistic party system: the relevance of anti-system parties, measured by their share of the vote.[38] In addition we will deal with the ideological distances between the other parties. In political systems characterised by the necessity to build coalition governments, as is the case in Germany, a third-party system property is highly important, namely segmentation, i.e. the degree to which the parties insulate themselves against each other concerning the building of coalitions.

The individual party system properties vary more or less over time. To characterise the amount and direction of these variations concerning the party system as a whole, one can differentiate between four distinctive levels of party system change:[39] temporary fluctuations (the normal ebbs and flows of party fortunes), restricted change (change of only one or a few properties), general change (several changes taking place at the same time) and transformation (altering of all properties, so that a completely new system comes into existence).

Party system change is determined by the same groups of factors which we have distinguished concerning the structural development of single parties. Among the factors defining the institutional framework, the most important ones are the respective electoral laws as well as the rules concerning the ban on parties and their financing. With respect to the factors influencing the demand side of party competition one has to consider the cleavage structure, already dealt with in the previous paragraph, and the issue structure of society. The issue structure consists of the current range of relevant political issues and the assignment of problem-solving competences to the parties by the citizens. The prevailing issue structure can actualise the underlying cleavage structure but also overlay it, and newly emerging social issues can lead to a change in the cleavage structure. The parties' leadership and basis are not only subject to developments in their institutional and social environment, however, but they actively influence this environment and thereby also change the party system properties. One therefore also has to take into account the factors shaping the supply side of party competition. Here, the most important factors are the organisational, personal and financial resources which the parties use, as well as their political behaviour, i.e. their programmes and problem-solving offers, their public presentation and their strategies towards their competitors.

Based on these theoretical considerations the next section will analyse the development of the German party system from its emergence in the 1860s up to the 1998 federal election.

## The development of the German party system

During Imperial Germany the German party system was marked by a rather high degree of fragmentation (see Figure 9.1), although ideologically the variety of parties could be grouped into the four main pillars already mentioned (Liberals, Conservatives, Catholics and Socialists). Some authors have suggested distinguishing three political 'camps', the Catholic, the Socialist and the national camp, with relatively high mobility of the voters within, but very low mobility between, the camps.[40] The parties of the national camp supported the authoritarian state, the Catholic Centre Party had certain reservations, but the only relevant anti-system party was the SPD. The SPD's share of the vote, which increases considerably in the course of time, therefore reflects the polarisation of the German party system during Imperial Germany (see Figure 9.2). Because of the structuring in the form of socio-cultural milieus, the society of Imperial Germany was highly segmented. To analyse the segmentation as a property of the party system, however, makes no sense, as parliament had no constitutional rights to build and control the government so that formal coalition building was not necessary.

Apart from the exceptional election of the 'national assembly' (*Nationalversammlung*) in 1919, the party system of the Weimar Republic was even more fragmented than that of Imperial Germany. Only with the increasing success of the NSDAP did a considerable process of concentration take place (see Figure 9.1). The share of the vote of the NSDAP was also the main reason for the extremely high polarisation scores of the party system at the end of the Weimar Republic (see Figure 9.2). The NSDAP was not the only anti-system party, however. There existed relevant parties at both extreme poles of the left–right spectrum. On the right the conservative DNVP at first half-heartedly supported the new parliamentary democracy, but soon openly stood up for the restoration of the monarchy. On the left not only the Communists, but also the short-lived left-socialist USPD, opposed the system. Although none of the other parties unreservedly and uniformly advocated a parliamentary democracy, the SPD supported the maintenance of the new form of government together with the Centre Party and the left-liberal DDP, whereas a

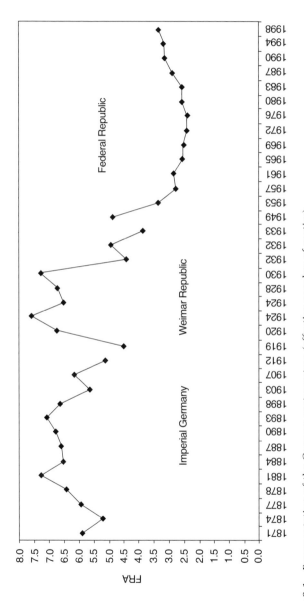

*Figure 9.1* Fragmentation of the German party system (effective number of parties)

*Source*: Own calculations based on official electoral statistics.

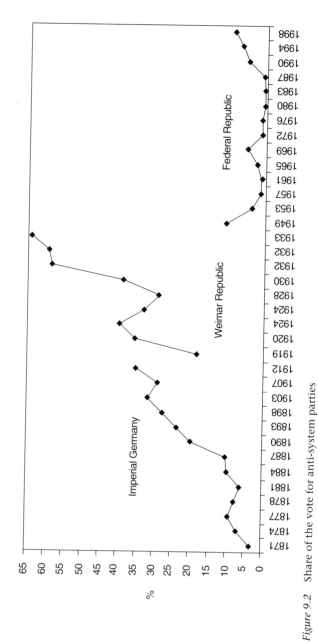

178

*Figure 9.2* Share of the vote for anti-system parties

*Source:* Own calculations based on official electoral statistics.

part of the national-liberal DVP sympathised with the former monar-chy. Until the rise of the NSDAP the party system of the Weimar Republic was moderately segmented. The KPD was the only relevant party excluded from coalition building; even the DNVP took part in two coalition governments between 1925 and 1928. The DNVP was the only party which since 1930 openly supported Adolf Hitler and even took part in a short-lived coalition with the NSDAP in 1933. Thereafter, the 'polarised pluralism' of the Weimar party system collapsed.

After the Second World War, the development of the party system of the Federal Republic from its beginning to date can be divided into three distinct developmental stages: the consolidation period of the 1950s, the period of the stable 'two-and-a-half' party system of the 1960s and 1970s and the period of pluralisation thereafter.[41]

Immediately after the war the newly formed party system was still relatively highly fragmented (see Figure 9.1). In the 1950s, however, a considerable process of concentration took place. This process was caused by a variety of factors belonging to the institutional framework, as well as to the demand and supply side of party competition. Firstly, the electoral law was altered: before 1953 a party gained parliamentary representation when it achieved more than 5 per cent of the vote in one of the *Länder*. Afterwards the parties had to exceed the 5 per cent barrier at the federal level. This barrier has a negative effect on the vote for small parties, because the voters have to fear that their votes are lost. On the supply side of the party competition, the polarising dynamic of the competition between the CDU/CSU and the SPD con-tributed to the concentration of votes on the two large parties. On the demand side, both the cleavage and the issue structure changed con-siderably. This change took place because: (1) the conflict line between the inhabitants of the Federal Republic and the expellees lost import-ance due to the positive economic development and compensatory payments, (2) regional conflicts eroded due to the great regional mobil-ity of the citizens forced by the war, and (3) Germany had a consider-able economic boom which was attributed to the governing parties, especially to the CDU/CSU. Parallel to the concentration process a con-siderable depolarisation process took place. On the one hand the party system lost its two relevant anti-system parties with the ban on the SRP (1952) and the KPD (1956) by the Federal Constitutional Court. On the other hand, the SPD became ideologically more moderate, which was manifested by the Godesberg Programme of 1959.

The consolidation process of the 1950s led to the relatively stable 'two-and-a-half' party system of the 1960s and 1970s, an example of 'moderate pluralism'[42] with the following core characteristics:

- A low fragmentation due to the existence of two big parties. The combined share of the vote held by the CDU/CSU and the SPD increased from more than 80 per cent at the beginning of the 1960s to more than 90 per cent in the mid-1970s. The relative size of the two parties fluctuated, however. The concentration process of the 1950s mainly benefited the CDU/CSU and led to a considerable asymmetry within the party system which was reduced in the 1960s as the SPD's programmatic change helped to increase its electoral support. Only once, in 1972, however, did the SPD succeed in becoming the strongest party in the Bundestag. Afterwards the CDU/CSU regained its leading position, and the SPD could once more outdo the CDU/CSU only in 1998.[43]
- A low polarisation due to moderate ideological distances between the democratic parties and low electoral support for anti-system parties. Most of the time the total vote share for anti-system parties[44] was below 1 per cent, and even during the peak of the second wave of organised right-wing extremism[45] at the end of the 1960s it was below 5 per cent.[46]
- No segmentation, as all the relevant parties in principle could build coalitions with one another. Until the mid-1960s there were only bourgeois coalitions led by the CDU/CSU, followed by a Grand Coalition of CDU/CSU and SPD between 1966 and 1969 and SPD–FDP coalitions in the 1970s.

In the 1980s the party system began to change. However, no party system transformation, for example a considerable change of all properties leading to a new type of system, took place. The change was relatively moderate although it affected all three party system properties in the form of a general pluralisation, that is an increase in the diversity of the system concerning the number, relative size and ideological distance of the relevant parties.

The erosion of the system stability especially affected the big parties which had increasing problems of mobilisation: since 1976 the total vote share for the CDU/CSU and the SPD decreased continuously. This development was not only due to the political behaviour of the parties but also due to long-term processes of social, economic and cultural change. The changing employment structure and processes of value change, secularisation and individualisation affected the demand side of party competition by reducing the importance of the traditional cleavages for the citizens' voting behaviour, thereby reducing the part of the party-in-the-electorate with long-range party identification. While the old cleavages were weakened, a new one emerged: the cleavage between the economy and ecology, which found its expression in the party system in form of the Greens. The appearance of this party, which took part in federal elections in 1980 for the first time, increased the fragmentation of the party system. In addition, the third wave of organised right-wing extremism in the form of the Republicans (REP) since the mid-1980s not only further increased the fragmentation but also contributed to the polarisation of the party system. Last but not least, the segmentation of the party system was also affected by the developments of the 1980s. In the 1960s and 1970s all the parties represented in the Bundestag could in principle build coalitions with each other. The emergence of the Greens changed this situation. In the beginning all other parties hesitated, but in 1985 the 'red–green' coalition at the Land level in Hesse demonstrated the possibility of coalitions between the SPD and the Greens, whereas coalitions between the bourgeois parties and the Greens remained politically impossible.

German unification in 1990 took place in this period of increasing pluralisation of the West German party system. In the German Democratic Republic a pluralistic party system did not exist. The constitution definitely laid down the supremacy of the SED. Therefore, the four other parties besides the SED, the so-called 'block-parties' – CDU, LDP, NDPD and DBD – were neither autonomous organisations nor did they compete for power with the SED in elections. If one can speak of a party system at all, it was a non-competitive hegemonic one. Between the autumn of 1989 and the autumn of 1990, however, a transformation into a pluralistic party system took place in four phases which can be characterised as bipolarisation, differentiation, adaptation and unification.[47]

The first phase, until the end of November 1989, was characterised by the open outbreak of the GDR's latent system crisis and the formation of a visible opposition to the regime, the pioneers being small groups which had developed since the end of the 1970s under the umbrella of the Protestant church. The second phase from December 1989 to January 1990 was mainly characterised by a dramatic increase in fragmentation because of three differentiation processes: the internal differentiation of the opposition, the foundation of new small parties without direct roots in the early opposition days but with considerable support from West German parties, and the emancipation of the 'block parties' from the SED. The SED itself, which changed its name to PDS in February 1990, went through severe crises but survived the regime change. The West German party elites at first perceived no incentives to intervene massively. When the internal and external conditions concerning unification dramatically changed in early 1990 and the first free parliamentary elections were under consideration, however, their reservedness gave way to a more and more intensive intervention. This led to the adaptation phase of the former GDR's party system which was characterised by concentration processes especially in the form of electoral alliances. The fourth phase of the former GDR's party system development began in May/June 1990 when the preparations for the unification of the GDR parties with their Western sister parties were intensified, and ended in early October of this year. Only the green and citizens movement did not unify until early 1993.

The inclusion of the GDR's party system reinforced the pluralisation process at the all-German level,[48] because the East German party system was considerably more fragmented and there existed a relevant anti-system party in the form of the PDS. Unification therefore produced fears of a return of 'Weimar conditions', that is a system transformation from moderate to polarised pluralism with all its politically disintegrative and ideologically radicalising effects.[49] Bonn (or Berlin) is not Weimar, however. Although the fragmentation has continuously increased after unification, the German party system is still characterised by a rather low degree of fragmentation, especially compared to the situation in the Weimar Republic before the rise of the NSDAP. Practically the same holds true for the degree of polarisation in the present German party system. Above all, due to the electoral success of the PDS in East Germany, where it is one of the three big parties, the total vote share for anti-system parties has considerably increased since 1987. Compared to the Weimar Republic, however, the polarisation of the present German party system is still very low. The third property of the party system, its segmentation, has also changed moderately, too. The success of the SPD in the 1998 federal election led to a 'red–green' coalition and even parts of the CDU leadership no longer rule out future coalitions with the Greens, so that this party is more and more accepted as a possible coalition partner. This is not the case, however, for the PDS, although at the East German Land level a SPD–PDS coalition already exists (in Mecklenburg–West Pomerania). But the non-acceptance of the PDS as a coalition partner at the federal level has increased the segmentation of the party system only to a very modest extent, because at this level the PDS is a small party not needed for coalition building.

All in all one can state that the merging of the West and East German party system has intensified the pluralisation process which had already started in West Germany before unification. This pluralisation, however, is a restricted party system change and up to 1998 has not altered the core characteristics of the West German party system. The return to 'Weimar' conditions, feared by some observers initially, has not taken place.

## Conclusion

At first sight there was not much institutional change in the German party sphere during recent decades. At the individual party level it is true that – with the Greens and the SED/PDS – two new parties emerged with a dominance structure between the subsystems concerning the performance of the party's system functions deviant from that of the 'established' parties. But in the course of time both parties adapted to the predominant type of party. Concerning the party system, neither the developments of the 1980s nor the unification process changed its core characteristics. If one takes a closer look, however, one discovers changes at both levels. At the individual party level there is a general decline of the functional relevance of the parties' bases. This may lead to a new type of party which resembles the party type predominant during the early stages of German party development. At the party system level a pluralisation process has taken place which up to now has not changed the party system type from moderate to polarised pluralism but which has not yet come to an end.

## Notes

1 Robert Michels, *Zur Soziologie des Parteiwesens in der modernen Demokratie*, reprint of the 2nd edn (Leipzig, 1911) ed. by W. Conze (Stuttgart: Kroener, 1957), pp. 370–1.
2 Frank J. Sorauf, 'Political Parties and Political Analysis', in William N. Chambers and Walter D. Burnham (eds), *The American Party Systems*, 2nd edn (New York: Oxford University Press, 1975), pp. 37–8.
3 Richard S. Katz and Peter Mair, 'The Evolution of Party Organizations in Europe: the Three Faces of Party Organization', in William Crotty (ed.), *Political Parties in a Changing Age*, Special Issue of *The American Review of Politics*, 14 (Conway, Ark.: University of Central Arkansas Press, 1993), pp. 594–601.

4 *Ibid.*, p. 597.
5 F. Sorauf (note 2), p. 38.
6 See Oskar Niedermayer, 'Das intermediäre System', in Max Kaase, Andreas Eisen, Oscar W. Gabriel, Oskar Niedermayer and Hellmut Wollmann (eds), *Politisches System: Berichte zum sozialen und politischen Wandel in Ostdeutschland*, vol. 3 (Opladen: Leske & Budrich, 1996), pp. 155–8.
7 E. E. Schattschneider, *Party Government* (New York: Holt, Rinehart & Winston, 1942), p. 35.
8 For a short history of the German parties see Robert Hofmann, *Geschichte der deutschen Parteien* (Munich: Piper, 1993), and Peter Lösche, *Kleine Geschichte der deutschen Parteien* (Stuttgart: Kohlhammer, 1993).
9 Seymour Martin Lipset and Stein Rokkan, 'Cleavage Structures, Party Systems, and Voter Alignments: an Introduction', in Seymour Martin Lipset and Stein Rokkan (eds), *Party Systems and Voter Alignments: Cross-National Perspectives* (New York: Free Press, 1967), p. 14.
10 On the socio-cultural milieus of Imperial Germany and the Weimar Republic see M. Rainer Lepsius, 'Parteiensystem und Sozialstruktur: zum Problem der Demokratisierung der deutschen Gesellschaft', in Wilhelm Abel and Knut Borchardt (eds), *Wirtschaft, Geschichte und Wirtschaftsgeschichte* (Stuttgart: Fischer, 1966), pp. 371–93.
11 R. Michels (note 1), pp. 370–1.
12 See Peter Lösche and Franz Walter, *Die SPD: Klassenpartei–Volkspartei–Quotenpartei* (Darmstadt: Wissenschaftliche Buchgesellschaft, 1992), pp. 174–8.
13 The research literature regarding the individual parties until the end of the 1980s is summarised in Oskar Niedermayer and Richard Stöss (eds), *Stand und Perspektiven der Parteienforschung in Deutschland* (Opladen: Westdeutscher Verlag, 1993). See also Alf Mintzel and Heinrich Oberreuter (eds), *Parteien in der Bundesrepublik Deutschland*, 2nd edn (Bonn: Bundeszentrale für politische Bildung, 1992).
14 In party system analyses the sister parties CDU and CSU are treated as one party, because they do not territorially compete with each other (the CSU is organised and stands for election only in Bavaria, the CDU in the rest of the federal territory) and have always been aligned in the national parliament. At the party level of analysis, however, they have to be treated as separate parties.
15 The real decision about the SPD's chancellor candidate in the 1998 federal election, Gerhard Schröder, was made by the voters in the preceding Land election in Lower Saxony where Schröder stood for re-election as minister-president.
16 Compared to the respective maximum, the CDU, SPD and the Greens until 1989 lost one-tenth, the FDP one-fourth of their members. After unification the downwards trend continued in the West of Germany. In Eastern Germany the CDU and FDP had to cope with a considerable decrease in their membership figures, the SPD stagnated on a low level and the Greens had less than 3,000 members at the end of 1995. See Oscar W. Gabriel and Oskar Niedermayer, 'Entwicklung und Sozialstruktur der Parteimitgliedschaften', in Oscar W. Gabriel, Oskar Niedermayer and Richard Stöss (eds), *Parteiendemokratie in Deutschland* (Bonn/Opladen:

Bundeszentrale für politische Bildung/Westdeutscher Verlag, 1997), pp. 280–1. One of the main reasons for the increasing difficulties in recruiting new members, especially young ones, is the fact that the widening of the citizens' repertory of political action during the 'participatory revolution' of the 1960s has exposed the parties to an increasing competition with other forms of political participation. See Max Kaase, 'The Challenge of the "Participatory Revolution" in Pluralist Democracies', *International Political Science Review*, 5 (1984), p. 299.

17  Until the end of the 1950s, the SPD was clearly dominated by the party's central office. See P. Lösche and F. Walter (note 12), pp. 181–4. The CDU for a long time was a bipolar party whose central office was considerably strengthened only in the 1970s. See Wulf Schönbohm, *Die CDU wird moderne Volkspartei* (Stuttgart: Klett-Cotta, 1985), p. 300.

18  Elmar Wiesendahl, 'Wie politisch sind politische Parteien? Zu einigen vernachlässigten Aspekten der Organisationswirklichkeit politischer Parteien', in Jürgen W. Falter, Christian Fenner and Michael Greven (eds), *Politische Willensbildung und Interessenvermittlung* (Opladen: Westdeutscher Verlag, 1984), pp. 81–3; Josef Schmid, *Die CDU* (Opladen: Leske & Budrich, 1990), pp. 276–84; Ulrich von Alemann, 'Party Research goes Politics. Ein Plädoyer gegen die Kapitulation der Parteienforscher vor der Mediengesellschaft', *Politische Vierteljahresschrift*, 38 (1997), p. 800.

19  See Thomas Poguntke, 'Der Stand der Forschung zu den Grünen: Zwischen Ideologie und Empirie', in O. Niedermayer and R. Stöss (note 13), pp. 199–202.

20  See Thomas Poguntke, 'Parteiorganisationen in der Bundesrepublik Deutschland: Einheit in der Vielfalt?', in O. W. Gabriel, O. Niedermayer and R. Stöss (note 16), pp. 275–6.

21  Gero Neugebauer and Richard Stöss, *Die PDS. Geschichte. Organisation. Wähler. Konkurrenten* (Opladen: Leske & Budrich), pp. 126–35.

22  See Peter Haungs, 'Plädoyer für eine erneuerte Mitgliederpartei. Anmerkungen zur aktuellen Diskussion über die Zukunft der Volksparteien', *Zeitschrift für Parlamentsfragen*, 25 (1994), pp. 108–15.

23  See Peter Radunski, 'Fit für die Zukunft?', *Sonde*, 24 (1991), pp. 3–8.

24  See Karl Friedrich Kindler, 'Der Antiparteienaffekt in Deutschland', *Gesellschaft – Staat – Erziehung*, (1958), p. 107.

25  See Hermann Scheer, *Partei kontra Bürger? Die Zukunft der Parteiendemokratie* (Munich: Piper, 1979), pp. 163–81.

26  See Ekkehart Krippendorff, 'Das Ende des Parteienstaates', *Der Monat*, 14, (1962), pp. 64–70.

27  Jürgen Dittberner and Rolf Ebbighausen, *Das Parteiensystem in der Legitimationskrise* (Opladen: Westdeutscher Verlag, 1973).

28  Alf Mintzel and Hermann Schmitt, 'Krise der Parteiendemokratie? Zu Funktionen, Leistungen und Defiziten der Parteien in der parlamentarischen Demokratie', *Politische Bildung*, 2 (1981), p. 15.

29  See Elmar Wiesendahl, 'Parteien in der Krise: Mobilisierungsdefizite, Integrations- und Organisationsschwächen der Parteien in Deutschland', *Sozialwissenschaftliche Informationen*, 22 (1993), p. 77.

30  See the contributions in Peter Haungs and Eckhard Jesse (eds), *Parteien in der Krise? In- und ausländische Perspektiven* (Köln: Verlag Wissenschaft und

Politik, 1987); Christian Graf von Krockow and Peter Lösche (eds), *Parteien in der Krise* (Munich: Beck, 1986).

31  Interview with Gunter Hofmann and Werner A. Perger, *Richard von Weizsäcker im Gespräch* (Frankfurt a.M.: Eichborn, 1992).

32  See, e.g., Hans-Herbert von Arnim, *Der Staat als Beute* (Munich: Knaur, 1993); Erwin K. Scheuch and Ute Scheuch, *Cliquen, Klüngel und Karrieren* (Reinbek b. Hamburg: Rowohlt, 1992).

33  Ulrich von Alemann and W. Tönnesmann, 'Die Dinosaurier werden immer trauriger. Ein kleiner Essay über große Parteien', *Perspektiven DS*, 1 (1992), pp. 15–16.

34  See Oskar Niedermayer, 'Zur systematischen Analyse der Entwicklung von Parteiensystemen', in Oskar W. Gabriel and Jürgen Falter (eds), *Wahlen und politische Einstellungen in westlichen Demokratien* (Frankfurt a.M.: Lang, 1996), pp. 20–31.

35  Douglas Rae, *The Political Consequences of Electoral Laws* (New Haven: Yale University Press, 1967), pp. 53–8.

36  Markku Laakso and Rein Taagepera, 'Effective Number of Parties: a Measure with Application to West Europe', *Comparative Political Studies*, 12 (1979), p. 4.

37  The effective number of parties is defined as 'the number of hypothetical equal-size parties that would have the same total effect on fractionalisation of the system as have the actual parties of unequal size'. See M. Laakso and R. Taagepera (note 36), p. 4. Therefore, the 'effective' and the real number of parties are identical when all parties have the same percentage of votes. The more unequal the distribution of the vote, the smaller is the effective compared to the real number, and in party systems clearly dominated by one party the index approaches the value 1.

38  See Giovanni Sartori, *Parties and Party Systems: A Framework for Analysis* (Cambridge: Cambridge University Press, 1976), p. 132.

39  See Gordon Smith, 'A System Perspective on Party System Change', *Journal of Theoretical Politics*, 1 (1989), p. 353.

40  See Karl Rohe, *Wahlen und Wählertraditionen in Deutschland* (Frankfurt a.M.: Suhrkamp, 1992), pp. 92–7.

41  The research literature concerning the development of the party system of the Federal Republic is summarised in Eva Kolinsky, 'Das Parteiensystem der Bundesrepublik: Forschungsthemen und Entwicklungslinien', in O. Niedermayer and R. Stöss (note 13), pp. 35–56; see also Eckhard Jesse, 'Die Parteien im westlichen Deutschland 1945 bis zur deutschen Einheit 1990', in O. W. Gabriel, O. Niedermayer and R. Stöss (note 16), pp. 59–83; Oskar Niedermayer, 'Der neue Faktor PDS. Die Zukunft des Parteiensystems', in Deutsches Institut für Fernstudienforschung (ed.), *Funkkolleg 'Deutschland im Umbruch'*, Studienbrief 3 (Tübingen: DIFF, 1997), pp. 10/7–10/14.

42  G. Sartori (note 38), pp. 173–85.

43  The 1998 federal election was the first election in the history of the Federal Republic of Germany in which the citizens voted the acting chancellor out of office. The SPD considerably increased its share of the vote and gained 40.9 per cent, the CDU/CSU clearly lost the election with 35.1 per cent (1994: 39.5 per cent), the FDP obtained 6.2 per cent, the Greens 6.7 per cent, the PDS for the first time overcame the 5 per cent barrier with 5.1 per

cent and the extreme right-wing parties (REP, DVU, NPD) together obtained 3.3 per cent.

44  To operationalise the group of anti-system parties we use the categories 'anti-democratic parties' and 'anti-capitalist parties' suggested by Richard Stöss, 'Einleitung: Struktur und Entwicklung des Parteiensystems der Bundesrepublik – Eine Theorie', in Richard Stöss (ed.), *Parteien-Handbuch*, vol. 1, *Sonderausgabe* (Opladen: Westdeutscher Verlag, 1986), pp. 239–65. Green-alternative parties are not treated as anti-system parties.

45  See Richard Stöss, *Die extreme Rechte in der Bundesrepublik* (Opladen: Westdeutscher Verlag, 1989), pp. 132–76.

46  The first wave of organised right-wing extremism was in the beginning of the 1950s, the second was due to the rise of the NPD, which failed to overcome the 5 per cent barrier in the federal election of 1969, however, and thereafter became a marginal party again.

47  See Oskar Niedermayer, 'Party System Change in East Germany', *German Politics*, 4 (1995), pp. 80–2.

48  On the development of the German party system after unification see Ulrich von Alemann, 'Die Parteien in den Wechsel-Jahren? Zum Wandel des deutschen Parteiensystems', *Aus Politik und Zeitgeschichte*, B 6/1996, pp. 3–8; Karlheinz Niclauss, *Das Parteiensystem der Bundesrepublik Deutschland* (Paderborn: Schöningh, 1995), and Oskar Niedermayer, 'Das gesamtdeutsche Parteiensystem', in O. W. Gabriel, O. Niedermayer and R. Stöss (note 16), pp. 106–30.

49  See Hans-Joachim Veen, 'Zwischen Rekonzentration und neuer Diversifizierung. Tendenzen der Parteienentwicklung fünf Jahre nach der deutschen Einheit', in Winand Gellner and Hans-Joachim Veen (eds), *Umbruch und Wandel in westeuropäischen Parteiensystemen* (Frankfurt a.M.: Lang, 1995), p. 117.

# 10
## Interest Groups: Continuity and Change of German Lobbyism since 1974

*Martin Sebaldt*

## Introduction

Lobbyism does not enjoy a good reputation in Germany. Since Theodor Eschenburg's critical essay 'Herrschaft der Verbände?',[1] published for the first time in 1955, the already-existing reservations concerning interest groups and their political work have never ceased, but were renewed by younger generations of politicians and social scientists. However, most of this negative judgements are based on merely impressionistic and exemplary insights into the matter, lacking a sound empirical analysis.

This chapter attempts to avoid some of these mistakes, focusing on the following aspects:

- How can the German system of interest groups as a whole be characterised, what segments does it consist of, and what internal structures can be found in there?
- How is lobbyism organised in practice, what is the nature of the system of interest mediation, and what rules of conduct are to be regarded there?
- What continuities and changes can be identified in the field of German lobbyism since the early 1970s?

## The German system of interest groups: continuity and change

The German system of interest groups has expanded considerably during recent decades. Although this judgement is accepted by most political scientists, hard data are lacking. In the 1970s Thomas Ellwein coined a rough formula, which estimated about three or four existing interest groups per 1,000 Germans.[2] Taking the 81,759,407 inhabitants of Germany counted in September 1995, today's German system of interest groups should consist of about 327,000 groups.

Concerning the politically active interest groups, which constitute the core of the German system of interest representation, data are also unsatisfactory. Jürgen Weber estimated that there were about 5,000 of them at the federal level and 20,000 including the regional sub-organisations – but his estimate also dates back to the early 1980s.[3] The only reliable information regarding the officially registered interest groups exists at the federal parliament, the German Bundestag: in 1972 the representatives decided against the background of US experience to make official registration compulsory for groups wishing to attend parliamentary hearings and deliver statements there. Since 1974 these 'lobbylists',[4] comprising the 'tip of the iceberg' of German interest groups, are published annually. At least this sector of interest groups can be quantified exactly (see Table 10.1):

The already-stated fact that the system of interest groups has expanded is backed by the numbers given in Table 10.1. In 1974 when the first lobbylist was published, only 635 interest groups were registered with the German Bundestag. A quarter-century later the number has more than doubled. No less than 1,673 groups constitute the list in

Table 10.1   Officially registered German interest groups, 1974–98

| Year | Number | Index of development |
| --- | --- | --- |
| 1974 | 635 | 100.0 |
| 1976 | 769 | 121.1 |
| 1978 | 889 | 140.0 |
| 1980 | 996 | 156.9 |
| 1982 | 1104 | 173.9 |
| 1984 | 1192 | 187.7 |
| 1986 | 1287 | 202.7 |
| 1988 | 1376 | 216.7 |
| 1990 | 1501 | 236.4 |
| 1992 | 1481 | 233.2 |
| 1994 | 1572 | 247.6 |
| 1996 | 1614 | 254.2 |
| 1998 | 1673 | 263.5 |

*Source*:  Lobbylists of the German Bundestag.

1998 and give a first impression of how lobbyism in Bonn has developed and expanded.

### Interest groups and society

These data permit only a first overview of the spectrum of interest groups: it is still unknown what kind of social development is responsible for this expansion. Generally, one can assume that the transformation of the map of German interest groups resembles that of German society as a whole. In the view of pluralist theory, interest groups come into being as a result of newly emerging social needs and can therefore be seen as a valuable indicator of societal change.[5] Looking at the German lobbyists this fact is confirmed.

First of all, these data mirror the economic transformation of German society. As documented in Table 10.2, the evolution of a post-industrial society with a dominating third sector[6] has affected the system of German interest groups considerably. Since 1974 the already-dominating tertiary sector has expanded further, reducing the shares of the primary and the secondary. Whereas in 1974 groups representing service branches accounted only for 61.7 per cent of the whole, 20 years later their share was 71.3 per cent. At the same time interest groups of the primary and the secondary sector dropped from 5.7 per cent to 4.3 per cent and from 28.7 per cent to 20.3 per cent, respectively. Only the numbers of large inter-sectoral umbrella organisations remained nearly on the same level.

So without any doubt a considerable economic change took place in German society, but the amount of *social* transformation is even more impressing. In 1986 Ulrich Beck published his widely recognised book about 'risk society'.[7] The core argument is that the structure of modern societies is severely affected by existing external risks (pollution, threat of atomic war, Third World crisis) and internal threats (lacking societal cohesion, social poverty, deprived social groups), which are produced by societies themselves. For that reason one can estimate that groups dedicated to the neutralisation of these risks should have grown exponentially in numbers during recent decades. Looking at the 'lobbylists', this hypothesis is also confirmed: Table 10.3 shows that the sectors of groups involved in fighting against the dangers of these external and internal risks are growing much faster than the overall number of interest groups.

Interest groups dedicated to environmental problems, neutralisation of war risks and elimination of global economic and political inequalities nearly quadrupled their number from 23 to 89. At the same time,

Table 10.2   German interest groups according to economic sectors (1974–94)

| Year | Represented economic sector | | | | | | | | | |
|---|---|---|---|---|---|---|---|---|---|---|
| | All sectors | | Primary | | Secondary | | Tertiary | | Total | |
| | No. | Percentage | No. | Percentage | No. | Percentage | No. | Percentage | No. | Percentage |
| 1974 | 25 | 3.9 | 36 | 5.7 | 182 | 28.7 | 392 | 61.7 | 635 | 100.0 |
| 1976 | 28 | 3.6 | 37 | 4.8 | 211 | 27.4 | 493 | 64.1 | 769 | 99.9 |
| 1978 | 37 | 4.2 | 42 | 4.7 | 234 | 26.3 | 576 | 64.8 | 889 | 100.0 |
| 1980 | 38 | 3.8 | 44 | 4.4 | 253 | 25.4 | 661 | 66.4 | 996 | 100.0 |
| 1982 | 41 | 3.7 | 44 | 4.0 | 269 | 24.4 | 750 | 67.9 | 1104 | 100.0 |
| 1984 | 43 | 3.6 | 53 | 4.4 | 282 | 23.7 | 814 | 68.3 | 1192 | 100.0 |
| 1986 | 48 | 3.7 | 54 | 4.2 | 291 | 22.6 | 894 | 69.5 | 1287 | 100.0 |
| 1988 | 51 | 3.7 | 60 | 4.4 | 297 | 21.6 | 968 | 70.3 | 1376 | 100.0 |
| 1990 | 58 | 3.9 | 71 | 4.7 | 317 | 21.1 | 1055 | 70.3 | 1501 | 100.0 |
| 1992 | 54 | 3.6 | 67 | 4.5 | 311 | 21.0 | 1049 | 70.8 | 1481 | 99.9 |
| 1994 | 64 | 4.1 | 68 | 4.3 | 319 | 20.3 | 1121 | 71.3 | 1572 | 100.0 |

*Source*: M. Sebaldt (note 5), pp. 85.

Table 10.3    German interest groups devoted to the neutralisation of external and internal societal risks (1974–94)

| Year | Types of societal risks | | | | | |
|------|---|---|---|---|---|---|
| | Interest groups devoted to external risks | | Interest groups devoted to internal risks | | All associations | |
| | No. | Index | No. | Index | No. | Index |
| 1974 | 23 | 100.0 | 46 | 100.0 | 635 | 100.0 |
| 1976 | 25 | 108.7 | 55 | 120.0 | 769 | 121.1 |
| 1978 | 33 | 143.5 | 70 | 152.2 | 889 | 140.0 |
| 1980 | 39 | 169.6 | 86 | 187.0 | 996 | 156.9 |
| 1982 | 42 | 182.6 | 98 | 213.0 | 1104 | 173.9 |
| 1984 | 51 | 221.7 | 112 | 243.5 | 1192 | 187.7 |
| 1986 | 65 | 282.6 | 126 | 273.9 | 1287 | 202.7 |
| 1988 | 72 | 313.0 | 140 | 304.3 | 1376 | 216.7 |
| 1990 | 83 | 360.9 | 155 | 337.0 | 1501 | 236.4 |
| 1992 | 82 | 356.5 | 155 | 337.0 | 1481 | 233.2 |
| 1994 | 89 | 387.0 | 159 | 345.7 | 1572 | 247.6 |

*Source*: M. Sebaldt (note 5), pp. 126–7.

groups devoted to internal risks more than tripled and underwent a very similar development: groups dealing with the problems of the disabled, broken families, poverty, physical and psychic diseases, etc. – often small in size and organised by those affected themselves – constitute without any doubt a new sector of the interest group system widely unknown 30 years ago.[8]

On the whole, 'risk society' implies a generally increased ability of social interests to organise in effective interest groups. Groups considered by Mancur Olson 30 years ago as being largely unable to be organised (consumers, patients etc.),[9] are very well organised nowadays, and the present system of interest groups mirrors this fact precisely. The general modernisation of German political culture seems to be the main reason for this fact: whereas Almond and Verba in the 1960s still described Germany's political culture as mainly 'subject'[10] with citizens passively waiting for the help of the state, the scene has changed dramatically since then: in Almond's and Verba's terms Germany can nowadays be characterised as a modern 'participant' society with individuals fighting for their rights instead of taking a benevolent state for granted.[11] The complex system of recently emerged citizens' initiatives and action groups, which constitute a totally new sector of interest groups, is the manifest consequence of this development.

### Hierarchy and anarchy in the system of German interest groups

Are there any structures in this very complex system of interest groups or must it be considered as an (un)organised anarchy which makes interest representation in Bonn an uncontrolled lobbyism without any rules and co-ordination between groups? Both are the case, and for that reason only some general conclusions can be drawn.

On the one hand, it is good tradition to organise German interest groups into a hierarchical system with umbrella organisations representing several small member associations, as Figure 10.1 shows. Interest groups in the economic sector in particular are organised that way: the *Bundesverband der Deutschen Industrie* (BDI), for example, is the overall umbrella organisation for all branches of German industry, being responsible for articulating and aggregating interests concerning all industrial employers.[12] But members are not individual persons or companies but *sectoral* umbrella organisations being responsible for a specific branch and performing the same task on a lower level. The *Bundesverband Steine und Erden*, for instance, represents membership associations of the mining sector and the raw material industry (e.g. *Deutscher Asphaltverband*). Apart from this vertical organisation there are regional sub-organisations on every level which make the whole system very complex.[13] At the top of the whole there are advisory co-ordinating councils such as the *Gemeinschaftsausschuß der Deutschen Gewerblichen Wirtschaft*, but they lack any competence.

This impressionistic picture can be very misleading if read the wrong way: one could assume that the whole system of German employer groups is organised hierarchically and systematically like a military organisation with the commander-in-chief at the top. Reality is far from that: the umbrella organisations are powerful only if authorised by their member organisations which finance and control them by funding. In cases without consensus among members each association works separately, and the umbrella organisation is forced to remain silent.[14] The system of German labour unions follows a similar pattern: the *Deutscher Gewerkschaftsbund* (DGB), umbrella organisation of the branch labour unions such as *IG Metall*, is only a co-ordinating organisation.[15] The real power rests with its member organisations which are the responsible partners in wage negotiations.

Other types of German interest groups are even less organised. The sector of traditional welfare-organisations, including groups such as the

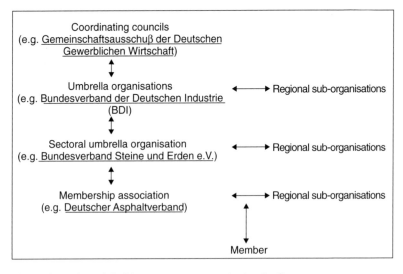

*Figure 10.1*　A model of interest group organisation in Germany

*Deutscher Paritätischer Wohlfahrtsverband* or the catholic *Caritas*, is co-ordinated by the *Bundesarbeitsgemeinschaft der Freien Wohlfahrtspflege e.V.*,[16] but this example constitutes an exception rather than the rule. Many other organisations, such as science, disabled, or leisure-time associations, are not co-ordinated by such umbrella organisations and therefore much less well organised than the interest groups of the economic sector.

### Interest groups and the state: pluralistic and neo-corporatist modes of interest mediation in competition

Faced with this very complex system of interest groups the state has to organise an appropriate mode of interest mediation, which reduces the complexity of interests without leaving important groups out in the cold. In Germany this has resulted in a system of institutionalised contacts between interest groups and the state, characterised as neo-corporatism.[17] Whenever possible the state tries to focus its contacts on the respective umbrella organisations, which – ideally – have already organised consensus among their members, to make the task of political co-operation with interest groups easier. It is for this reason that the state promotes the idea of creating such umbrella organisations systematically.[18] As mentioned above, this task is not always managed successfully. Usually umbrella organisations and member associations perform their lobby work in Bonn simultaneously. The desired neo-corporatistically structured mode of interest mediation is therefore permanently pluralised. Pluralistic and neo-corporatist modes are in permanent conflict and competition with each other.[19]

Government cannot force interest groups to organise hierarchically to ensure that 'pure' neo-corporatism can be practised. But it can offer opportunities and situations in which close and long-lasting contacts with interest groups can be established; and so it did: Table 10.4 lists the different legally codified types of institutionalised contacts accounting for the importance which German lobbyists attach to them.[20]

The most prominent institutionalised contacts between the government and interest groups are without any doubt the legally *mandatory hearings* concerning federal legislation, conducted by the individual federal ministries. Groups affected by a planned measure are invited to comment on early drafts of bills while they are prepared in the responsible department.[21] A maximum of influence concerning the contents of a given measure can be issued there, and consequently the estimated importance of this instrument (1.53) is very high. Legally mandatory hearings concerning *federal governmental orders* are almost of the same importance: it is widely known that effectiveness and substance of legislation are eventually fixed by orders, which have to adapt abstract legislation to practical work and to operationalise it. This work is

Table 10.4   Institutionalised contacts between the government and interest groups and their importance in lobbyists' views

| Type of institutionalised contact | Average importance |
|---|---|
| Legally mandatory hearings concerning federal legislation, conducted by federal ministries | 1.53 |
| Legally mandatory hearings concerning federal governmental orders, conducted by federal ministries | 1.90 |
| Hearings of the German Bundestag | 1.93 |
| Advisory councils and committees of federal ministries | 2.24 |
| Types of 'Konzertierte Aktion' | 3.14 |

*Legend*: 1: very important; 5: unimportant.

*Source*: M. Sebaldt (note 5), p. 271.

usually done behind the scenes and performed in close contact between government officials and closely affected lobbyists.

*Hearings of the Bundestag* take place at a later stage of the legislative decision-making process, following the stages of intra-governmental consensus-building. For that reason the contents of a draft are fixed, and the chances to alter it on the parliamentary stage are limited. Hearings of the Bundestag, organised by the responsible committee, therefore often degenerate into a 'show' with carefully selected groups defending the government point of view on one side and interest groups representing the views of the opposition on the other. This *ritualistic* type of communication reduces the importance of parliamentary hearings considerably.[22]

There are at least two other types of institutionalised contacts worth mentioning. *Advisory councils and committees of federal ministries* constitute a very important institutional device for interest group lobbying, as the latter are very much a part of them. The *Beirat für Innere Führung* of the department of defence, for instance, embraces scientists and politicians, but – besides other lobbyists – also members of the *Bundeswehrverband* and the *Verband der Reservisten der Bundeswehr*, the leading soldier associations. The importance of these councils lies in the permanent influence associations can exert there, and for that reason membership is desired by groups.

The *'Konzertierte Aktion'* (concerted action) – a special type of permanent council of politicians, government officials and leading economic umbrella organisations created in the era of the Grand Coalition 1966–69, and originally designed to solve conflicts in tripartite co-operation between government, employers and labour unions – never worked efficiently and eventually collapsed in 1977.[23] Only in the medical sector is a *'Konzertierte Aktion'* between physicians' associations and health insurance companies to fix fees still operating.[24] For that reason the overall importance of this type of institutionalised contact is considered to be quite low.

But the development of the *'Konzertierte Aktion'* demonstrates well that in the history of the Federal Republic of Germany each mode of interest mediation has had its ups and downs. Generally speaking, the vision of a neo-corporatistic system of interest groups closely connected with the state was *en vogue* during the 1960s and the early 1970s and culminated in the project of *'Globalsteuerung'*[25] of the Grand Coalition and the government of Willy Brandt. The architects of that policy plan tried to optimise the already-existing hierarchical system of interest groups in order to be able to create a whole system of 'concerted actions'. A long-term planned and controlled tripartist system of interest mediation was the target, and the creation of an advisory Economic and Social Council (*Bundeswirtschafts- und Sozialrat*) like the respective body of the European Community was publicly discussed.[26]

However, neither the Council nor the system of global planning was ever established. Ongoing European integration and the already-described economic and social changes in Germany destroyed the vision of global planning and the idea of a hierarchical system of interest groups organised by the state. The growing transfer of political competences from the member states to the European Union in the 1980s and 1990s eroded the political sovereignty of the individual member states, but this sovereignty had been the main fundament of a concept of global planning.

The consequences are obvious: since the 1980s the planned or partly established system of neo-corporatism has eroded considerably and given way to a more pluralistic mode of interest mediation. Institutionalised contacts between state and interest groups still constitute an important element of neo-corporatism, but they take place in a much more pluralised political environment than 20 years ago.

### Does unification matter? The German system of interest groups since 1990

As German unification came suddenly, political and social integration of Eastern Germany could not be planned systematically but had to be implemented in a short time. On a theoretical level two models of integration were possible: first, to reunite Germany, but to secure the regional identity of the East by preserving as many of the former GDR institutions and associations as possible; secondly, to get a homogeneous unified Germany by exporting the already-existing political and social structures to the East.

Political reality set the pace and made theoretical discussions on the best mode of integration obsolete: a rapid 'transfer of institutions'[27] took place and prevented the evolution of specific new types of democratic institutions in the new Länder. Parliamentary systems were established in the newly created Länder, and West German parties moved to the East simply by taking over old 'bloc-party' organisations or by founding new regional sub-organisations. Only the PDS, successor of the former SED, modified the general pattern and gave the party system of East Germany a specific shape.

The evolution of German interest groups in the East took place in a very similar way: in most of the cases already-existing West German associations moved to the new Länder as soon as possible and founded new regional sub-organisations. As early as 1991 the *Bundesverband der Deutschen Industrie* (BDI) succeeded, for instance, in establishing branches in the new Bundesländer, and many of its member organisations took the same route.[28] Seven years later this 'transfer of institutions' is fully completed: the BDI is now composed of 16 regional sub-organisations, each representing one Land, and organisational differences between East and West are minimal.

Apart from some specific regional organisations East German interests were rarely able to organise in newly created nationwide associations. The *Volkssolidarität*, for instance, former mass organisation of the GDR, was transformed into a welfare association of the West German type, but preserving the existing infrastructure. Despite its nationwide claim, it is still mainly operating in the new Länder.

But what are the consequences of German unification for the system of interest groups as a whole? Is there only a transfer of institutions without any modification of the existing spectrum of interest groups? This picture would also be misleading, ignoring the growing *complexity* of the individual groups: more than ever the task of reaching compromise among members and member organisations is a difficult one. The *pluralising* effect of German unification on the system of interest groups is obvious, weakening co-ordinating umbrella organisations and strengthening the position of members simply by growing numbers and the regional diversity of the latter. The traditional neo-corporatist type of interest mediation is thus eroded once again.

## Lobbyism in Germany: the nature of interest groups' political work

### The basics of lobbyism: interest mediation as a political market-system

Traditional views on interest groups often interpret lobbying as a one-way process: interest groups, keen on political influence and committed to securing political privileges for their members, would pressurise politicians as long as such favours are granted. However, political reality is much more complex. The best way to characterise the system of interest mediation between lobbyists and politicians and government officials is to describe it as a political market with two types of participants offering specific political goods valuable and necessary for the other.[29]

The system of interest mediation may indeed be seen as a communication network with equal participants offering equal goods: on the one hand, politicians desperately need specific information concerning a variety of political subjects. Only in rare cases are they experts in the concerned field of legislation, and lobbyists can provide the information required, thereby creating a solid basis for public policy decision-making. On the other hand, politicians are able to give hints to interest groups about hidden political projects at an early stage of policy planning and to create considerable advantages in political competition for such groups. The remaining goods can be seen as products of this information exchange system: interest groups treated favourably by the government will normally back it by showing political loyalty, especially by advising their members to vote for the government in future elections; government in exchange offers political privileges for such groups or secures an already-existing favourable *status quo*. Thus, the picture that emerges is one of a permanent communication process, conducted by political *partners* on equal terms.[30]

### Political lobby-networks: the nature of interest groups' political environment

What is the specific nature of this network? As discussed above, contacts between government departments and interest groups are of the utmost importance because they are necessary for providing politicians and government officials with information about potential consequences of planned measures, and because they are legally mandatory. German lobbyists, asked for their opinion about the importance of specific types of other political actors for their lobbyist work, confirm this fact (see Table 10.5).

Several conclusions can be drawn from this: first, government departments both at the federal and the state level are very important for lobbyist work – much more important on the whole than parliamentary institutions. If necessary, lobbyists concentrate their efforts on the responsible committees or the working groups of the parliamentary party groups. In both cases government representatives are more important than opposition members. This is a consequence of the fact that the German Bundestag is organised as a 'working parliament' with a complex division of labour system:[31] lobbyists need to know who is responsible for a specific political matter, and they usually do.

Still, lobbyists consider contacts with the media and other 'friendly' groups more valuable than those with parliament, and the reasons for this are quite obvious: in a media democracy public presentation and marketing of interests are very important factors of success. The efforts of interest groups to keep close contacts with journalists and to organise professional public relations are the results. Close coalitions

Table 10.5   Other political actors and their importance for the lobby work of German interest groups

| Political actor | Average importance |
| --- | --- |
| Federal ministries | 1.61 |
| Media | 1.76 |
| Associations with similar or identical interests | 1.83 |
| Committees of the German Bundestag | 2.04 |
| Ministries of the Länder | 2.18 |
| Government party groups in the Bundestag | 2.25 |
| Lower public administration | 2.25 |
| Ministers personally | 2.27 |
| Institutions of the European Union | 2.30 |
| Opposition party groups in the Bundestag | 2.41 |
| Research organisations | 2.44 |
| Land governments | 2.49 |
| Other international organisations | 2.83 |
| Bundesrat | 2.95 |
| Associations with contending interests | 2.98 |
| Land parliaments | 2.99 |
| Central party-offices of government parties | 3.06 |
| Federal chancellery | 3.11 |
| Central party-offices of opposition parties | 3.12 |
| Local administration | 3.21 |
| Chancellor personally | 3.64 |
| Jurisdictional courts | 3.64 |
| Administration of the German Bundestag | 3.87 |

*Legend*: 1: very important; 5: unimportant.

*Source*: M. Sebaldt (note 5), pp. 255.

between groups with similar interests can ease this work: several interest groups standing together and acting as a political 'bloc' display more political news value than a single one, and of course more power.

But also the lobbying process itself can be optimised by such coalitions, as it enables the participating groups to create a division of labour system by focusing their efforts on influencing their political 'favourites'.[32] In welfare matters, for instance, the *Arbeiterwohlfahrt* as a traditionally working-class-oriented association usually concentrates it lobby work on the Social Democrats, while *Caritas* and *Diakonisches Werk*, as catholic and protestant organisations respectively, mainly lobby the CDU/CSU.

Of the remaining actors only the most important will be addressed here: central party offices, perhaps surprising at first sight, are only of secondary importance, because their political work is rarely specific and project-oriented enough to be of major interest for lobbyists. Legislation is done by government departments and parliaments, not by party organisations. Ideally, the latter concentrate on the conceptualisation of long-term political strategies, and therefore their function is that of a political think tank – usually not too interesting for a lobbyist. On the other hand, institutions of the European Union are becoming ever more important. Especially since the Treaty of Maastricht, 1993, interest groups have doubled their lobby work to influence national and European political actors simultaneously.[33] Many of them have already established offices in Brussels and Strasbourg to achieve direct contact with officials of the EU Commission and members of the European Parliament. The newly emerging problem for interest groups today is to co-ordinate the work of their several offices: lobbyists in Bonn, Berlin, and Brussels should speak with one voice.

### Lobbyism as a profession: techniques and methods of political work

What are the 'rules of the game'? How is lobbyism organised in practice, and what rules of conduct are of importance? German lobbyists, asked for their opinion, described a clear set of such rules necessary for performing good lobby work.[34] The most frequent notion lobbyists made in interviews is that display of competence and respectability is the main key to success: only if government officials, parliamentarians, etc. obtain the impression that projects and wishes articulated by interest group representatives are realistic and politically reasonable, will they spend time thinking them over. Open-mindedness, discretion and social competence of lobbyists will ease this process. 'Lone wolves' without communicative capabilities are not appropriate for such a job, and neither are incompetent small-talkers. The profile of a successful lobbyist is therefore clear, and German lobbyists unanimously emphasise that newcomers have to undergo a careful 'training on the job' to internalise these rules of the game. For that reason 'lobbyism as a profession' is a fitting characterisation of the whole case.

## Conclusions

Several conclusions can be drawn from the above analysis:

- The system of German interest groups has changed considerably over recent decades. Today more and more groups are representing the tertiary sector, while the number of interest groups in the primary and secondary sectors is on the decline, symbolising the turn towards a post-industrial society. Simultaneously, Germany has become a 'risk society', facing socially dangerous external and internal risks. Consequently, many interest groups designed to face them emerged, and therefore established a completely new sector of lobbyism.

- Although it is good German tradition to establish neo-corporatistic modes of interest mediation by creating a hierarchical organised system of interest groups with overall and sectoral umbrella organisations, political reality of lobbyism is much more pluralistic and dynamic than any textbook description of neo-corporatism. This is mainly because, in many cases, these umbrella organisations are not able to organise consensus among their members who, as a consequence, lobby individually. But a proven system of legally obligatory contacts between politicians, government officials and lobbyists ensures that some order is maintained in this complex pluralistic interest mediation process.

- The network of lobbyism is mainly based on close contacts between government agencies and lobbyists. Parliamentary lobbyism is of only secondary importance; much more effective are contacts with the media, other groups with similar interests, and institutions of the European Union. This network is held together by strong two-sided needs of politicians and lobbyists for information and political support, constituting a political market with participants offering those goods necessary for the other. This market system is conducted by a set of rules to be followed by both sides: open-mindedness, competence, seriousness and a sound social competence constitute the most important qualities.

- The future of German lobbyism will be strongly affected by the ongoing process of European integration: as more and more political decisions are made in Brussels, negotiated by 15 member states and their respective interest groups, national lobbyism will decline in importance. The need for co-ordination of interest groups' political work at the European level will increase dramatically, and the dominant mode of interest mediation at Brussels, Strasbourg, etc. will be a pluralistic one.[35] European umbrella associations are even less able to force their member organisations into a tight neo-corporatistic system than are their German counterparts nowadays. The fact that many European associations accept individual persons as well as firms as members favours the emergence of an anarchical pluralism lacking any neo-corporatist signs of order.

• As a consequence the future German system of interest groups will also be a pluralistic one: the already-weakened German umbrella associations will lose even more of their political power, unable to aggregate the interests of their members appropriately and to play the role of a monopolistic German lobbyist at the European Union. The described economic and social changes, accompanied by an ongoing modernisation of political culture, will further increase the diversity of interest groups in Germany.

## Notes

1  Theodor Eschenburg, *Herrschaft der Verbände?*, 2nd edn (Stuttgart: DVA, 1963).
2  Thomas Ellwein, 'Die großen Interessenverbände und ihr Einfluß', in E.-B. Blümle and P. Schwarz (eds), *Wirtschaftsverbände und ihre Funktion* (Darmstadt: Wissenschaftliche Buchgesellschaft, 1985) (1st edn 1973), pp. 239–77.
3  Jürgen Weber, *Die Interessengruppen im politischen System der Bundesrepublik Deutschland*, 2nd rev. edn (Munich: BLZ, 1981), p. 91.
4  The official title of these lists is: *Öffentliche Liste über die Registrierung von Verbänden und deren Vertretern*. They are published annually by the official report journal of the federal government, the *Bundesanzeiger*.
5  See Martin Sebaldt, *Organisierter Pluralismus: Kräftefeld, Selbstverständnis und politische Arbeit deutscher Interessengruppen* (Opladen: Westdeutscher Verlag, 1997), p. 38.
6  See Daniel Bell, *Die nachindustrielle Gesellschaft: Aus dem Amerikanischen von Siglinde Summerer und Gerda Kurz* (Frankfurt a.M./ New York: Campus, 1989).
7  Ulrich Beck, *Risikogesellschaft. Auf dem Weg in eine andere Moderne* (Frankfurt a.M.: Suhrkamp, 1986).
8  For a detailed description of methods and data see M. Sebaldt (note 5), pp. 391–405.
9  Mancur Olson, *Die Logik des kollektiven Handelns: Kollektivgüter und die Theorie der Gruppen*, 3rd edn (Tübingen: Mohr, 1992) (1st edn 1965), pp. 163–4.
10  Gabriel Almond and Sidney Verba, *The Civic Culture: Political Attitudes and Democracy in Five Nations* (Princeton, NJ: Princeton University Press, 1963).
11  See Martin Greiffenhagen, *Politische Legitimität in Deutschland* (Bonn: Bundeszentrale für politische Bildung, 1998), pp. 358–64.
12  See Siegfried Mann, *Macht und Ohnmacht der Verbände. Das Beispiel des Bundesverbandes der Deutschen Industrie e.V. (BDI) aus empirisch-analytischer Sicht* (Baden-Baden: Nomos, 1994).
13  See J. Weber (note 3), pp. 95–104.
14  Martin Sebaldt, 'Verbände und Demokratie: Funktionen bundesdeutscher Interessengruppen in Theorie und Praxis', *Aus Politik und Zeitgeschichte*, B 36–37/1997, pp. 35–6.
15  See Ulrich von Alemann (ed.), *Neokorporatismus* (Frankfurt a.M./New York: Campus, 1981), pp. 81–90.

16  See J. Weber (note 3), p. 157.

17  See U. von Alemann (note 15); Peter J. Williamson, *Corporatism in Perspective: An Introductory Guide to Corporatist Theory* (London: Sage, 1989).

18  See Gerhard Lehmbruch, 'Concertation and the Structure of Corporatist Networks', in John Goldthorpe (ed.), *Order and Conflict in Contemporary Capitalism* (Oxford: Clarendon Press, 1984), pp. 60–80.

19  See M. Sebaldt (note 5), p. 73.

20  Twenty-four lobbyists of different types of associations, working in Bonn, were interviewed in 1994 to get data concerning their professional self-conception and their political working style. Methods are described in M. Sebaldt (note 5), pp. 400–4.

21  See Wolfgang Rudzio, *Das politische System der Bundesrepublik Deutschland: Eine Einführung*, 3rd rev. edn (Opladen: Leske & Budrich, 1991), p. 81.

22  See Wolfgang Ismayr, *Der Deutsche Bundestag: Funktionen, Willensbildung, Reformansätze* (Opladen: Leske & Budrich, 1992), pp. 478–85.

23  See Helmut Willke, 'Zur Integrationsfunktion des Staates. Die Konzertierte Aktion als Paradigma in der neuen staatstheoretischen Diskussion', *Politische Vierteljahresschrift*, 20 (1979), pp. 221–40.

24  See Helmut Wiesenthal, *Die Konzertierte Aktion im Gesundheitswesen: Ein Beispiel für Theorie und Politik des modernen Korporatismus* (Frankfurt a.M./New York: Campus, 1981).

25  Dieter Grosser, 'Das Verhältnis von Staat und Wirtschaft in der Bundesrepublik Deutschland', in Dieter Grosser (ed.), *Der Staat in der Wirtschaft der Bundesrepublik* (Opladen: Leske & Budrich/UTB, 1985), pp. 48–51.

26  See Rudolf Steinberg, 'Zur Institutionalisierung des Verbandseinflusses in einem Bundeswirtschafts- und Sozialrat', *Die Öffentliche Verwaltung*, 25 (1972), pp. 837–45.

27  Helmut Wiesenthal, 'Einleitung: Grundlinien der Transformation Ostdeutschlands und die Rolle korporativer Akteure', in Helmut Wiesenthal (ed.), *Einheit als Interessenpolitik: Studien zur sektoralen Transformation Ostdeutschlands* (Frankfurt a.M./New York: Campus, 1995), p. 10.

28  See Jürgen Bauer, 'Aktivitäten des BDI in den neuen Bundesländern', *Aus Politik und Zeitgeschichte*, B 13/1991, pp. 12–19.

29  See Michael T. Hayes, *Lobbyists and Legislators: A Theory of Political Markets* (New Brunswick, NJ: Rutgers University Press, 1981).

30  This interpretation is widely confirmed by the 24 interviewed German lobbyists (see note 20).

31  See W. Ismayr (note 22).

32  See M. Sebaldt (note 5), pp. 291–6.

33  See Beate Kohler-Koch, *Die Gestaltungsmacht organisierter Interessen*, in Beate Kohler-Koch and Markus Jachtenfuchs (eds), *Europäische Integration* (Opladen: Leske & Budrich, 1996), pp. 193–222.

34  See M. Sebaldt (note 5), p. 255.

35  See Wolfgang Streeck and Phillip C. Schmitter, 'From National Corporatism to Transnational Pluralism: Organized Interests in the Single European Market', in Volker Eichener and Helmut Voelzkow (eds), *Europäische Integration und verbandliche Interessenvermittlung* (Marburg: Metropolis, 1994), pp. 181–215.

# Bibliography

Aberbach, J. D., Putnam, R. D. and Rockman, B. A., *Bureaucrats and Politicians in Western Democracies* (Cambridge, Mass.: Harvard University Press, 1981).

Abromeit, H., 'Mehrheitsdemokratische und konkordanzdemokratische Elemente im politischen System der Bundesrepublik Deutschland', *Österreichische Zeitschrift für Politikwissenschaft*, 18 (1989), pp. 165–80.

Abromeit, H., *Der verkappte Einheitsstaat* (Opladen: Leske & Budrich, 1992).

Abromeit, H., *Interessenvermittlung zwischen Konkurrenz und Konkordanz* (Opladen: Leske & Budrich, 1993).

Alemann, U. von (ed.), *Neokorporatismus* (Frankfurt a.M./New York: Campus, 1981).

Alemann, U. von, *Organisierte Interessen in der Bundesrepublik*, 2nd edn (Opladen: Leske & Budrich, 1989).

Alemann, U. von, 'Die Parteien in den Wechsel-Jahren? Zum Wandel des deutschen Parteiensystems', *Aus Politik und Zeitgeschichte*, B6/1996, pp. 3–8.

Alemann, U. von, 'Party Research goes Politics. Ein Plädoyer gegen die Kapitulation der Parteienforscher vor der Mediengesellschaft', *Politische Vierteljahresschrift*, 38 (1997), pp. 797–803.

Alemann, U. von and Tönnesmann, W., 'Die Dinosaurier werden immer trauriger. Ein kleiner Essay über große Parteien', *Perspektiven DS*, 1 (1992), pp. 15–23.

Almond, G. and Verba, S., *The Civic Culture: Political Attitudes and Democracy in Five Nations* (Princeton, NJ: Princeton University Press, 1963).

Amphoux, J., *Le Chancellier Fédéral dans le Régime Constitutionnel de la République Féderal d´Allemagne* (Paris: Pichon, 1962).

Andeweg, R. and Nijzink, L., 'Beyond the Two-Body-Image: Relations Between Ministers and MPs', in H. Döring (ed.), *Parliaments and Majority Rule in Western Europe* (Frankfurt a.M./New York: Campus/St Martin's Press, 1995), pp. 152–76.

Arnim, H.-H. von, *Der Staat als Beute* (Munich: Knaur, 1993).

Arnim, H.-H. von, 'Reformblockade der Politik? Ist unser Staat noch handlungsfähig?', *Zeitschrift für Rechtspolitik*, 31 (1998), pp. 138–47.

Arnold, R., 'L'union monétaire européenne et la Constitution allemande', *Revue du droit public et de la science politique en France et a étranger*, 3 (1998), pp. 649–57.

Bagehot, W., *The English Constitution* (London: Collins, 1963) (1st edn 1867).

Balkhausen, D., *Gutes Geld & schlechte Politik: Der Report über die Bundesbank* (Dusseldorf: Econ, 1992).

Bannas, G., 'Adenauers "Geschwätz von gestern" heißt bei Schröder "Alles hat seine Zeit"', *Frankfurter Allgemeine Zeitung*, 28 January 1999, p. 3.

Batt, H.-L., *Die Grundgesetzreform nach der deutschen Einheit* (Opladen: Leske & Budrich, 1996).

Bauer, J., 'Aktivitäten des BDI in den neuen Bundesländern', *Aus Politik und Zeitgeschichte* B 13/1991, pp. 12–19.

Baum, L., *The Supreme Court*, 6th edn (Washington, DC: Congressional Quarterly Press, 1998).

Beck, U., *Risikogesellschaft: Auf dem Weg in eine andere Moderne* (Frankfurt a.M.: Suhrkamp, 1986).

Beck, U., *Die Erfindung des Politischen* (Frankfurt a.M.: Suhrkamp, 1993).

Bell, D., *Die nachindustrielle Gesellschaft: Aus dem Amerikanischen von Siglinde Summerer und Gerda Kurz* (Frankfurt a.M./New York: Campus, 1989).

Berger, H., *Konjunkturpoltik im Wirtschaftswunder: Handlungsspielräume und Verhaltensmuster von Bundesbank und Regierung in den 1950er Jahren* (Tübingen: Mohr Siebeck, 1997).

Berger, H. and Schneider, F., 'Does the Bundesbank Give Way in Conflicts with the West German Government?', *University of Linz Working Paper* 9716 (1997).

Beyme, K. von, 'The Genesis of Constitutional Review in Parliamentary Systems', in C. Landfried (ed.), *Constitutional Review and Legislation: An International Comparison* (Baden-Baden: Nomos, 1988), pp. 21–38.

Beyme, K. von, *Die politische Klasse im Parteienstaat* (Frankfurt a.M.: Suhrkamp, 1993).

Beyme, K. von *Das politische System der Bundesrepublik Deutschland*, 8th edn (Munich: Piper, 1996).

Beyme, K. von, 'Interest Groups in the German Bundestag', *Government & Opposition*, 33 (1998), pp. 38–55.

Beyme, K. von, *The Legislator: German Parliament as a Centre of Decision-Making* (Aldershot: Ashgate, 1998).

Beyme, K. von, *Parlament und Regierung: Die Demokratisierung der parlamentarischen Systeme* (Opladen: Westdeutscher Verlag, 1999).

Bickerich, W., *Die D-Mark: Eine Biographie* (Berlin: Rowohlt, 1998).

Billing, W., 'Der Kampf um die Besetzung des höchsten Staatsamtes', *Zeitschrift für Parlamentsfragen*, 25 (1995), pp. 595–620.

Blankenburg, E., 'Changes in Political Regimes and Continuity of the Rule of Law in Germany', in H. Jacob (ed.), *Courts, Law, and Politics in Comparative Perspective* (New Haven/London: Yale University Press, 1996), pp. 249–314.

Blankenburg, E., 'Die Verfassungsbeschwerde – Die Nebenbühne der Politik und Klagemauer von Bürgern', *Kritische Justiz*, 31 (1998), pp. 203–18.

Borchardt, K., 'Währung und Wirtschaft', in Deutsche Bundesbank (eds), *Deutsches Geld- und Bankwesen in Zahlen 1876–1975* (Frankfurt a.M.: Fritz Knapp, 1976), pp. 3–55.

Braun, D., 'Der bundesdeutsche Föderalismus an der Wegscheide. Interessenkoalitionen, Akteurskonflikte und institutionelle Lösungen', *Staatswissenschaften und Staatspraxis*, 7 (1996), pp. 101–35.

Bredthauer, R., *Das Wahlsystem als Objekt von Politik und Wissenschaft: Die Wahlsystemdiskussion in der BRD 1967/68 als politische und wissenschaftliche Auseinandersetzung* (Meisenheim am Glan: Hain, 1973).

Broszat, M., Dübber, U., Hofer, W., Möller, H., Oberreuter, H., Schmädeke, J. and Treue, W. (eds), *Deutschlands Weg in die Diktatur* (Berlin: Siedler, 1983).

Brünneck, A. von, 'Constitutional Review and Legislation in Western Democracies', in C. Landfried (ed.), *Constitutional Review and Legislation* (Baden-Baden: Nomos, 1988), pp. 219–60.

Brünneck, A. von, *Verfassungsgerichtsbarkeit in den westlichen Demokratien* (Baden-Baden: Nomos, 1992).

Buchheim, C., 'Die Errichtung der Bank deutscher Länder und die Währungsreform in Westdeutschland', in Deutsche Bundesbank (ed.), *Fünfzig Jahre Deutsche Mark: Notenbank und Währung in Deutschland seit 1948* (Munich: Beck, 1998), pp. 91–138.

Bücking, H.-J., 'Der Streit um Grundmandatsklausel und Überhangmandate', in E. Jesse and K. Löw (eds), *Wahlen in Deutschland* (Berlin: Duncker & Humblot, 1998), pp. 141–215.

Bull, H. P., 'Hierarchie als Verfassungsgebot? Zur Demokratietheorie des Bundesverfassungsgerichts', in M. Th. Greven, H. Münkler and R. Schmalz-Bruns (eds), *Bürgersinn und Kritik: Festschrift für Udo Bermbach zum 60. Geburtstag* (Baden-Baden: Nomos, 1998), pp. 241–56.

Bulmahn, T., 'Vereinigungsbilanzen. Die deutsche Einheit im Spiegel der Sozialwissenschaften', *Aus Politik and Zeitgeschichte*, B 40–41/1997, pp. 29–37.

Bundesministerium der Justiz (ed.), *Entlastung des Bundesverfassungsgerichts: Bericht der Kommission* (Bonn, 1998).

Burmeister, J. (ed.), *Verfassungsstaatlichkeit: Festschrift für Klaus Stern zum 65. Geburtstag* (Munich: Beck, 1997).

Busch, A., *Preisstabilitätspolitik. Politik und Inflationsraten im internationalen Vergleich* (Opladen: Leske & Budrich, 1995).

Clemens, C., 'Party Management as a Leadership Resource: Kohl and the CDU/CSU', *German Politics*, 7 (1998), pp. 91–119.

Cohen, J. E., *Presidential Responsiveness and Public Policy-Making: The Public and the Policies that Presidents Choose* (Ann Arbor: University of Michigan Press, 1997).

Cole, A., 'Political Leadership in Western Europe: Helmut Kohl in Comparative Context', *German Politics*, 7 (1998), pp. 120–45.

Colliard, J.-C., *Les Régimes parlementaires contemporaines* (Paris: Fondation Nationale des sciences Politiques, 1978).

Conradt, D. P., 'Electoral Law Politics in West Germany', *Political Studies*, 18 (1970), pp. 341–56.

Cortell, A. P. and Peterson, S., 'Altered States: Explaining Domestic Institutional Change', *British Journal of Political Science*, 29 (1999), pp. 177–203.

Cullen, P. J. and Goetz, K. H., 'Concluding Theses on Constitutional Policy in Unified Germany', in K. H. Goetz and P. J. Cullen (eds), *Constitutional Policy in Unified Germany* (special issue of *German Politics*, 3 (1994), no. 3), pp. 162–76.

Czada, R., 'Vereinigungskrise und Standortdebatte. Der Beitrag der Wiedervereinigung zur Krise des westdeutschen Modells', *Leviathan*, 26 (1998), pp. 24–59.

Czada, R. and Lehmbruch, G. (eds), *Transformationspfade in Ostdeutschland: Beiträge zur sektoralen Vereinigungspolitik* (Frankfurt a.M.: Campus, 1998).

Danter, K., 'Entlastung des Bundesverfassungsgerichts durch Regionalisierung von Kompetenzen zu den Landesverfassungsgerichten', *Die Öffentliche Verwaltung*, 51 (1998), pp. 239–43.

Deeg, R., 'Economic Globalization and the Shifting Boundaries of German Federalism', *Publius: The Journal of Federalism*, 26 (1996), pp. 27–52.

Derlien, H. U., 'Repercussions of Government Change on the Career Civil Service in West Germany: the Cases of 1969 and 1982', *Governance*, 1 (1988), pp. 50–78.

Derlien, H.-U., 'Institutionalising Democracy in Germany: From Weimar to Bonn and Berlin', in M. Heper, A. Kazancigil and B. A. Rockman (eds) *Institutions and Democratic Statecraft* (Boulder, Col.: Westview Press, 1997), pp. 145–70.

Deutsche Bundesbank, *Die Geldpolitik der Bundesbank* (Frankfurt a.m.: Deutsche Bundesbank, 1995).

Deutsche Bundesbank, 'Der Zentralbankrat vor fünfzig Jahren', *Deutsche Bank Monatsbericht März 1998*, pp. 17–31.

Dickhaus, M., *Die Bundesbank im westeuropäischen Wiederaufbau: die internationale Währungspolitik der Bundesrepublik Deutschland 1948 bis 1958* (Munich: Oldenbourg, 1996).

Dittberner, J. and Ebbighausen, R. (eds), *Das Parteiensystem in der Legitimationskrise* (Opladen: Westdeutscher Verlag, 1973).

Dönhoff, M. Gräfin, 'Autorität auch ohne Macht', *Zeit–Punkte*, no. 2 (1994), pp. 94–7.

Döring, W., *Wie die Krise des Föderalismus überwunden werden kann* (Stuttgart: FDP, Landesverband Baden-Württemberg, 1998).

Duverger, M., *La Monarchie Républicaine* (Paris: Robert Laffont, 1974).

Edinger, L. J. and Nacos, B. L., 'From the Bonn to the Berlin Republic: Can a Stable Democracy Continue?', *Political Science Quarterly*, 113 (1998), pp. 179–91.

Ehrmann, H. W., 'Judicial Activism in a Divided Society: the Rule of Law in the Weimar Republic', in J. R. Schmidhauser (ed.), *Comparative Judicial Systems: Challenging Frontiers in Conceptual and Empirical Analysis* (London: Butterworths, 1987), pp. 75–92.

Elbe, F. and Kiessler, R., *A Round Table with Sharp Corners: The Diplomatic Path to German Unity* (Baden-Baden: Nomos, 1996).

Elgie, R., *Political Leadership in Liberal Democracies* (London: Macmillan, 1995).

Ellul, J., *Propagandes* (Paris: Armand Colin, 1962).

Ellul, J., 'Propagande et personnalisation du pouvoir', in L. Hamon and A. Mabileau (eds), *La Personnalisation du Pouvoir* (Paris: Presses Universitaires de France, 1964), pp. 331–41.

Ellwein, Th., 'Die großen Interessenverbände und ihr Einfluß', in E.-B. Blümle and P. Schwarz (eds), *Wirtschaftsverbände und ihre Funktion* (Darmstadt: Wissenschaftliche Buchgesellschaft, 1985), pp. 239–77.

Ellwein, Th. and Hesse, J. J., 'Thesen zur Reform der öffentlichen Verwaltung in Deutschland', *Staatswissenschaften und Staatspraxis*, 7 (1996), pp. 469–78.

Eschenburg, Th., *Herrschaft der Verbände?* (Stuttgart: DVA, 1963).

Escher, H., 'Ländermitwirkung und der Ausschuß der Ständigen Vertreter (AStV)', in F. H. U. Borkenhagen (ed.), *Europapolitik der deutschen Länder* (Opladen: Leske & Budrich, 1998), pp. 51–68.

Faber, H., *Wirtschaftsplanung und Bundesbankautonomie* (Baden-Baden: Nomos, 1969).

Farrell, D., *Comparing Electoral Systems* (London: Prentice Hall/Harvester Wheatsheaf, 1997).

Faupel, R., 'Das Bundesverfassungsgericht in Nöten. Die Vorschläge der Kommission zur Entlastung des BVerfG', *Neue Justiz*, 52 (1998), pp. 57–62.

Fenske, H., *Wahlrecht und Parteiensystem: Ein Beitrag zur deutschen Parteiengeschichte* (Frankfurt a.M.: Athenäum, 1972).

Filmer, W. and Schwan, H. (eds), *Richard von Weizsäcker* (Dusseldorf/Vienna: Econ, 1984).

Fischer, W., 'Forderungen der Länder zur Regierungskonferenz 1996/97', in F. H. U. Borkenhagen (ed.), *Europapolitik der deutschen Länder* (Opladen: Leske & Budrich, 1998), pp. 9–27.

Folz, H.-P., *Demokratie und Integration: Der Konflikt zwischen Bundesverfassungsgericht und Europäischem Gerichtshof über die Kontrolle der Gemeinschaftskompetenzen* (Berlin: Springer, 1999).

Fraenkel, E., *Deutschland und die westlichen Demokratien*, 7th edn (Frankfurt a.M.: Suhrkamp, 1991).

Frey, B. S. and Schneider, F., 'Central Bank Behaviour: a Positive Empirical Analysis', *Journal of Monetary Economics*, 7 (1981), pp. 291–315.

Friedrich-Naumann-Stiftung, *Wider die Erstarrung in unserem Staat – für eine Erneuerung des Föderalismus* (Königswinter: Friedrich-Naumann-Stiftung, 1998).

Fromme, F. K., 'Wenn der Bundespräsident nicht unterschreiben will', *Frankfurter Allgemeine Zeitung*, 29 June 1981.

Fromme, F. K., 'Bundesverfassungsgericht', in W. Weidenfeld and K.-R. Korte (eds), *Handbuch zur deutschen Einheit* (Bonn: Bundeszentrale für politische Bildung, 1996), pp. 84–95.

Frowein, J., 'Die Rechtsprechung des Bundesverfassungsgerichts zum Wahlrecht', *Archiv des öffentlichen Rechts*, 99 (1974), pp. 72–110.

Fuchs, D., 'Wohin geht der Wandel der demokratischen Institutionen in Deutschland? Die Entwicklung der Demokratievorstellungen der Deutschen seit ihrer Vereinigung', in G. Göhler (ed.), *Institutionenwandel* (Leviathan Sonderheft 16/1996) (Opladen: Westdeutscher Verlag, 1996), pp. 253–84.

Gabriel, O. W. and Niedermayer, O., 'Entwicklung und Sozialstruktur der Parteimitgliedschaften', in O. W. Gabriel, O. Niedermayer and R. Stöss (eds) *Parteiendemokratie in Deutschland* (Bonn/Opladen: Bundeszentrale für politische Bildung/Westdeutscher Verlag, 1997), pp. 277–300.

Geiger, W., *Gesetz über das Bundesverfassungsgericht* (Berlin: Franz Vahlen, 1951).

Goetz, K. H., 'National Governance and European Integration: Intergovernmental Relations in Germany', *Journal of Common Market Studies*, 33 (1995), pp. 91–116.

Goetz, K. H., 'The Federal Constitutional Court', in G. Smith, W. Paterson and S. Padgett (eds), *Developments in German Politics, vol. 2* (London: Macmillan, 1996), pp. 96–116.

Goetz, K. H. and Cullen, P., 'The Basic Law after Unification: Continued Centrality or Declining Force?', in K. H. Goetz and P. J. Cullen (eds) *Constitutional Policy in Unified Germany* (special issue of *German Politics*, 3 (1994), no. 3), pp. 5–46.

Göhler, G., 'Wie verändern sich Institutionen? Revolutionärer und schleichender Institutionenwandel', in G. Göhler (ed.), *Institutionenwandel* (Leviathan Sonderheft 16/1996) (Opladen: Westdeutscher Verlag, 1996), pp. 21–56.

Golsch, L., *Die politische Klasse im Parlament: Politische Professionalisierung von Hinterbänklern im Deutschen Bundestag* (Baden-Baden: Nomos, 1998).

Gramlich, L., *Bundesbankgesetz, Währungsgesetz, Münzgesetz: Kommentar* (Cologne/Berlin: Carl Heymanns, 1988).

Greiffenhagen, M., *Politische Legitimität in Deutschland* (Bonn: Bundeszentrale für politische Bildung, 1998).

Grimm, D., 'Blockade kann nötig sein', *Die Zeit*, 10 October 1998, pp. 14–15.

Grosser, A., 'Les Elections allemandes. Le Plébiscite du 15e Septembre 1957', *Revue française de science politique*, 7 (1957), pp. 838–64.

Grosser, D., 'Das Verhältnis von Staat und Wirtschaft in der Bundesrepublik Deutschland', in D. Grosser (ed.), *Der Staat in der Wirtschaft der Bundesrepublik* (Opladen: Leske & Budrich/UTB, 1985), pp. 13–59.

Guggenberger, B., 'Die Rechtsprechung des Bundesverfassungsgerichts und die institutionelle Balance des demokratischen Verfassungsstaates', in B. Guggenberger and Th. Würtenberger (eds), *Hüter der Verfassung oder Lenker der Politik? Das Bundesverfassungsgericht im Widerstreit* (Baden-Baden: Nomos, 1998), pp. 202–32.

Häberle, P., 'Die Verfassungsbeschwerde im System der bundesdeutschen Verfassungsgerichtsbarkeit', *Jahrbuch des öffentlichen Rechts*, 45 (1997), pp. 89–135.

Hall, P. and Taylor, R., 'Political Science and the Three New Institutionalisms', *Political Studies*, 44 (1996), pp. 936–57.

Hanrieder, W., *West German Foreign Policy, 1949–1963: International Pressure and Domestic Response* (Stanford: Stanford University Press, 1967).

Hartmann, J. and Kempf, U., *Staatsoberhäupter in westlichen Demokratien* (Opladen: Westdeutscher Verlag, 1989).

Hartwig, M., 'Die zukünftige Position des Bundesverfassungsgerichts im staatsrechtlichen Gefüge der Bundesrepublik Deutschland', in M. Piazzolo (ed.), *Das Bundesverfassungsgericht: Ein Gericht im Schnittpunkt von Recht und Politik* (Mainz/Munich: v. Hase & Koehler, 1996), pp. 165–88.

Hasse, R. H., *Die Europäische Zentralbank: Perspektiven für eine Weiterentwicklung des Europäischen Währungssystems* (Gütersloh: Bertelsmann Stiftung, 1989).

Haungs, P., 'Plädoyer für eine erneuerte Mitgliederpartei. Anmerkungen zur aktuellen Diskussion über die Zukunft der Volksparteien', *Zeitschrift für Parlamentsfragen*, 25 (1994), pp. 108–15.

Haungs, P. and Jesse, E. (eds), *Parteien in der Krise? In- und ausländische Perspektiven* (Cologne: Verlag Wissenschaft und Politik, 1987).

Häußler, R., *Der Konflikt zwischen Bundesverfassungsgericht und politischer Führung: Ein Beitrag zur Geschichte und Rechtsstellung des Bundesverfassungsgerichts* (Berlin: Duncker & Humblot, 1994).

Hayes, M. T., *Lobbyists and Legislators: A Theory of Political Markets* (New Brunswick, NJ: Rutgers University Press, 1981).

Heinze, R. G., *Die blockierte Gesellschaft: Sozioökonomischer Wandel und die Krise des "Modell Deutschland"* (Opladen: Westdeutscher Verlag, 1998).

Helms, L., '"Machtwechsel" in der Bundesrepublik Deutschland. Eine vergleichende empirische Analyse der Regierungswechsel von 1966, 1969 und 1982', *Jahrbuch für Politik*, 4 (1994), pp. 225–48.

Helms, L., 'Das Amt des deutschen Bundeskanzlers in historisch und international vergleichender Perspektive', *Zeitschrift für Parlamentsfragen*, 27 (1996), pp. 697–711.

Helms, L., 'Executive Leadership in Parliamentary Democracies: the British Prime Minister and the German Chancellor Compared', *German Politics*, 5 (1996), pp. 101–20.

Helms, L., *Wettbewerb und Kooperation: Zum Verhältnis von Regierungsmehrheit und Opposition im parlamentarischen Gesetzgebungsverfahren in der Bundesrepublik Deutschland, Großbritannien und Österreich* (Opladen: Westdeutscher Verlag, 1997).

Helms, L., 'Keeping Weimar at Bay: the German Federal Presidency since 1949', *German Politics and Society*, 16 (1998), pp. 50–68.

Helms, L., 'Perspectives on Government and Opposition in Unified Germany', *Politics*, 18 (1998), pp. 151–8.

Helms, L., 'Gibt es eine Krise des Parteienstaates in Deutschland?', in W. Merkel and A. Busch (eds) *Demokratie in Ost und West: Festschrift für Klaus von Beyme* (Frankfurt a.M.: Suhrkamp, 1999), pp. 435–54.

Hennis, W., 'Die Chance einer ganz anderen Republik', in W. Hennis, *Auf dem Weg in den Parteienstaat* (Stuttgart: Reclam, 1998), pp. 93–106.

Hentschel, V., 'Die Entstehung des Bundesbankgesetztes, 1949–1957: Politische Kontroversen und Konflikte' (Teil I und Teil II), *Bankhistorisches Archiv. Zeitschrift zur Bankengeschichte*, 14 (1988), pp. 3–31 and 79–115.

Hentschel, V., *Ludwig Erhardt: Ein Politikerleben* (Munich: Olzog, 1996).

Hermens, F. A., 'Evaluating Electoral Systems', in M. Kaase (ed.), *Politische Wissenschaft und politische Ordnung: Analysen zu Theorie und Empirie demokratischer Regierungsweise. Festschrift zum 65. Geburtstag von Rudolf Wildenmann* (Opladen: Westdeutscher Verlag, 1986), pp. 233–53.

Herzog, D., 'Der moderne Berufspolitiker. Karrierebedingungen und Funktion in westlichen Demokratien', *Der Bürger im Staat*, 40 (1990), pp. 9–16.

Hesse, J. J. and Ellwein, Th., *Das Regierungssystem der Bundesrepublik Deutschland* 8th edn (Opladen: Westdeutscher Verlag, 1997).

Hesse, K., *Der unitarische Bundesstaat* (Karlsruhe: C. F. Müller, 1962).

Hesse, K., 'Verfassungsrechtsprechung im geschichtlichen Wandel', *Juristen Zeitung*, 32 (1995), pp. 265–73.

Hesse, K., 'Stufen der Entwicklung der deutschen Verfassungsgerichtsbarkeit', *Jahrbuch des Öffentlichen Rechts der Gegenwart*, 46 (1998), pp. 1–23.

Hoecker, B., 'Zwischen Macht und Ohnmacht: Politische Partizipation von Frauen in Deutschland', in B. Hoecker (ed.), *Handbuch politische Partizipation von Frauen in Europa* (Opladen: Leske & Budrich, 1996), pp. 65–90.

Höffe, O., *Vernunft und Recht: Bausteine zu einem interkulturellen Rechtsdiskurs* (Frankfurt a.M.: Suhrkamp, 1996).

Hofmann, G., 'Die Versuchs-Regierung', *Die Zeit*, 28 January 1999, p. 3.

Hofmann, G. and Perger, W. A., *Richard von Weizsäcker im Gespräch* (Frankfurt a.M.: Eichborn, 1992).

Hofmann, R., *Geschichte der deutschen Parteien* (Munich: Piper, 1993).

Holtfrerich, C.-L., 'Geldpolitik bei festen Wechselkursen (1948–1970)', in Deutsche Bundesband (ed.), *Fünfzig Jahre Deutsche Mark: Notenbank und Währung in Deutschland seit 1948* (Munich: Beck, 1998), pp. 347–438.

Horst, P., 'Präsident der Bundesrepublik Deutschland', *Zeitschrift für Parlamentsfragen* 25 (1995), pp. 586–95.

Hrbek, R., 'Die Auswirkungen der EU–Integration auf den Föderalismus in Deutschland', *Aus Politik und Zeitgeschichte* B 24/1997, pp. 12–21.

Hutton, W., *The State We're In* (London: Vintage, 1996).

Ismayr, W., *Der Deutsche Bundestag. Funktionen, Willensbildung, Reformansätze* (Opladen: Leske & Budrich, 1992).

Jäger, W., 'Von der Kanzlerdemokratie zur Koordinationsdemokratie', *Zeitschrift für Politik*, 35 (1988), pp. 15–32.

James, H., 'Die Reichsbank 1876 bis 1945', in Deutsche Bundesbank (ed.), *Fünfzig Jahre Deutsche Mark: Notenbank und Währung in Deutschland seit 1948* (Munich: Beck, 1998), pp. 29–91.

Jann, W., 'Politische Willensbildung und Entscheidungsstrukturen im Prozeß der deutschen Einigung – Im Osten nichts Neues?', in G. Lehmbruch (ed.), *Einigung und Zerfall: Deutschland und Europa nach dem Ende des Ost–West–Konflikts* (Opladen: Leske & Budrich, 1995), pp. 55–71.

Jeffery, C., 'The Non-Reform of the German Federal System after Unification', *West European Politics*, 18 (1995), pp. 252–72.

Jesse, E., *Wahlrecht zwischen Kontinuität und Reform: Eine Analyse der Wahlsystemdiskussion und der Wahlrechtsänderungen in der Bundesrepublik Deutschland 1949–1983* (Düsseldorf: Droste, 1985).

Jesse, E., 'The West German Electoral System: the Case for Reform, 1949–1987', *West European Politics*, 10 (1987), pp. 434–48.

Jesse, E., 'Split-voting in the Federal Republic of Germany: an Analysis of the Federal Elections from 1953 to 1987', *Electoral Studies*, 7 (1988), pp. 109–24.

Jesse, E., *Elections: The Federal Republic of Germany in Comparison* (New York/Oxford: Berg, 1990).

Jesse, E., 'Die institutionellen Rahmenbedingungen der Bundestagswahl vom 2. Dezember 1990', in H.-D. Klingemann and M. Kaase (eds), *Wahlen und Wähler: Analysen aus Anlaß der Bundestagswahl 1990* (Opladen: Westdeutscher Verlag, 1994), pp. 15–41.

Jesse, E., 'Die Parteien im westlichen Deutschland 1945 bis zur deutschen Einheit 1990', in O. W. Gabriel, O. Niedermayer and R. Stöss (eds), *Parteiendemokratie in Deutschland* (Bonn/Opladen: Bundeszentrale für politische Bildung/Westdeutscher Verlag, 1997), pp. 59–83.

Jesse, E., 'Grundmandatsklausel und Überhangmandate. Zwei wahlrechtliche Eigentümlichkeiten in der Kritik', in M. Kaase and H.-D. Klingemann (eds), *Wahlen und Wähler: Analysen aus Anlaß der Bundestagswahl 1994* (Opladen: Westdeutscher Verlag, 1998), pp. 15–41.

Johnson, N., 'The Federal Constitutional Court: Facing up to the Strains of Law and Politics in the New Germany', *German Politics*, 3 (1994), pp. 131–48.

Jung, M. and Roth, D., 'Wer zu spät geht, den bestraft der Wähler. Eine Analyse der Bundestagswahl 1998', *Aus Politik und Zeitgeschichte*, B 52/1998, pp. 3–18.

Jung, O., 'Wahlen und Abstimmungen im Dritten Reich 1933–1938', in E. Jesse and K. Löw (eds), *Wahlen in Deutschland* (Berlin: Duncker & Humblot, 1998), pp. 69–97.

Kaase, M., 'Personalized Proportional Representation: the "Model" of the West German Electoral System', in A. Lijphart and B. Grofman (eds), *Choosing an Electoral System: Issues and Alternatives* (New York: Praeger, 1984), pp. 155–64.

Kaase, M., 'The Challenge of the "Participatory Revolution" in Pluralist Democracies', *International Political Science Review*, 5 (1984), pp. 299–318.

Kaiser, A., 'Types of Democracy: from Classical to New Institutionalism', *Journal of Theoretical Politics*, 9 (1997), pp. 419–44.

Kaltefleiter, W., *Die Funktionen des Staatsoberhauptes in der parlamentarischen Demokratie* (Cologne/Opladen: Westdeutscher Verlag, 1970).

Kaltefleiter, W., 'Die Wahl des Bundespräsidenten durch Plebiszit?', in G. Rüther (ed.) *Repräsentative oder plebiszitäre Demokratie – eine Alternative?* (Baden-Baden: Nomos, 1996), pp. 160–9.

Kaltenthaler, K., 'The Restructuring of the German Bundesbank: the Politics of Institutional Change', *German Politics and Society*, 14 (1996), pp. 23–48.

Katz, R. S. and Mair, P., 'The Evolution of Party Organizations in Europe: the Three Faces of Party Organization', in W. Crotty (ed.), *Political Parties in a Changing Age*, (special issue of *The American Review of Politics*, 14) (Conway, Ark.: University of Central Arkansas Press, 1993), pp. 593–617.

Katzenstein, P., *Policy and Politics in West Germany: The Growth of a Semisovereign State* (Philadelphia: Temple University Press, 1987).

Kazancigil, A., 'Connecting Political Institutions to Democracy', in M. Heper, A. Kazancigil and B. A. Rockman (eds), *Institutions and Democratic Statecraft* (Boulder, Col.: Westview Press, 1997), pp. 299–307.

Kennedy, E., *The Bundesbank: Germany's Central Bank in the International Monetary System* (New York: Council on Foreign Relations Press, 1991).

Kilper, H. and Lhotta, R., *Föderalismus in der Bundesrepublik Deutschland* (Opladen: Leske & Budrich, 1996).

Kindler, K. F., 'Der Antiparteienaffekt in Deutschland', *Gesellschaft – Staat – Erziehung* (1958), pp. 107–21.

King, A., 'The British Prime Minister in the Age of the Career Politician', in G. W. Jones (ed.), *West European Prime Ministers* (London: Frank Cass, 1991), pp. 25–47.

King, A., '"Chief Executives" in Western Europe', in I. Budge and D. McKay (eds), *Developing Democracy: Comparative Research in Honour of J. F. P. Blondel* (London: Sage, 1994), pp. 150–63.

Klages, A. and Paulus, P., *Direkte Demokratie in Deutschland: Impulse aus der deutschen Einheit* (Marburg: Schüren, 1996).

Klatt, H., 'Reform und Perspektiven des Föderalismus in der Bundesrepublik Deutschland. Stärkung der Länder als Modernisierungskonzept', *Aus Politik und Zeitgeschichte*, B 28/1986, pp. 3–21.

Knies, W., 'Auf dem Weg in den "verfassungsgerichtlichen Jurisdiktionsstaat"? Das Bundesverfassungsgericht und die gewaltenteilende Kompetenzordnung des Grundgesetzes', in J. Burmeister (ed.), *Verfassungsstaatlichkeit: Festschrift für Klaus Stern zum 65. Geburtstag* (Munich: Beck, 1997), pp. 1155–82.

Koch, S., 'Die Wahl der Richter des BVerfG', *Zeitschrift für Rechtspolitik*, 29 (1996), pp. 41–4.

Kohler-Koch, B., *Die Gestaltungsmacht organisierter Interessen*, in B. Kohler-Koch and M. Jachtenfuchs (eds), *Europäische Integration* (Opladen: Leske & Budrich, 1996), pp. 193–222.

Kohler-Koch, B., 'Bundeskanzler Kohl – Baumeister Europas. Randbemerkungen zu einem zentralen Thema', mimeo, Mannheim, 1998.

Kolinsky, E., 'Das Parteiensystem der Bundesrepublik: Forschungsthemen und Entwicklungslinien', in O. Niedermayer and R. Stöss (eds), *Stand und Perspektiven der Parteienforschung in Deutschland* (Opladen: Westdeutscher Verlag, 1993), pp. 35–56.

Kommers, D. P., *The Constitutional Jurisprudence of the Federal Republic of Germany*, 2nd edn (Durham/London: Duke University Press, 1997).

König, K., *Modernisierung von Staat und Verwaltung* (Baden-Baden: Nomos, 1997).

Korte, K.-R., 'Kommt es auf die Person des Kanzlers an? Zum Regierungsstil von Helmut Kohl in der "Kanzlerdemokratie" des deutschen "Parteienstaates"', *Zeitschrift für Parlamentsfragen*, 29 (1998), pp. 387–401.

Krippendorff, E., 'Das Ende des Parteienstaates', *Der Monat*, 14 (1962), pp. 64–70.

Krockow, C. Graf von and Lösche, P. (eds), *Parteien in der Krise* (Munich: Beck, 1986).

Kropp, S. and Sturm, R., *Koalitionen und Koalitionsvereinbarungen. Theorie, Analyse und Dokumentation* (Opladen: Leske & Budrich, 1998).

Kutscha, M., 'Das Bundesverfassungsgericht und der Zeitgeist', *Neue Justiz*, 50 (1998), pp. 171–5.

Laakso, M. and Taagepera, R., 'Effective Number of Parties. A Measure with Application to West Europe', *Comparative Political Studies*, 12 (1979), pp. 3–27.

Landfried, C., 'Constitutional Review and Legislation: in the Federal Republic of Germany', in C. Landfried (ed.) *Constitutional Review and Legislation. An International Comparison* (Baden-Baden: Nomos, 1988), pp. 147–67.

Landfried, C., 'The Judicialisation of Politics in Germany', *International Political Science Review*, 15 (1994), pp. 113–24.

Landfried, C., *Bundesverfassungsgericht und Gesetzgeber*, 2nd edn (Baden-Baden: Nomos, 1996).

Lane, J.-E., MacKay, D. and Newton, K., *Political Data Handbook: OECD Countries*, 2nd edn (Oxford: Oxford University Press, 1997).

Lang, G. and Welzel, P., 'Budgetdefizite, Wahlzyklen und Geldpolitik: Empirische Ergebnisse für die Bundesrepublik Deutschland 1962–1989', *Institut für Volkswirtschaftslehre der Universität Augsburg*, Beitrag no. 63 (1991).

Lange, E. H. M., *Wahlrecht und Innenpolitik: Entstehungsgeschichte und Analyse der Wahlgesetzgebung und Wahlrechtsdiskussion im westlichen Nachkriegsdeutschland, 1945–1956* (Meisenheim am Glan: Hain, 1975).

Laufer, H., 'Verfassungsordnung und Verfassungsentwicklung', in F. Schneider (ed.), *Der Weg der Bundesrepublik von 1945 bis zur Gegenwart* (Munich: Beck, 1985), pp. 154–76.

Leaman, J., 'The Bundesbank. Unelected Government of Germany and Europe?', *Debatte*, 1 (1993), pp. 8–32.

Lehmbruch, G., *Parteienwettbewerb im Bundesstaat* (Stuttgart: Kohlhammer, 1976).

Lehmbruch, G., 'Concertation and the Structure of Corporatist Networks', in J. Goldthorpe (ed.), *Order and Conflict in Contemporary Capitalism* (Oxford: Clarendon Press, 1984), pp. 60–80.

Lehmbruch, G., *Parteienwettbewerb im Bundesstaat. Regelsysteme und Spannungslagen im Institutionengefüge der Bundesrepublik Deutschland*, 2nd edn (Opladen: Westdeutscher Verlag, 1998).

Leicht, R., 'Die Mauern eines Amtes', *Zeit–Punkte*, no. 2 (1994), pp. 5–7.

Lenz, C., 'Die Wahlrechtsgleichheit und das Bundesverfassungsgericht', *Archiv des öffentlichen Rechts*, 121 (1996), pp. 337–58.

Lenz, C., 'Grundmandatsklausel und Überhangmandate vor dem Bundesverfassungsgericht', *Neue Juristische Wochenschrift*, 50 (1997), pp. 1534–7.

Lepsius, M. R., 'Parteiensystem und Sozialstruktur zum Problem der Demokratisierung der deutschen Gesellschaft', in W. Abel and K. Borchardt, (eds) *Wirtschaft, Geschichte und Wirtschaftsgeschichte* (Stuttgart: Fischer, 1966), pp. 371–93.

Ley, R., 'Die Wahl der Mitglieder des Bundesverfassungsgerichtes. Eine Dokumentation anläßlich des 40jährigen Bestehens', *Zeitschrift für Parlamentsfragen*, 22 (1991), pp. 420–49.

Lietzmann, H. J., *Das Bundesverfassungsgericht. Eine sozialwissenschaftliche Studie* (Opladen: Leske & Budrich, 1985).

Lietzmann, H. J. '"Reflexiver Konstitutionalismus" und Demokratie. Die moderne Gesellschaft überholt die Verfassungsrechtsprechung', in B. Guggenberger and Th. Würtenberger (eds), *Hüter der Verfassung oder Lenker der Politik? Das Bundesverfassungsgericht im Widerstreit* (Baden-Baden: Nomos, 1998), pp. 233–61.

Lijphart, A., *Democracies: Patterns of Majoritarian and Consensus Government in Twenty-One Countries* (New Haven/London: Yale University Press, 1984).

Lijphart, A. (ed.), *Parliamentary versus Presidential Government* (Oxford: Oxford University Press, 1992).

Lipset, S. M. and Rokkan, S., 'Cleavage Structures, Party Systems, and Voter Alignments: an Introduction', in S. M. Lipset and S. Rokkan (eds), *Party Systems and Voter Alignments: Cross-National Perspectives* (New York: Free Press, 1967), pp. 1–64.

Loewenberg, G., *Parlamentarismus im politischen System der Bundesrepublik Deutschland* (Tübingen: Wunderlich, 1969).

Lohmann, S., 'Designing a Central Bank in a Federal System: the Deutsche Bundesbank, 1957–1992', P. Syklos (ed.), *Varieties of Monetary Reforms: Lessons and Experiences on the Road to Monetary Union* (Boston: Kluwer Academic Publishers, 1994), pp. 247–77.

Lösche, P., *Kleine Geschichte der deutschen Parteien* (Stuttgart: Kohlhammer, 1993).

Lösche, P. and Walter, F., *Die SPD: Klassenpartei–Volkspartei–Quotenpartei* (Darmstadt: Wissenschaftliche Buchgesellschaft, 1992).

Lowi, Th. J., 'American Business, Public Policy, Case Studies, and Political Theory', *World Politics*, 17 (1964), pp. 677–715.

Lowndes, V., 'Varieties of New Institutionalism: a Critical Appraisal', *Public Administration*, 74 (1996), pp. 181–97.

Luthardt, W., 'Europäischer Integrationsprozeß, deutscher Föderalismus und Verhandlungsprozesse in einem Mehrebenensystem: Beteiligungsföderalismus als Zukunftsmodell', *Staatswissenschaften und Staatspraxis*, 7 (1996), pp. 293–316.

Mahrenholz, E. G., 'Das richterliche Sondervotum', in W. Hoppe, W. Krawietz and M. Schulte (eds), *Rechtsprechungslehre – 2. Internationales Symposium Münster 1988* (Cologne: Carl Heymanns, 1992), pp. 167–71.

Mann, S., *Macht und Ohnmacht der Verbände: Das Beispiel des Bundesverbandes der Deutschen Industrie e.V. (BDI) aus empirisch-analytischer Sicht* (Baden-Baden: Nomos, 1994).

Manow, Ph., 'Informalisierung und Parteipolitisierung – Zum Wandel exekutiver Entscheidungsprozesse in der Bundesrepublik', *Zeitschrift für Parlamentsfragen*, 27 (1996), pp. 96–107.

Maor, M., *Political Parties and Party Systems. Comparative Approaches and the British Experience* (London: Routledge, 1997).

March, J. G. and Olsen, J. P., *Democratic Governance* (New York: Free Press, 1995).

Marsh, D., *Die Bundesbank: Geschäfte mit der Macht* (Munich: Bertelsmann, 1995).

Mattson, I., 'Private Members' Initiatives and Amendments', in H. Döring (ed.), *Parliaments and Majority Rule in Western Europe* (Frankfurt a.m./New York: Campus/St Martin's Press, 1995), pp. 448–87.

McKay, J., 'Berlin–Brandenburg? Nein danke! The Referendums on the Proposed *Länderfusion*', *German Politics*, 5 (1996), pp. 485–502.

Meyer, H., *Wahlsystem und Verfassungsordnung: Bedeutung und Grenzen wahlsystematischer Gestaltung nach dem Grundgesetz* (Frankfurt a.m.: Metzner, 1973).

Meyer, H., 'Wahlgrundsätze und Wahlverfahren', in J. Isensee and P. Kirchhof (eds), *Handbuch des Staatsrechts der Bundesrepublik Deutschland*, vol. 2 (Heidelberg: C. F. Müller, 1987), pp. 269–311.

Meyer, H., 'Der Überhang und anderes Unterhaltsames aus Anlaß der Bundestagswahl 1994', *Kritische Vierteljahresschrift für Gesetzgebung und Rechtswissenschaft*, 77 (1994), pp. 312–62.

Michels, R., *Zur Soziologie des Parteiwesens in der modernen Demokratie*, reprint of the 2nd edn (Leipzig, 1911), ed. by W. Conze (Stuttgart: Kroener, 1957).

Milatz, A., 'Reichstagswahlen und Mandatsverteilung 1871 bis 1918. Ein Beitrag zu Problemen des absoluten Mehrheitswahlrechts', in G. A. Ritter (ed.), *Gesellschaft, Parlament und Regierung: Zur Geschichte des Parlamentarismus in Deutschland* (Düsseldorf: Droste, 1974), pp. 207–33.

Mintzel, A. and Oberreuter, H. (eds), *Parteien in der Bundesrepublik Deutschland*, 2nd edn (Bonn: Bundeszentrale für politische Bildung, 1992).

Mintzel, A. and Schmitt, H., 'Krise der Parteiendemokratie? Zu Funktionen, Leistungen und Defiziten der Parteien in der parlamentarischen Demokratie', *Politische Bildung* (1981), pp. 3–16.

Möller, H., 'Die Westdeutsche Währungsreform von 1948', in Deutsche Bundesbank (ed.), *Währung und Wirtschaft in Deutschland, 1876–1975* (Frankfurt a.M.: Fritz Knapp Verlag, 1976), pp. 433–83.

Morsey, R., *Heinrich Lübke* (Paderborn: Ferdinand Schöningh, 1996).

Müller, W. C. and Strøm, K., 'Koalitionsregierungen in Westeuropa – eine Einleitung, in W. C. Müller and K. Strøm (eds), *Koalitionsregierungen in Westeuropa: Bildung, Arbeitsweise und Beendigung* (Vienna: Signum, 1997), pp. 9–45.

Müller-Rommel, F., 'The Chancellor and His Staff', in S. Padgett (ed.), *Adenauer to Kohl: The Development of the German Chancellorship* (London: Hurst & Company, 1994), pp. 106–26.

Münch, I. von (ed.), *Grundgesetzkommentar*, vol. 2 (Munich: Beck, 1976).

Murswieck, A., 'Parlament, Regierung und Verwaltung. "Parlamentarisches Regierungssystem" oder "Politisches System"?', in S. von Bandemer and G. Wewer (eds), *Regierungssystem und Regierungslehre: Fragestellungen, Analysekonzepte und Forschungsstand eines Kernbereichs der Politikwissenschaft* (Opladen: Leske & Budrich, 1989), pp. 149–57.

Neugebauer, G. and Stöss, R., *Die PDS: Geschichte. Organisation. Wähler. Konkurrenten* (Opladen: Leske & Budrich, 1996).

Neumann, M. J. M., 'Geldwertstabilität: Bedrohung und Bewährung', in Deutsche Bundesbank (ed.), *Fünfzig Jahre Deutsche Mark: Notenbank und Währung in Deutschland seit 1948* (Munich: Beck, 1998), pp. 309–46.

Niclauss, K., *Kanzlerdemokratie – Bonner Regierungspraxis von Konrad Adenauer bis Helmut Kohl* (Stuttgart: Kohlhammer, 1988).

Niclauss, K., 'Le Gouvernement fédéral', *Pouvoirs*, no. 66 (1993), pp. 99–120.

Niclauss, K., *Das Parteiensystem der Bundesrepublik Deutschland* (Paderborn: Schöningh, 1995).

Niclauss, K., *Der Weg zum Grundgesetz. Demokratiegründung in Westdeutschland 1945–1949* (Paderborn: Schöningh, 1998).

Niedermayer, O., 'Party System Change in East Germany', *German Politics*, 4 (1995), pp. 75–91.

Niedermayer, O., 'Das intermediäre System', in M. Kaase, A. Eisen, O. W. Gabriel, O. Niedermayer and H. Wollmann (eds), *Politisches System: Berichte zum sozialen und politischen Wandel in Ostdeutschland*, vol. 3 (Opladen: Leske & Budrich, 1996), pp. 155–230.

Niedermayer, O., 'Zur systematischen Analyse der Entwicklung von Parteiensystemen', in O. W. Gabriel and J. W. Falter (eds), *Wahlen und politische Einstellungen in westlichen Demokratien* (Frankfurt a. M.: Lang, 1996), pp. 19–49.

Niedermayer, O., 'Das gesamtdeutsche Parteiensystem', in O. W. Gabriel, O. Niedermayer and R. Stöss (eds), *Parteiendemokratie in Deutschland* (Bonn/Opladen: Bundeszentrale für politische Bildung/Westdeutscher Verlag, 1997), pp. 106–130.

Niedermayer, O., 'Der neue Faktor PDS. Die Zukunft des Parteiensystems', in Deutsches Institut für Fernstudienforschung (ed.), *Funkkolleg 'Deutschland im Umbruch'*, Studienbrief 3 (Tübingen: DIFF, 1997), pp. 10/1–10/40.

Niedermayer, O. and Stöss, R. (eds), *Stand und Perspektiven der Parteienforschung in Deutschland* (Opladen: Westdeutscher Verlag, 1993).

Nohlen, D., *Wahlsysteme der Welt: Daten und Analysen. Ein Handbuch* (Munich: Piper, 1978).

Nohlen, D. *Wahlrecht und Parteiensystem* (Opladen: Leske & Budrich, 1986).

Nohlen, D., *Elections and Electoral Systems*, 2nd edn (New Dehli: Macmillan India Limited, 1996).

Oberreuter, H. (ed.), *Parlamentsreform* (Passau: Passavia, 1981).

Olsen, J. P., 'Analysing Institutional Dynamics', *Staatswissenschaften und Staatspraxis*, 3 (1992), pp. 247–71.

Olson, M., 'The Principle of "Fiscal Equivalence". The Division of Responsibilities between Different Levels of Government', *American Economic Review*, 59 (1969), pp. 479–87.

Olson, M., *Die Logik des kollektiven Handelns: Kollektivgüter und die Theorie der Gruppen*, 3rd edn (Tübingen: Mohr, 1992).

Padgett, S., 'The Chancellor and his Party', in S. Padgett (ed.), *Adenauer to Kohl: The Development of the German Chancellorship* (London: Hurst & Company, 1994), pp. 44–77.

Padgett, S., 'Introduction: Chancellors and the Chancellorship', in S. Padgett (ed.), *Adenauer to Kohl: The Development of the German Chancellorship* (London: Hurst & Company, 1994), pp. 1–19.

Padgett, S., 'Interest Groups in the Five New Länder', in G. Smith, W. Paterson and S. Padgett (eds), *Developments in German Politics 2* (London: Macmillan, 1996), pp. 233–47.

Pappi, F. U., 'Die Abwahl Kohls. Hauptergebnis der Bundestagswahl 1998', *Zeitschrift für Politik*, 46 (1999), pp. 1–29.

Parkes, S., *Understanding Contemporary Germany* (London/New York: Routledge, 1997).

Paterson, W. E., 'Helmut Kohl, the Vision Thing and Escaping the Semi-Sovereignty Trap', *German Politics*, 7 (1998), pp. 18–35.

Patzelt, W. 'Deutsche Politik unter Reformdruck', in R. Hettlage and K. Lenz (eds), *Deutschland nach der Wende: Eine Zwischenbilanz* (Munich: Beck, 1995), pp. 68–92.

Pehle, H., 'Ist das Wahlrecht in Bund und Ländern reformbedürftig? Eine Bilanz seiner Mängel und Ungereimtheiten nach 50 Jahren', *Gegenwartskunde*, 48 (1999), pp. 233–56.

Pestalozza, C., *Verfassungsprozeßrecht. Die Verfassungsgerichtsbarkeit des Bundes und der Länder mit einem Anhang zum Internationalen Rechtsschutz*, 3rd edn (Munich: Beck, 1991).

Peters, B. G., 'Political Institutions, Old and New', in R. E. Goodin and H.-D. Klingemann (eds), *A New Handbook of Political Science* (Oxford: Oxford University Press, 1996), pp. 205–20.

Piazzolo, M. (ed.), *Das Bundesverfassungsgericht. Ein Gericht im Schnittpunkt von Recht und Politik* (Mainz: v. Hase & Koehler, 1996).

Pieper, S. U., *Verfassungsrichterwahlen* (Berlin: Duncker & Humblot, 1998).

Poguntke, Th., 'Der Stand der Forschung zu den Grünen: Zwischen Ideologie und Empirie', in O. Niedermayer and R. Stöss (eds), *Stand und Perspektiven der Parteienforschung in Deutschland* (Opladen:Westdeutscher Verlag, 1993), pp. 187–210.

Poguntke, Th., 'Parteiorganisationen in der Bundesrepublik Deutschland. Einheit in der Vielfalt?', in O. W. Gabriel, O. Niedermayer and R. Stöss (eds), *Parteiendemokratie in Deutschland* (Bonn/Opladen: Bundeszentrale für politische Bildung/Westdeutscher Verlag, 1997), pp. 257–76.

Pulzer, P., 'Germany', in V. Bogdanor and D. Butler (eds), *Democracy and Elections. Electoral Systems and their Political Consequences* (Cambridge: Cambridge University Press, 1983), pp. 84–109.

Pulzer, P., 'Stabilität und Immobilität', in W. Bleek and H. Maull (eds), *Ein ganz normaler Staat? Perspektiven nach 40 Jahren Bundesrepublik* (Munich: Piper, 1989), pp. 117–27.

Radunski, P., 'Fit für die Zukunft?', *Sonde*, 24 (1991), pp. 3–8.

Rae, D., *The Political Consequences of Electoral Laws* (New Haven: Yale University Press, 1967).

Rau, C., *Selbst entwickelte Grenzen in der Rechtsprechung des United States Supreme Court und des Bundesverfassungsgerichts* (Berlin: Duncker & Humblot, 1996).

Rausch, H., *Der Bundespräsident* (Munich: Bayerische Landeszentrale für politische Bildungsarbeit, 1979).

Reissenberger, M., 'Wer bewacht die Wächter? Zur Diskussion um die Rolle des Verfassungsgerichts', *Aus Politik und Zeitgeschichte*, B 15/1997, pp. 11–20.

Reißig, R., 'Transformationsforschung: Gewinne, Desiderate und Perspektiven', *Politische Vierteljahresschrift*, 39 (1998), pp. 301–28.

Rensing, M., *Geschichte und Politik in den Reden der deutschen Bundespräsidenten 1949–1984* (Münster/New York: Waxmann, 1996).

Renzsch, W., *Finanzverfassung und Finanzausgleich: Die Auseinandersetzungen um ihre politische Gestaltung in der Bundesrepublik Deutschland zwischen Währungsreform und deutscher Vereinigung (1948–1990)* (Bonn: Dietz, 1991).

Renzsch, W., 'Föderative Problembewältigung: Zur Einbeziehung der neuen Länder in einen gesamtdeutschen Finanzausgleich ab 1995', *Zeitschrift für Parlamentsfragen* 25 (1994), pp. 116–38.

Rieger, G., '"Parteienverdrossenheit" und "Parteienkritik" in der Bundesrepublik Deutschland', *Zeitschrift für Parlamentsfragen*, 25 (1994), pp. 459–71.

Riggs, F. W., 'Presidentialism versus Parliamentarism: Implications for Representativeness and Legitimacy', *International Political Science Review*, 18 (1997), pp. 253–78.

Rinck, H.-J., 'Die Vorprüfung der Verfassungsbeschwerde', *Neue Jursitische Wochenschrift*, 12 (1959), pp. 169–216.

Roberts, G. K., 'The Federal Republic of Germany', in S. E. Finer (ed.), *Adversary Politics and Electoral Reform* (London: Anthony Wigram, 1975), pp. 203–22.

Roberts, G. K., 'The "Second–vote" Strategy of the West German Free Democratic Party', *European Journal of Political Research*, 16 (1988), pp. 317–37.

Rockman, B. A., 'Entrepreneur in the Constitutional Marketplace: the Development of the Presidency', in P. F. Nardulli (ed.), *The Constitution and American Political Development: An Institutional Perspective* (Urbana/Chicago: University of Illinois Press, 1992), pp. 97–120.

Rockman, B. A., 'Institutions, Democratic Stability, and Performance, in M. Heper, A. Kazancigil and B. A. Rockman (eds), *Institutions and Democratic Statecraft* (Boulder,Col.: Westview Press, 1997), pp. 11–34.

Roeper, H. and Weimer, W., *Die D-Mark: eine deutsche Wirtschaftsgeschichte* (Frankfurt a.M.: Societäts-Verlag, 1996).

Rohe, K., *Wahlen und Wählertraditionen in Deutschland* (Frankfurt a.M.: Suhrkamp, 1992).

Rose, R., 'Governments against Sub-Governments: a European Perspective on Washington', in R. Rose and E. N. Suleiman (eds), *Presidents and Prime Ministers* (Washington, DC: American Enterprise Institute, 1980), pp. 284–347.

Roth, R. and Rucht, D. (eds), *Neue soziale Bewegungen in der Bundesrepublik Deutschland*, 2nd edn (Bonn: Bundeszentrale für politische Bildung, 1991).

Rothstein, B., 'Political Institutions: an Overview', in R. E. Goodin and H.-D. Klingemann (eds), *A New Handbook of Political Science* (Oxford: Oxford University Press, 1996), pp. 133–66.

Rudzio, W., 'Informelle Entscheidungsmuster in Bonner Koalitionsregierungen', in H.-H. Hartwich and G. Wewer (eds), *Regieren in der Bundesrepublik II* (Opladen: Leske & Budrich, 1991), pp. 125–41.

Rudzio, W., 'Der demokratische Verfassungsstaat als Beute der Parteien?', in W. Gellner and H.-J. Veen (eds), *Umbruch und Wandel in westeuropäischen Parteiensystemen* (Frankfurt a.M.: Lang, 1995), pp. 1–15.

Rudzio, W., *Das politische System der Bundesrepublik Deutschland. Eine Einführung*, 4th edn (Opladen: Leske & Budrich/UTB, 1996).

Rudzio, W., 'Freiheitliche demokratische Grundordnung und wehrhafte Demokratie', in P. Massing (ed.), *Das Demokratiemodell der Bundesrepublik Deutschland* (Schwalbach: Wochenschau, 1996), pp. 11–22.

Rupp, H. H., 'Ausschaltung des Bundesverfassungsgerichts durch den Amsterdamer Vertrag?', *Juristen Zeitung*, 53 (1998), pp. 213–17.

Rusconi, G. E., 'Quale "democrazia costituzionale"? La corte federale nella politica tedesca e il problema della costituzione europea', *Rivista Italiana di Scienza Politica*, 27 (1997), pp. 272–306.

Saalfeld, Th., *Parteisoldaten und Rebellen: Fraktionen im Deutschen Bundestag 1949–1990* (Opladen: Leske & Budrich, 1995).

Saalfeld, Th., 'The German Bundestag: Influence and Accountability in a Complex Environment', in Ph. Norton (ed.), *Parliaments and Governments in Western Europe* (London: Frank Cass, 1998), pp. 44–72.

Säcker, H., 'Gesetzgebung durch das Bundesverfassungsgericht? Das Bundesverfassungsgericht und die Legislative', in M. Piazzolo (ed.), *Das Bundesverfassungsgericht: Ein Gericht im Schnittpunkt von Recht und Politik* (Mainz/Munich: v. Hase & Koehler, 1996), pp. 189–225.

Sartori, G., *Parties and Party Systems: A Framework for Analysis* (Cambridge: Cambridge University Press, 1976).

Sartori, G., 'Neither Presidentialism nor Parliamentarism', in J. J. Linz and A. Valenzuela (eds), *The Failure of Presidential Democracy: Comparative Perspectives* (Baltimore/London: Johns Hopkins University Press, 1994), pp. 106–18.

Scarrow, S., 'Party Competition and Institutional Change. The Expansion of Direct Democracy in Germany', *Party Politics*, 3 (1997), pp. 451–91.

Schanbacher, E., *Parlamentarische Wahlen und Wahlsystem in der Weimarer Republik: Wahlgesetzgebung und Wahlreform im Reich und in den Ländern* (Düsseldorf: Droste, 1982).

Scharpf, F. W., 'Die Politikverflechtungsfalle', *Politische Vierteljahresschrift*, 26 (1985), pp. 323–56.

Scharpf, F. W., *Optionen des Föderalismus in Deutschland und Europa* (Frankfurt a.M.: Campus, 1994).

Scharpf, F. W. and Benz, A., *Kooperation als Alternative zur Neugliederung? Zusammenarbeit zwischen den norddeutschen Ländern* (Baden-Baden: Nomos, 1991).

Scharpf, F. W., Reissert, B. and Schnabel, F., *Politikverflechtung: Theorie und Empirie des kooperativen Föderalismus in der Bundesrepublik*, 2 vols (Kronberg/Ts.: Scriptor, 1976/77).

Schattschneider, E. E., *Party Government* (New York: Holt, Rinehart and Winston, 1942).

Schäuble, Th., 'Gewaltenteilung und Bundesverfassungsgericht', *Recht und Politik*, 32 (1996), pp. 66–70.

Schäuble, W., *Der Vertrag: Wie ich über die deutsche Einheit verhandelte* (Stuttgart: DVA, 1991).

Scheer, H., *Parteien kontra Bürger? Die Zukunft der Parteiendemokratie* (Munich: Piper, 1979).

Scheuch, E. K. and Scheuch, U., *Cliquen, Klüngel und Karrieren* (Reinbek b. Hamburg: Rowohlt, 1992).

Schindler, P., *Datenhandbuch zur Geschichte des Deutschen Bundestages, 1949–1982* (Baden-Baden: Nomos, 1983).

Schindler, P., *Datenhandbuch zur Geschichte des Deutschen Bundestages, 1983–1991* (Baden-Baden: Nomos, 1994).

Schlaich, K., 'Die Funktionen des Bundespräsidenten im Verfassungsgefüge', in J. Isensee and P. Kirchhof (eds), *Handbuch des Staatsrechts der Bundesrepublik Deutschland*, vol. 2 (Heidelberg: C. F. Müller, 1987), pp. 541–84.

Schlaich, K., *Das Bundesverfassungsgericht. Stellung, Verfahren, Entscheidungen*, 4th edn (Munich: Beck, 1997).

Schmalz-Bruns, R., *Reflexive Demokratie* (Baden-Baden: Nomos, 1995).

Schmid, J., *Die CDU* (Opladen: Leske & Budrich, 1990).

Schmid, P., 'Monetary Policy: Targets and Instruments', in S. Frowen and R. Pringle (eds), *Inside the Bundesbank* (London: Macmillan, 1998), pp. 32–44.

Schmidt, M. G., 'Allerweltsparteien in Westeuropa? Ein Beitrag zu Kirchheimers These vom Wandel des westeuropäischen Parteiensystems', *Leviathan*, 13 (1985), pp. 376–97.

Schmidt, M. G., 'Learning from Catastrophes: West Germany's Public Policy', in F. G. Castles (ed.), *The Comparative History of Public Policy* (Cambridge: Cambridge University Press, 1989), pp. 56–99.

Schmidt, M. G., *Regieren in der Bundesrepublik Deutschland* (Opladen: Leske & Budrich, 1992).

Schmidt, M. G., 'The Parties-Do-Matter-Hypothesis and the Case of the Federal Republic of Germany', *German Politics*, 4 (1995), pp. 1–21.

Schmidt, M. G., 'Germany: the Grand Coalition State', in J. M. Colomer (ed.), *Political Institutions in Europe* (London/New York: Routledge, 1995), pp. 62–98.

Schmidt, U., 'Sieben Jahre nach der Einheit. Die ostdeutsche Parteienlandschaft im Vorfeld der Bundestagswahlen 1998', *Aus Politik und Zeitgeschichte*, B 1-2/1998, pp. 37–53.

Schmitt Glaeser, W., 'Das Bundesverfassungsgericht als "Gegengewalt" zum verfassungsändernden Gesetzgeber? – Lehren aus dem Diäten-Streit 1995', in J. Burmeister (ed.), *Verfassungsstaatlichkeit. Festschrift für Klaus Stern zum 65. Geburtstag* (Munich: Beck, 1997), pp. 1183–99.

Schmitt, C., 'Der Hüter der Verfassung', *Archiv des öffentlichen Rechts*, 55 (1928), pp. 161–237.

Schmitt-Beck, R., 'Denn sie wissen nicht, was sie tun ... Zum Verständnis des Verfahrens der Bundestagswahl bei westdeutschen und ostdeutschen Wählern', *Zeitschrift für Parlamentsfragen*, 24 (1993), pp. 393–415.

Schneider, H.-P. and Zeh, W., 'Koalitionen, Kanzlerwahl und Kabinettsbildung', in H.-P. Schneider and W. Zeh (eds), *Parlamentsrecht und Parlamentspraxis in der Bundesrepublik Deutschland* (Berlin/New York: de Gruyter, 1989), pp. 1297–324.

Schoen, H., 'Stimmensplitting bei Bundestagswahlen: eine Form taktischer Wahlentscheidung?', *Zeitschrift für Parlamentsfragen*, 29 (1998), pp. 223–43.

Scholz, G., *Die Bundespräsidenten*, 2nd edn (Heidelberg: Decker Müller, 1992).

Scholz, R., 'Die Befugnisse des Kanzlers haben an Substanz verloren', *Die Welt*, 5 April 1989.

Schönbohm, W., *Die CDU wird moderne Volkspartei* (Stuttgart: Klett-Cotta, 1985).

Schreckenberger, W., 'Veränderungen im parlamentarischen Regierungssystem: Zur Oligarchie der Spitzenpolitiker der Parteien', in K. D. Bracher, P. Mikat, K. Repgen, M. Schumacher and H.-P. Schwarz (eds), *Staat und Parteien: Festschrift für Rudolf Morsey zum 65. Geburtstag* (Berlin: Duncker & Humblot, 1992), pp. 133–57.

Schreckenberger, W., 'Informelle Verfahren der Entscheidungsvorbereitung zwischen der Bundesregierung und den Mehrheitsfraktionen: Koalitionsgespräche und Koalitionsrunden', *Zeitschrift für Parlamentsfragen*, 25 (1994), pp. 29–346.

Schultze, R.-O., 'Wieviel Asymmetrie verträgt der Föderalismus?', in D. Berg-Schlosser, G. Riescher and A. Waschkuhn (eds), *Politikwissenschaftliche Spiegelungen: Festschrift für Theo Stammen* (Opladen: Westdeutscher Verlag, 1998), pp. 199–216.

Schulze-Fielitz, H., 'Das Bundesverfassungsgericht in der Krise des Zeitgeists. Zur Metadogmatik der Verfassungsinterpretation', *Archiv des öffentlichen Rechts*, 122 (1997), pp. 1–31.

Sebaldt, M., *Organisierter Pluralismus: Kräftefeld, Selbstverständnis und politische Arbeit deutscher Interessengruppen* (Opladen: Westdeutscher Verlag, 1997).

Sebaldt, M., 'Verbände und Demokratie: Funktionen bundesdeutscher Interessengruppen in Theorie und Praxis', *Aus Politik und Zeitgeschichte*, B 36-37/1997, pp. 27-37.

Seibel, W., 'Historische Analyse und politikwissenschaftliche Institutionenforschung', in A. Benz and W. Seibel (eds), *Theorieentwicklung in der Politikwissenschaft – eine Zwischenbilanz* (Baden-Baden: Nomos, 1997), pp. 357–76.

Shepsle, K. A., 'Representation and Governance: the Great Legislative Trade-Off', *Political Science Quarterly*, 103 (1988), pp. 461–84.

Simon, H., 'Verfassungsgerichtsbarkeit', in E. Benda, W. Maihofer and H.-J. Vogel (eds), *Handbuch des Verfassungsrechts der Bundesrepublik Deutschland*, 2nd edn (Berlin/New York: de Gruyter, 1994), pp. 1637-77.

Simonis, G. (ed.), *Deutschland nach der Wende. Neue Politikstrukturen* (Opladen: Leske & Budrich, 1998).

Smith, G., 'A System Perspective on Party System Change', *Journal of Theoretical Politics*, 1 (1989), pp. 349–64.

Smith, G., 'Structures of Government', in G. Smith, W. E. Paterson and P. H. Merkl (eds), *Developments in West German Politics* (London: Macmillan, 1989), pp. 24–39.

Smith, G., 'The Party System at the Crossroads', in G. Smith, W. Paterson and S. Padgett (eds), *Developments in German Politics 2* (London: Macmillan, 1996), pp. 55–75.

Sorauf, F. J., 'Political Parties and Political Analysis', in W. N. Chambers and W. D. Burnham (eds), *The American Party Systems*, 2nd edn (New York: Oxford University Press, 1975), pp. 33–55.

Southern, D., 'The Chancellor and the Constitution', in S. Padgett (ed.), *Adenauer to Kohl: The Development of the German Chancellorship* (London: Hurst & Company, 1994), pp. 20–41.

Spindler, J. von, Becker, W. and Starke, E., *Die Deutsche Bundesbank: Grundzüge des Notenbankwesens und Kommentar zum Gesetz über die Deutsche Bundesbank* (Stuttgart: Kohlhammer, 1973).

Steinberg, R., 'Zur Institutionalisierung des Verbandseinflusses in einem Bundeswirtschafts- und Sozialrat', *Die Öffentliche Verwaltung*, 25 (1972), pp. 837–45.

Steininger, R., *Deutsche Geschichte, 1945–61*, vol. 1 (Frankfurt a.M.: Fischer, 1983).

Stern, K., 'Die Notenbank im Staatsgefüge', in Deutsche Bundesbank (ed.), *Fünfzig Jahre Deutsche Mark: Notenbank und Währung in Deutschland seit 1948* (Munich: Beck, 1998), pp. 141–98.

Stoiber, E., *Föderaler Wettbewerb: Deutschlands Stärke – Bayerns Chance, Regierungserklärung des Bayerischen Ministerpräsidenten vom 4.2.1998 im Bayerischen Landtag* (Munich: Press release, 1998).

Stöss, R., 'Einleitung: Struktur und Entwicklung des Parteiensystems der Bundesrepublik – Eine Theorie', in R. Stöss (ed.), *Parteien–Handbuch*, vol. 1, *Sonderausgabe* (Opladen: Westdeutscher Verlag, 1986), pp. 17–309.

Stöss, R., *Die extreme Rechte in der Bundesrepublik* (Opladen: Westdeutscher Verlag, 1989).

Streeck, W. and Schmitter, P. C., 'From National Corporatism to Transnational Pluralism: Organized Interests in the Single European Market', in V. Eichener and H. Voelzkow (eds), *Europäische Integration und verbandliche Interessenvermittlung* (Marburg: Metropolis, 1994), pp. 181–215.

Sturm, R., 'The Changing Territorial Balance', in G. Smith, W. Paterson and S. Padgett (eds), *Developments in German Politics 2* (London: Macmillan, 1996), pp. 119–34.

Sturm, R., 'The States as Laboratories', in F. Gress, D. Fechtner and M. Hannes (eds), *The American Federal System: Federal Balance in Comparative Perspective* (Frankfurt a.M.: Lang, 1994), pp. 141–5.

Sturm, R., 'The Constitution under Pressure: Emerging Asymmetrical Federalism in Germany?'. Paper, IPSA Congress Berlin, 1994, to be published in B. Agranoff (ed.), *Asymmetrical Federalism* (Baden-Baden: Nomos, 1999) (forthcoming).

Sturm, R., 'Party Competition and the Federal System: the Lehmbruch Hypothesis Revisited', in C. Jeffery (ed.), *Recasting German Federalism: The Legacies of Unification* (London/New York: Pinter, 1999), pp. 197–216.

Sturm, R., 'Multi-level Politics of Regional Development in Germany', *European Planning Studies*, 6 (1998), pp. 525–36.

Stüwe, K., 'Der "Gang nach Karlsruhe". Die Opposition im Bundestag als Antragsstellerin vor dem Bundesverfassungsgericht', *Zeitschrift für Parlamentsfragen*, 28 (1997), pp. 545–57.

Teufel, E., *Rede des Vorsitzenden der Ministerpräsidentenkonferenz der Länder beim Festakt '50 Jahre Rittersturz–Konferenz' am 9. Juli in Koblenz* (Staatsministerium Baden-Württemberg: Press release, 1998).

Tietmeyer, H., 'The Bundesbank: Committed to Stability', in S. Frowen and R. Pringle (eds), *Inside the Bundesbank* (London: Macmillan, 1998), pp. 1–10.

Töller, A. E., *Europapolitik im Bundestag. Eine empirische Untersuchung zur europapolitischen Willensbildung im EG–Ausschuß des 12. Deutschen Bundestages* (Frankfurt a.M.: Lang, 1995).

Vallinder, T., 'The Judicialization of Politics – a World-wide Phenomenon: Introduction', *International Political Science Review*, 15 (1994), pp. 91–9.

Vaubel, R., 'Eine Public-Choice-Analyse der Deutschen Bundesbank und ihre Implikationen für die Europäische Währungsunion', in D. Duwendag and J. Siebke (eds), *Europa vor dem Eintritt in die Wirtschafts- und Währungsunion* (Berlin: Duncker & Humblot, 1993), pp. 23–79.

Veen, H.-J., 'Zwischen Rekonzentration und neuer Diversifizierung. Tendenzen der Parteienentwicklung fünf Jahre nach der deutschen Einheit', in W. Gellner and H.-J. Veen (eds), *Umbruch und Wandel in westeuropäischen Parteiensystemen* (Frankfurt a.M.: Lang, 1995), pp. 117–33.

Wahl, R., 'Quo Vadis – Bundesverfassungsgericht? Zur Lage von Verfassungsgerichtsbarkeit und Staatsdenken', in B. Guggenberger and Th. Würtenberger (eds), *Das Bundesverfassungsgericht im Widerstreit* (Baden-Baden: Nomos, 1998), pp. 81–120.

Wandel, E., *Die Entstehung der Bank deutscher Länder und die deutsche Währungsreform 1948: Die Rekonstruktion des westdeutschen Geld- und Währungssystems 1945–1948 unter Berücksichtigung der amerikanischen Besatzungspolitik* (Frankfurt a.M.: Fritz Knapp, 1980).

Wassermann, R., 'Zur gegenwärtigen Krise des Bundesverfassungsgerichts', *Recht und Politik*, 32 (1996), pp. 61–5.

Weber, J., *Die Interessengruppen im politischen System der Bundesrepublik Deutschland*, 2nd edn (Munich: BLZ, 1981).

Wehler, W., 'Der Staatsgerichtshof für das Deutsche Reich: Die politische Rolle der Verfassungsgerichtsbarkeit in der Zeit der Weimarer Republik', PhD-dissertation, University of Bonn (1979).

Wengst, U., 'Vom Reichspräsidenten zum Bundespräsidenten', in Bundeszentrale für politische Bildung (ed.), *Deutsche Verfassungsgeschichte 1849–1919–1949*, (Bonn: without publisher), pp. 77–81.

Wenner, U., *Sperrklauseln im Wahlrecht der Bundesrepublik Deutschland* (Frankfurt a.M.: Peter Lang, 1986).

Werner, C., 'Das Dilemma parlamentarischer Opposition', in Dietrich Herzog, Hilke Rebenstorf and Bernhard Weßels (eds), *Parlament und Gesellschaft: Eine Funktionsanalyse der repräsentativen Demokratie* (Opladen: Westdeutscher Verlag, 1993), pp. 184–217.

Wewer, G., 'Das Bundesverfassungsgericht – eine Gegenregierung? Argumente zur Revision einer überkommenen Denkfigur', in B. Blanke and H. Wollmann (eds), *Die alte Bundesrepublik: Kontinuität und Wandel* (*Leviathan* Sonderheft 12/1991) (Opladen: Westdeutscher Verlag, 1991), pp. 310–35.

Wiedemeyer, W., *Roman Herzog* (Munich/Landsberg: Olzog, 1994).

Wiesendahl, E., 'Wie politisch sind politische Parteien? Zu einigen vernachlässigten Aspekten der Organisationswirklichkeit politischer Parteien', in J. W. Falter, C. Fenner and M. Greven (eds), *Politische Willensbildung und Interessenvermittlung* (Opladen: Westdeutscher Verlag, 1984), pp. 78–88.

Wiesendahl, E., 'Parteien in der Krise: Mobilisierungsdefizite, Integrations- und Organisationsschwächen der Parteien in Deutschland', *Sozialwissenschaftliche Informationen*, 22 (1993), pp. 77–87.

Wiesenthal, H., *Die Konzertierte Aktion im Gesundheitswesen. Ein Beispiel für Theorie und Politik des modernen Korporatismus* (Frankfurt a.M./New York: Campus, 1981).

Wiesenthal, H., 'Einleitung: Grundlinien der Transformation Ostdeutschlands und die Rolle korporativer Akteure', in W. Helmut (ed.), *Einheit als Interessenpolitik: Studien zur sektoralen Transformation Ostdeutschlands* (Frankfurt a.M./New York: Campus, 1995), pp. 8–33.

Wildenmann, R., 'Die Rolle des Bundesverfassungsgerichts und der Deutschen Bundesbank in der politischen Willensbildung: Ein Beitrag zur Demokratietheorie', *Veröffentlichungen der Universität Mannheim*, vol. 23 (1969), pp. 3–19.

Williamson, P. J., *Corporatism in Perspective: An Introductory Guide to Corporatist Theory* (London: Sage, 1989).

Willke, H., 'Zur Integrationsfunktion des Staates. Die Konzertierte Aktion als Paradigma in der neuen staatstheoretischen Diskussion', *Politische Vierteljahresschrift*, 20 (1979), pp. 221–40.

Wittkowski, R., 'Das Maastricht-Urteil des Bundesverfassungsgerichts vom 12.10.1993 als "Solange III"-Entscheidung?', *Bayerische Verwaltungsblätter*, 40 (1994), pp. 359–63.

Young, B., 'The Strong German State and the Weak Feminist Movements', *German Politics*, 7 (1998), pp. 128–50.

# Index